T0320045

A Research Agenda for Economic Crime and Development

Elgar Research Agendas outline the future of research in a given area. Leading scholars are given the space to explore their subject in provocative ways, and map out the potential directions of travel. They are relevant but also visionary.

Forward-looking and innovative, Elgar Research Agendas are an essential resource for PhD students, scholars and anybody who wants to be at the forefront of research.

For a full list of Edward Elgar published titles, including the titles in this series, visit our website at www.e-elgar.com.

A Research Agenda for Economic Crime and Development

Edited by

BARRY RIDER OBE

Professorial Fellow, Centre of Development Studies, University of Cambridge, UK

Elgar Research Agendas

Cheltenham, UK • Northampton, MA, USA

Published by
Edward Elgar Publishing Limited
The Lypiatts
15 Lansdown Road
Cheltenham
Glos GL50 2JA
UK

Edward Elgar Publishing, Inc.
William Pratt House
9 Dewey Court
Northampton
Massachusetts 01060
USA

A catalogue record for this book
is available from the British Library

Library of Congress Control Number: 2023939587

This book is available electronically in the **Elgar**online
Law subject collection
http://dx.doi.org/10.4337/9781802201383

ISBN 978 1 80220 137 6 (cased)
ISBN 978 1 80220 138 3 (eBook)

Printed and bound by CPI Group (UK) Ltd, Croydon, CR0 4YY

Contents

Contributors

Dr Rohan Clarke, BSc (UWI, Mona), LLB (Nottingham), MILP (Canterbury, NZ), PhD (Cantab), FSALS.

Fellow, Yale University Global Justice Programme, Lord Denning Scholar at the Honourable Society of Lincoln's Inn and formerly Diplomatic Service, Government of Jamaica.

Dr Rohan Clarke is a Fellow at Yale University's Global Justice Program and an international consultant on illicit finance. He received his PhD from Jesus College, University of Cambridge, where he was a Commonwealth (Cambridge) Scholar. His most recent academic work, *Illicit Finance and the Law in the Commonwealth Caribbean: The Myth of Paradise*, has been published by Routledge in its Law of Financial Crimes book series (2022). It drew on journalistic exposés such as the Paradise and Panama Papers as a backdrop to critically unpack the treatment of small states and offshore financial centres in transnational legal, regulatory and policy discourses on anti-money laundering, anticorruption, tax evasion, and combating the financing of terrorism. His academic work has also appeared in respectable peer-reviewed journals such as the *Journal of Financial Crime* and *The Company Lawyer*.

Dr Clarke spent over a decade in the Jamaican Diplomatic Service, during which he had the notable distinction of serving at the Embassy of Jamaica and Mission to the European Union in Brussels. He also held diplomatic accreditation to the Organisation for the Prohibition of Chemical Weapons in the Hague, UNESCO in Paris, as well as to Belgium, France, Luxembourg, Monaco, Netherlands, Portugal, and Spain. In the field of illicit finance, he has consulted for Palladium Group (UK) and the Global Initiative against Transnational Organized Crime (Geneva).

Dr Clarke is currently a Lord Denning Scholar at the Honourable Society of Lincoln's Inn, where he intends to be called to the Bar of England and Wales.

Dr Dayanath Jayasuriya PC, LLB (Hons)(Ceylon), PhD (Colombo), FICA, Hon FSALS, Advocate (Sri Lanka).

Managing Partner of Asian Pathfinder Legal Consultancy and Drafting Services, Sri Lanka.

Dr Dayanath Jayasuriya has a LL.B. from the University of Ceylon and a PhD in Law from the University of Colombo. In 1973 he was admitted as an Advocate of the Supreme Court of Sri Lanka and was later conferred the title of President's Counsel. He has been elected as a Fellow of the International Compliance Association (UK), Honorary Fellow of the Society for the Advanced Study of Law, and Fellow of the International Federation of Adjusting Associations.

He joined the Attorney-General's Department in February 1974 and left in 1983 as a Senior State Counsel. He handled many fundamental rights cases for the state. Until 1999, Dr Jayasuriya worked in Geneva, Vienna, Bangkok and New Delhi, and later from 2003–04, where he held senior positions within the United Nations and WHO, including that as Head, the UNAIDS Secretariat, Pakistan and Chief Technical Adviser to the UN International Drug Control Programme covering South Asia and the Central Asian Republics. He has been a UN adviser to countries in Europe, Central Asian Republics, Asia, Africa, South America and the South Pacific on regulatory aspects.

From 2000–03 he served as the Director-General of the Securities and Exchange Commission and Insurance Board of Sri Lanka and as the Chairman of both from 2004–05. He is the Founder President of the South Asian Insurance Regulators' Forum. In 2005 he served as the Chairman of the IOSCO President's Committee. He is an adviser on corporate governance, risk management and compliance to a number of multinational, regional and domestic companies.

As Chairman of the Insurance Board of Sri Lanka, he coordinated with insurance and reinsurance companies the settlement of tsunami-related claims and developed guidelines for entertaining, assessing and settling such claims in the future.

Dr Jayasuriya has been a Visiting Professor of Mercantile Law at the University of the Free State in South Africa; Visiting Scholar at Harvard University; and has delivered guest lectures at many universities, including in Oxford, Cambridge, London, New South Wales, Tasmania, Montreal and Delaware. He is a Distinguished Visitor at the Georgetown Law School, Washington, DC, and acts as an academic adviser to numerous universities in southern Africa, the UK, Ireland and Sri Lanka. He is the Coordinator for South Asia for the

International Association of Anti-Corruption Agencies, the headquarters of which is based in Doha/Beijing.

For 10 years he served as Chairman of Orient Finance PLC, a central bank regulated leading finance company. He was a Founder Director of the International Financing Facility for Immunization Co. in the UK, one of the largest charities in the country.

Dr Jayasuriya has written more than 20 books, 25 monographs and published over 250 articles. His books have been cited in judgments of the United States Appeal Courts and some are standard works of reference for professional and postgraduate courses in many countries. He is on the editorial board of several British journals, such as *The Company Lawyer, Journal of Qualitative Research in Financial Markets, Journal of Money Laundering Control, Journal of Financial Crime, International Journal of Islamic and Middle Eastern Finance and Management*, and *Roundtable*.

Dr Ingrida Kerusauskaite, PhD (Cantab), MPhil (Cantab), BA (SOAS, University of London).

Senior Fellow, Center for Anti-Corruption & Democratic Trust, International Foundation for Electoral Systems (IFES), Founder and CEO, AIMSustain, Guest lecturer, Centre for Development Studies, University of Cambridge.

Ingrida has worked with government agencies, judiciary, law enforcement, private sector and NGOs to improve approaches to counter financial crime, corruption and serious organized crime; improve approaches to irregular migration; and to support progress towards ESG goals. She has led various multi-million-pound programmes in a range of environments from the Caribbean to Eastern, Western and Southern Africa to Eastern and Western Europe, the Balkans, the Middle East and China.

When working with KPMG's forensic team in London, she supported governments', multilateral organizations' and financial sector's (large banks and real estate agencies to small fin-techs) anti-money laundering, anti-bribery and corruption, and broader compliance framework design and rollout. She has led programmes on behalf of some of the largest development assistance providers, and has now founded her own firm, Aim Sustain, focused on accountability, integrity, mobility and sustainability work.

Her research focuses on international development, financial crime, rule of law, transnational philanthropic capital flows and irregular migration. She published a book on anti-corruption with Routledge in 2018. Ingrida continues to lecture at the University of Cambridge, Centre for Development Studies.

She is also delivering a research project under an MOU with the Centre for Strategic Philanthropy at the Judge Business School, University of Cambridge, on the proportionality of regulation of cross-border private philanthropic flows.

Professor Louis de Koker, B.Iuris, LLB, LLM (UFS), LLM (Cantab), LLD (UFS), FSALS.

Professor of Law, La Trobe Law School, La Trobe University, Australia.

Louis de Koker holds a chair in law at the La Trobe Law School (Australia), where he is Associate Dean: Research and Industry Engagement and the coordinator and RegTech programme leader of the La Trobe LawTech research group. He is also a senior financial crime policy consultant to Consultative Group to Assist the Poor (CGAP), an independent think tank housed at the World Bank promoting financial inclusion.

Louis, the former director of the Centre for the Study of Economic Crime of the University of Johannesburg, has authored a range of articles, chapters and books on financial crime. Recent books include Goldbarsht and De Koker (eds) *Financial Technology and the Law: Combating Financial Crime* (Springer, 2022) and De Koker et al (eds) *Money Laundering and Terrorist Financing: Law and Compliance in South Africa* (LexisNexis South Africa, 2022).

He has advised on a range of laws and regulations in countries such as Jordan, Kyrgyzstan, Namibia, South Africa, Uganda, and Vietnam, and his research on integrity laws and their impact on financial inclusion has been cited in publications of the various international bodies, including the World Bank, IMF, the Financial Action Task Force (FATF) and the Basel Committee on Banking Supervision. He was a member of a World Bank team that researched financial crime controls relating to mobile money, a member of the core team that designed the World Bank tool for national money laundering risk assessment, and a member of the FATF project group that drafted their guidance papers on aligning financial inclusion and financial integrity and digital identity guidance.

From 2014–19 he was the national programme leader of the A$1.8 million Law and Policy research programme of the Australian government-funded Data to Decisions Cooperative Research Centre. This programme considered the legal and policy aspects relating to big data analysis and Australian national security objectives.

Professor Antonello Miranda JD (Palermo), LLD (Palermo), CL (LSE), DL (City Polytechnic, Lond), FSALS, Advocate (Italy).

Full Professor of Comparative Law and Director of the Centre of Advanced Studies, University of Palermo, and honorary member of the Italian judiciary.

Antonello Miranda is a Full Professor of Comparative Law and European Private Law. He has been teaching Comparative Legal Systems and European Private Law since 1983. He also teaches International Law and Conflict of Laws. He was the dean responsible for graduate degrees in political sciences and international relations at the University of Palermo and was Director of the Department of European and Comparative Studies (CISECOM) of the master's course in Comparative and European Law. He served as Dean of the Faculty of Political Science of the University of Palermo for a number of years. He is also a deputy rector of the university responsible for international and diplomatic relations and chairman of the Institute of African Studies – for the development and cooperation with African (and Asiatic) countries. Antonello is also the Director of the Centre of Advanced Studies of the university.

He has visited and taught at a number of other universities and research institutes, including New York University, Sydney University, Brisbane University, the University of Cambridge, Loyola University, University of New Orleans, the University of Malta and the Institute of Advanced Legal Studies of the University of London. He has also served as an examiner for many universities, including the University of London and BPP University.

He is a member of the International Society of Family Law, General Secretary of the Italian Association of Comparative Law, a Fellow of the Society for Advanced Legal Studies and Member of the International Academy of Comparative Law.

He is the author of more than 70 published studies and books, most of them in English, on specific subjects of private comparative law (property and land law, family law, succession, contract, torts, right of information, compliance, human rights) especially directed to a comparison with the English and common law experience, and studies and books on the evolution and harmonization of the European substantive law, human trafficking, competition law, consumer protection, family law, compliance, mediation, and, recently, on a treaty in English on 'The Italian Legal System'.

Professor Chizu Nakajima, BA (Keio), MA (Keio), PhD (Lond), FSALS.

Professor of International and Comparative Law, BPP University; Emeritus Professor of Corporate Law and Governance at London Metropolitan

University; Visiting Professor of ESG Integration, University of Osaka, Japan; and Chair, British Japanese Law Association, UK.

Professor Chizu Nakajima has extensive experience in advising intergovernmental and governmental organizations on legal and policy issues relating to governance and integrity, and chairs a bilateral law association of the Law Society for England and Wales. Chizu is Professor of International and Comparative Law at BPP University and Emeritus Professor of Corporate Law and Governance, former head of the Business and Law Department of London Metropolitan University, and was the Director of the Centre for Financial Regulation at City, University of London. She supervises research students at the Universities of Cambridge and London, and as a visiting professor of the Graduate School of International Public Policy, Osaka University, she is currently advising public and private sector bodies on ESG integration. As Senior Associate Research Fellow, she continues to conduct legal research at the Institute of Advanced Legal Studies, University of London. Chizu has also worked for a number of financial institutions and has served on the governing body of a livery company in the City of London.

Patrick Rappo BA (Oxford), MA (Oxford), Barrister ((England and Wales).

Partner, DLA Piper.

Patrick's practice focuses on a range of corporate and white-collar crime matters, international bribery, corruption, money laundering, fraud, and sanctions issues. Patrick represents companies and individuals, and has been involved with a number of high-profile investigations and prosecutions – including Global Investigations Review's 'Most Important Case of 2020': SFO v Barclay's Bank. He works across high-risk sectors and high-risk jurisdictions.

Professor Barry Rider OBE, LLB (Lond)(Hons), MA (Cantab), MCL (Palermo), PhD (Lond), PhD (Cantab), LLD (Hon)(UFS), LLD (Hon)(Penn State, USA), FRSA, Hon FSALS, FIPI, Barrister (England and Wales).

Professorial Fellow, Centre of Development Studies, University of Cambridge.

Professor Barry Rider has taught law within the University of Cambridge since 1976, when he was elected as a Fellow of Jesus College, Cambridge. He is currently a Professorial Fellow in the Centre of Development Studies of the University of Cambridge and holds a number of substantive, honorary and visiting professorial and senior research appointments at a number of universities around the world, including a chair in comparative law at Renmin University in China. He served as Director of the Institute of Advanced Legal Studies, from 1994 to 2002. He has also practised as a lawyer in the City of London and a number of other jurisdictions, including as counsel to a leading international US law firm. He is a Master of the Bench of the Inner Temple.

In parallel to his academic career, Professor Rider has also worked for a number of governmental and intergovernmental agencies in a number of countries. He has served as a special adviser to select committees of the House of Commons. He was appointed as an Officer of the Most Excellent Order of the British Empire, by Her Majesty Queen Elizabeth II in 2014 for his work in combating economic crime. His contribution to the fight against serious crime and subversion has also been recognized by a number of other governments.

Professor Rider has been a prolific author and researcher and has – alone or in collaboration with others – authored over 40 books and a great many articles in learned journals. He has also been commissioned to undertake studies for many governments and international organizations. He established and serves as general editor of the *Journal of Financial Crime*, the *Journal of Money Laundering Control* and *The Company Lawyer*. He has been involved in establishing a large number of similar publications and sits on the editorial boards of many publications across the world. He is the founder and Executive Director of the Cambridge International Symposium on Economic Crime, which is now in its 40th year and attracts well over 2,000 participants annually to Jesus College.

Dr Dominic Thomas-James LLB (Hons)(KCL), MPhil, PhD (Cantab), FRSA, Barrister (England and Wales).

Postdoctoral Research Associate, Fitzwilliam College, University of Cambridge; Global Justice Fellow, Yale University; Consultant and Director of Publications, ICC FraudNet; and Barrister, Goldsmith Chambers, London.

Dr Dominic Thomas-James is a Research Associate at Fitzwilliam College, University of Cambridge and is a Global Justice Fellow at Yale University. He is Tutor in International Relations and International Development at the University of Cambridge Institute of Continuing Education and lectures in Justice and Development at the Centre of Development Studies at the Department of Politics and International Studies at the University of Cambridge. Dr Thomas-James is a Barrister at Goldsmith Chambers, London and is a qualified civil and commercial mediator accredited by the ADR Group. He is Director of Publications and Consultant to ICC FraudNet, the specialised asset recovery division of the International Chamber of Commerce, where he serves as editor of the Global Annual Report on Fraud and Asset Recovery. He has consulted to various intergovernmental and international organisations, and is a Senior Organiser of the annual Cambridge International Symposium on Economic Crime at Jesus College, Cambridge. Dr Thomas-James earned his Ph.D and M.Phil from Queens' College, Cambridge and his LL.B from King's College London, before being called to the Bar of England and Wales by the Honourable Society of the Inner Temple. He is author of the book *Offshore Financial Centres and the Law: Suspect Wealth in British Overseas Territories* (2021, Routledge).

Foreword

In popular parlance, development is viewed as a metaphor for the ongoing and ever upward progress of humankind, from the millennia of hunter gatherers to the twenty-first century of space travel, autonomous vehicles, virtual life, and digital everything. In reality, however, development is not a steady, forward state. It is a complex process, encumbered by strong countervailing forces, including economic downturns, political turmoil, forced migration, environmental security, pandemics, and the omnipresent, but often ignored, spectre of economic crime.

Economic crime poses both an existential and a supranational threat, impacting every nation, but some to a much greater degree than others. It represents the theft of riches and resources which are the rightful property of citizens and nations. The effect is to undermine confidence in the institutions of the state, corporations, and ultimately, the rule of law.

Corruption, by example, is a global problem, with responsibility lying in many places. Where corruption is endemic, there can be little effective development. The vulnerable become more vulnerable. The rich become richer, and the poor become poorer. Women and children and all those seeking basic amenities, education, and medical services are disproportionately affected.

In 2003, the nations of the world adopted the *United Nations Convention Against Corruption*, the first and only global initiative to combat this scourge. For those present during its negotiating sessions, optimism was the flavour of the day. And yet, 20 years later, questions are being asked: is corruption on the decline, has the human condition changed for the better, or is progress only illusory?

Economic crime, as we see in this timely book, is a multifaceted hydra which affects all nations of the world. It shows no favourites. Although a plague in many financially strapped nations, it is industrialized countries which often serve as the repositories for ill-gotten gains, plundered and stolen from the former. In many cases, economic crime and organized crime exist in parallel universes.

Many international and global initiatives, made in good faith and intended to suppress economic crime, have had negative consequences in those parts of the world where development is most needed. The Financial Action Task Force has produced a set of recommendations which all countries are expected to follow in combatting money laundering and terrorist financing. The recommendations have become normative standards; however, their impact is uneven. The targeting of small jurisdictions providing financial services to international clients belie those more powerful jurisdictions which do precisely the same thing and are not chastised.

As described in this book, development is closely aligned to the need for good governance. The United Nations recognized this with its Sustainable Development Goals, and in particular the need for corporations around the world to transition from a model which emphasizes shareholder primacy to one which reflects a form of corporate governance that views the corporation as a vital cog in dealing with environmental, social, and governance issues. But the 'new' corporation cannot exist if the global community imposes unrealistic expectations upon it, such as excessive financial reporting, which has the effect of stunting innovation and profits.

The foregoing quickly leads to an even more esoteric but equally important discussion – that of sovereignty. Nation states, and the concept of national sovereignty, developed many centuries ago, but in recent times have been partially displaced by larger and wealthier nations imposing unrealistic demands on the smaller and less wealthy, oftentimes exerting a form of economic sovereignty which strips the less advantaged of their independence. The issues surrounding development are indeed profound.

It is unfortunate that in both the 'real' world of government, business, and finance, and in the cloistered halls of academia, too few are examining the intersect between development and economic crime. The paucity of published academic material and courses on the dark side of development is a product of this chasm.

Recognizing the need for greater and more informed discussion, Professor Barry Rider, an international leader in this discussion, who teaches one of the few courses on development and crime, has attracted academics and practitioners who tackle this issue from a variety of perspectives. The agenda they produce in this text is intended to lift the dark cloud of economic crime from development. If those with political or bureaucratic will take the time to explore the plethora of ideas in this volume, they may well find the underpinnings for a global strategy.

The contributors to this book, all experts in the field, seek to exorcise the problem from their unique perspectives in a variety of nations and continents. The chapters implore those in power to undertake evidence-based approaches to dealing with economic crime in development. They advocate transparency in government, harnessing technology to create a level playing field through a process of digitization, influencing social norms in a positive direction, and investigating suspect wealth, among other initiatives. They also seek to disabuse us of the notion that the problem resides elsewhere, such as in the ubiquitous 'offshore'. The problem belongs to all of us.

Development should connote a better life and the realization of unfulfilled dreams. Too many citizens of the world live for today, with no realistic opportunity for a better day. This should not be. If one life is changed by what is written in the pages that follow, this book will be a success. If, however, it sparks study, discussion, and new strategies to deal with the seemingly intractable issue of economic crime in the sphere of development, it will have made a real difference.

Dr Peter M. German, KC, OOM
Barrister and Solicitor, President, International Centre for Criminal Law
Reform and Chair, Advisory Committee, Vancouver Anti-Corruption Institute
Vancouver, Canada

Preface

Whether development studies is simply an amalgam to topics viewed from different and disparate disciplines or a cohesive and integrated intellectual discipline itself is debateable. Of course, there are those who can see clearly an area of study focusing on development which brings together issues and, through its own intellectual perceptions and understanding, contributes more than the sum total of its content. Others are minded to dismiss its contribution as simply a 'rag bag' of topics which to a greater or lesser degree have relevance in discussing developmental concerns. There is probably a degree of justification in either view, and certainly, there is scope for better and more focused examination of what we mean by the subject area in the first place. There would be a limited value in simply looking at development, whatever this means, as a fact – without regard to its context and relevance. Indeed, there is a profound philosophical discussion to be had as to whether development is positive or merely and essentially a political aspiration. Even if we grasp development as a progression that is dynamic and produces or at least facilitates the attainment of economic, social and political advantages, much will depend upon who judges and the objectivity and applicability of their assessment. As we now see so clearly in the context of our environment, one man's development can easily, perhaps almost inevitably, be another's problem. For the last 30 or so years, I have attempted to grapple with, at least, some of these issues through an equally flawed prism – justice, in a course within the MPhil in Development Studies at the University of Cambridge.

Whether my students actually learn anything that my colleagues recognise as being within what they consider to be development studies is questionable. However, over the years a good many have gone into work directly related to promoting not simply economic and social development, in what we used to arrogantly describe as deprived societies, but in advancing stability and arguably the security of such. While their employers' and their own job titles often invoke development, and especially that even more controversial notion of sustainability, at best their contribution would seem pragmatic and possibly partisan. Consequently, it is pertinent to ask if in training these worthy individuals we are not merely, in very general terms, perpetuating the very uncertainties and dilemmas faced by those who attended the precursor to our courses in Cambridge which were conceived for the purpose of running an Empire.

Of course, this might be unfair and arguably a gross oversimplification. Nonetheless, after so many years offering advice, whether requested or not, to governments in the less developed parts of the world on issues more or less relevant to integrity, corruption and governance, I become more and more unclear as to whether so many of the real issues that we all face are peculiarly pertinent to 'developing countries'. The fundamental problem is invariably access to sufficient, appropriate and competent resources. But looking at the recent record of government in, for example, the UK in promoting integrity and thus, according to our wisdom, stability, it is not obvious that such resources are available or useable even in such a privileged environment.

The vulnerability of societies manifests itself in many ways. However, having walked such an unsure path in my attempt to contribute to the study and advancement of 'development', I have taken what many – perhaps most – will consider to be a personal liberty. In putting together this 'research agenda' I have persuaded a number of my eminent colleagues to write on development from a perspective that focuses on the threats to stability and sustainability presented by economically motivated crime and misconduct – in other words, looking at the dark side of development. Of course, in a work of this nature, discussion cannot be as comprehensive as the threat deserves and inevitably reflects the perspectives and interests of our distinguished authors. As with my own course, what is presented is eclectic and perhaps has a random quality about it. On the other hand, the specific topics that we address in this work are relevant, in practice to many of the inhibitors of economic and social advancement and stability.

In the first chapter, I seek to justify in rather more detail the importance that I attach to discouraging economically relevant and motivated criminals from undermining the integrity, efficacy and stability of economies. The primary driver of this concern and initiative was not to better facilitate the protection of one's own economy through the standardisation of rules and provision of more meaningful cooperation, but a genuine, perhaps politically naïve, wish to confront the real damage that many forms of economically motivated crime can do to the operation and advancement of economies – whether developed or otherwise. It does not take much to cause profound economic and political problems even in a relatively stable and highly developed economy, as the brief premiership of Liz Truss MP so dramatically illustrated in the UK. Indeed, in regard to some issues, it does not necessarily follow that relatively well-resourced and more mature systems are always better able to confront and contain threats. Obviously the character and extent of a threat will depend to a large extent on its context, and in some underdeveloped economies the potential for real damage is limited by the realities of the economy. On the other hand, fragility and narrow leadership can undermine recovery and possibly result in relative terms in more profound and lasting harm.

The emphasis that today we place on interventions within the economy to disrupt criminals, terrorists and isolate those who we politically disapprove of has redefined the front line in combating criminal and subversive threats. The focus on criminalising money laundering and generating financial intelligence has fundamentally altered the risks facing those who mind other people's wealth. In trying to improve the efficacy of these measures, it could be argued we have disproportionately burdened our financial institutions and moved away, to some degree, from our traditional approach to the rule of law. All this has implications in particular for those still building their economies. Such concerns are addressed by several of my colleagues in this work, and in particular by Professor Louis de Koker in Chapter 8. Whatever the cost benefits of focusing on the financial aspects of crime and terror, there is clearly a well-established and at this point in time non-negotiable commitment by the world's leading economies to this strategy. There are those who question whether this strategy is something of a 'Trojan horse' allowing dominant governments to better pursue agendas not simply related to 'clipping the wings' of criminals and terrorists – for example, facilitating the collection of tax! Nonetheless, a more or less determined commitment to pursue this approach has led to a confrontation with those economies that have pursued an offshore path. Dr Dominic Thomas-James and Dr Rohan Clarke in their chapters address these and related issues.

In an introduction of this nature, it would be unhelpful to do more than whet the appetite of the reader. In a nutshell, what we all try to do is raise issues from the perspective of those concerned with development, pertaining to activity of a criminal or at least negative nature, which directly or indirectly inhibit stability and advancement. While many of us hold or have held academic appointments, in my opinion of greater importance is that we have also been involved, in a variety of ways, in practice – actually trying to put often high-sounding principles in place – often in the most difficult of circumstances. This has given our academic work a perspective which might otherwise be lacking.

The series of which this book is proudly part seeks to identify further research topics primarily for those in the academy. However, as we have emphasised, useful and valued research does not exist in a vacuum. My own commitment to this project is very much based on the concern that I know exists in government – that there is a paucity of independent experts before whom policy can be tested and refined. Consequently, these books are not intended to present a comprehensive analysis of even the areas upon which they focus. They are properly reflective of the experience and perspectives of the various authors and ideally sufficiently interesting – indeed, controversial, to encourage others to deepen their own interest and learning. That there is a real need for much more intelligent thought, deliberation and research in the areas we touch upon is hopefully, if not self-evident, underlined in our discussions.

I personally am indebted to my colleagues for their commitment to this project and the excellent material that they have prepared on a topic which remains beyond the horizon of so many in the academy!

Professor Barry Rider OBE

1 Introduction to *A Research Agenda for Economic Crime and Development*

Barry Rider

This is not the place to attempt to trace the origins of development studies as a separate academic discipline. In my own university, Cambridge, it had a rather drawn-out gestation and protracted birth – starting as Professor Peter Nolan, the eminent development economist and China expert and first direc- tor of the University of Cambridge's Centre of Development Studies, used to describe to new students as a programme for young colonial administrators where pith helmets and shorts were the order of the day! Of course, Professor Nolan's jocular comments only reflect part of the story and today Britain's colonial past is a topic, at least in the academy, that one raises with a degree of trepidation.[1] Again, this is certainly not the place to debate the advantages and disadvantages of our imperial heritage – suffice it to say that a good many of the issues that properly face those concerned with promoting sustainable

---

[1]   On the other hand, Shridath Ramphal observed "to speak of international co-operation and development is to speak of the past no less than the present – and of the future also." "International Co-operation and Development; the Role of Universities," 17 *Journal of Modern African Studies*, (1979) 183. There were spe- cialized training courses for officers in the Colonial Service at the universities of Oxford and Cambridge and the London School of Economics, see A Kirk-Green, The Colonial Service Training Courses and generally at britishempire.co.uk/ ralphdolignon-furse.htm, and M Misra, *Colonial Officer and Gentleman: the British Empire and globalization tradition*, (2008), Cambridge University Press. The military also had specialist courses within the University of Cambridge and certain of its colleges; these persisted until quite recently. See generally L James, *The Rise and Fall of the British Empire*, (1994), Abacus; J Lloyd, *Empire, A history of the British Empire*, (2006), Hambledon; R Hyam, *Understanding the British Empire*, (2010), Cambridge University Press; K Kwarteng, *Ghosts of Empire, Britain's Legacy in the Modern World*, (2012), Bloomsbury; P Levine, *The British Empire: Sunrise to Sunset*, (2007), Pearson, and in particular C Elkins, *Legacy of Violence – a history of the British Empire*, (2022), Bodley Head.

development have a history and sometimes one that is rightly contested and questioned.

Development and law

Having regard to the very broad canvas upon which we paint our concerns about development,[2] apart from the more established areas of development economics and perhaps international relations, there is a tendency to personalize agendas for study and discussion around one's own experience – perhaps inevitably, for a discipline that is relatively new and lacking the rigidity of its more established cousins. Lawyers, of which the author is one, have a limited interest in, and some would argue few skills, to bring to the study of development[3] as opposed to, for example, the protection of the environment. Those that have taken an academic interest have often stumbled into the area from international and humanitarian law – much fewer, from finance and in particular international financial law. Historically, others have contributed from the perspective of constitutional law.[4] Given the importance of law from so many perspectives – normative, empowerment, protection, facilitation and security – many other areas of legal knowledge have proved important in promoting sustainable development and security. Adherence to some notion of the rule of law, albeit its content may be debated,[5] is widely regarded as necessary for

---

[2]   See generally D Clark, *Visions of Development: A Study of Human Values*, (2002), Elgar; M Cowen and R Shenton, *Doctrines of Development*, (2008), Routledge; P Hopper, *Understanding Development*, (2nd ed, 2018), Polity; Ha-Joon Chang, *Kicking Away the Ladder: Development Strategy in Historical Perspective*, (2022), Anthem; A Sen, *Development as Freedom*, (1999), Oxford University Press, and in particular, UNSD, *Sustainable Development Goals Report*, (2017), United Nations, particularly goal 16.

[3]   But see T Scheepers, *A Practical Guide to Law and Development in South Africa*, (2000), Juta.

[4]   The study of corruption has to some degree provided a bridge between disciplines, although most of the running has been made by non-lawyers, see in particular, R Fisman and M Golden, *Corruption, What everyone needs to know*, (2017), Oxford University Press, and generally B Rider (ed), *The Enemy Within*, (1997), Kluwer.

[5]   See generally F Pirie, *The Rule of Laws*, (2021), Profile Books, and T Bingham, *The Rule of Law*, (2010), Penguin. But see R Dworkin, *Law's Empire*, (1998), Hart, at 93. See also L Berg and D Desai, *Overview on the Rule of Law and Sustainable Development for the Global Dialogue on Rule of Law and Post 2015 Development Agenda*, (2013), position paper.

sound development.[6] Whether this be in a very weak form perhaps involving little more than observance of formal rules,[7] with little or no concern for substantive justice, to a system which goes beyond the substantive legal system to provide access and equity, regularity and predictability, adherence to the rule of law promotes security and stability.[8] Indeed, there will inevitably be a degree of tension between formal justice and its application to specific circumstances. However, the existence of and application of rules facilitates a level of expectation which fosters relationships, whether commercial or domestic, that tend towards stability.[9] In conceiving, developing and maintaining such a process, a broad spectrum of legal skills is required. While the application of such skills is much better when it takes adequate account of the circumstances within which those rules and procedures will be needed, many do not see this as being essentially different in a society that is underdeveloped.[10]

---

[6] See for example, P Atiyah, *Law and Modern Society*, (1995), Opus; P Allott, *The Health of Nations – Society and Law beyond the State*, (2002), Cambridge, and M Kramer, *Objectivity and the Rule of Law*, (2007), Cambridge. See also J Stone, *Human Law and Human Justice*, (1965), Stevens, and R Posner, *Overcoming Law*, (1995), Harvard University Press.

[7] As for example in China, see W Hurst, *Ruling before the Law*, (2018), Cambridge, and R Peerenboom, *China's Long March towards the Rule of Law*, (2002), Cambridge.

[8] See P Nolan, *China and the West: Crossroads of Civilization*, (2019), Routledge.

[9] It is said that businesspeople favour certainty over the substance of justice, hence justification for the operation of pragmatic rules, such as the so-called postal-acceptance rule in English contract law, see *Adams v. Lindsell* (1818) 106 ER 250 (KB) and in particular Thesiger LJ in *Household Fire and Carriage Accident Insurance Co Ltd v. Grant* (1879) 4 Ex D 216 at 223 and generally R Goode, *Commercial Law*, (3rd ed, 2004), Penguin, see also B Rider, "The virtue of certainty," 30 *The Company Lawyer*, (2009) 225. The more certain the situation, the easier it is to obtain insurance and order one's affairs. Indeed, the UK government extolled the virtues of pragmatism in the English commercial law to China in the context of its Prosperity Programme, see B Rider, *The Rule of Law in China, potential for UK China legal co-operation*, (2017), Report for the Prosperity Fund, Great Britain China Centre. Of course, attitudes have changed towards China and the so-called 'golden years' have long passed, see G Grylls, "Truss will declare China an official threat for the first time" and Leader Comment, "Back away from Beijing," 29 August 2022, *The Times*. China's human rights record, while of concern for many years, has now become a pressing international issue, see for example, C Philip, "China could face the Hague for the first time over Uighurs," 2 September 2022, *The Times*, and in particular, *Report of UN High Commissioner for Human Rights, Assessment Xinjiang Uyghur Autonomous Region*, 31 August 2022, UN, (but not also the UN Human Rights Council's refusal to discuss it, J Keaten, 6 October 2022, *The Diplomat*).

[10] Of course, the 'elephant in the room' will always be access to resources. As we shall see, this is not merely an issue for underdeveloped economies, see for

Another important contribution from those engaged with and in the law is the provision of rules and their installation. Again in practice there is not an obvious divide between the experience of developed and less developed societies, save in their ability to resource this process.[11] In practice there are many examples of legal systems looking to the experience of other jurisdictions in the crafting of their rules.[12] The study of comparative legal systems and laws can play a significant role in better facilitating this process. However, in practice, comparative study of law, at least in the common law tradition, is quite limited and rarefied.[13] This is not to say that within the common law, regard is not had to the experience of other jurisdictions and very occasionally systems of law.[14] However, as Lord Denning MR pointed out, there is appropriately caution as to the suitability of a rule and its application that has grown up in one legal environment being transported to another, which might prove less hospitable.[15] Of course, in the complex and highly inter-related world of today, all legal

---

example, R Kelly and M Dilworth, "Britain is £3bn fraud capital of the world," 27 June 2022, *Daily Mail*, and in particular, *Economic Crime, responses to the Committee's Eleventh Report, House of Commons Treasury Committee, 8th Special Report of 2021–22*, House of Commons, 25 April 2022, and J Turner, "It's frightening when the police give up on crime," 27 August 2022, *The Times*, in regard to the UK. See also *ibid* at n 49.

[11]   Our expectations of workable legal systems are such that even micro-states require a full range of laws invariably not too dissimilar to the largest states. In addition, their legal systems must be capable of interacting with the international community and observing required international standards. On the other hand, access to drafting and other legislative skills will be exceedingly limited and expensive to acquire, see *ibid* at note 77.

[12]   It is arguable that this is one of the factors that has, since early history, promoted the need for comparative study of legal systems and their norms, see M Reimann and R Zimmermann, *The Oxford Handbook of Comparative law*, (2006), Oxford at p 4 *et seq*. See also B Rider, "A gentleman and scholar" in A Miranda (ed), *Modernita del pensiero Giuridico di G Criscoli e dirrito comparato*, Parte 111, (2015), Giappichelli, 3.

[13]   While an established and respected discipline, it tends to be populated by those with a civilian background, see generally, J Gordley and A Von Mehren, *An Introduction to the Comparative Study of Private Law, Readings, Cases and Materials*, (2006), Cambridge, and K Zweigert and H Kotz, *An Introduction to Comparative Law*, (3rd ed, 1977), Cambridge.

[14]   See for example, see Lord Goff in *White v Jones* [1995] UKHL 5, and S Banakas, 'Tort duties under Contract's shadow – Are English and German Law converging?" in *Un giurista di successo: Studi in onore di Antonio Gambaro*, (2017), Giuffre.

[15]   "Just as with the English oak, so with the English common law: one could not transplant it to the African continent and expect it to retain the tough character which it had in England. It had many principles of manifest justice and good sense which could be applied with advantage to peoples of every race and color

systems require a more or less full toolset of law and institutions to operate. This process has been spurred on by globalization, but also various initiatives, often of arguably more practical significance to developed countries, such as the various 'crusades' against corruption, money laundering, terrorist finance and even insider dealing![16] The imperative to standardize laws and meet a similar expectation, often sanctioned, in their administration is a powerful argument in favour of 'borrowing' the laws and attempting to transplant the experience of others. This is something we shall return to, as it raises issues for developing countries and in particular the smaller and less well-resourced ones.

A personal focus – security and stability

Consequently the interest and involvement of lawyers across the legal spectrum in development is in practice far greater and more meaningful than is indicated by the rather limited, possibly even pedestrian, level of legal involvement in the academy. The present writer's interest and involvement in development studies at the University of Cambridge, and later other institutions, was similarly pragmatic. It derived from work primarily concerned with security and the threats presented by organized criminals[17] in undermining the

---

all the world over, but it had also many refinements, subtleties and technicalities which were not suited to other folk. These off-shoots must be cut away. In those far-off lands the people must have a law which they understood and which they would respect" per Lord Denning in *Nyali Ltd v Attorney-General* (1956) Court of Appeal. See also A Allott, *The Limits of Law*, (1980), Butterworths, especially Ch 1.

[16]   See *Report on Financial Crime and Development*, International Development Committee, Eleventh Report, House of Commons, 15 November 2011, Ch 3, and B Rider, 'Blindman's Bluff – a Model for Securities Regulation?' in J Norton and M Andenas (eds), *Emerging Financial Markets and the Role of International Financial Organisations*, (1996), Kluwer; B Rider, 'The War on Terror and Crime and the Offshore Centres: The 'New' Perspective?' in D Masciandaro (ed), *Global Financial Crime, Terrorism, Money Laundering and Offshore Centres*, (2004), Ashgate; B Rider, 'Pursuing Corruption,' in *Legal Studies in the Global Era: Legal issues beyond the Borders*, (2011), Chuo University, and B Rider, Insider Trading – smoke and mirrors," 1 *International and Comparative Corporate Law Journal*, (1999) 271.

[17]   See B Rider (ed), *A Research Agenda for Organised Crime*, (2023), Elgar, and see generally, B Rider, in *Organised Crime, Minutes of Evidence and Memoranda*, Home Affairs Committee, HC Session 1994, 16 November 1994, HMSO at 193. A personalized focus on development, given its vague boundaries, is not uncom-

integrity and thereby arguably the stability of economies. Initially, this work was focused on Hong Kong, the Philippines[18] and China, but later became far more international. Through this prism, it was then very clear that many of the goals for development, whether economic, social or political, could and were in a number of instances being wholly undermined by adverse forces capable of being categorized as organized crime, but often involving even more insidious and dangerous elements.[19] For example, take Hong Kong in

---

mon, see for example, the comments of S Corbridge in his *Development Studies – A Reader*, (1995), Arnold, at ix. See also generally, O Johnson (ed), *Financial Risks, Stability and Globalization*, (2002), IMF.

[18]   To some no doubt surprisingly, adequate regulation of insider abuse and trading was (and to some degree still is) considered a relatively important factor in promoting stability in the financial markets, see B Rider, S Bazley, K Alexander and J Bryant, *Market Abuse and Insider Dealing*, (4th ed, 2022), Bloomsbury, Ch 1. In the context of Hong Kong, at the time, promoting confidence in the integrity (fairness?) of the markets was viewed as an important issue, see B Rider, "The Regulation of Insider Trading in Hong Kong,"17 *Malaya Law Review*, 310 continued 1. *Malaya Law Review*, (1976) 157, and see also B Rider, "Insider Trading – Hong Kong Style," 128 *New Law Journal*, (1978) 897. In practice the emphasis was placed rather more on maintaining orderly markets than eradicating insider trading. Indeed, one American judge (Judge Owen, Southern District, New York) in an important case doubted how serious the authorities were in Hong Kong in penalising insider dealing and commented it was the sort of thing that they gave you a knighthood for – see at the Hong Kong end – *Nanus Asia Co Inc v Standard Chartered Bank* [1990] 11 HKLR 396, but see also *R v Hong Kong Dragon Co Ltd*, (Crim App No 889 of 1971) Hong King Court of Appeal, 12 April 1972, for a strong condemnation of 'white collar' crime and the reputation of the Crown Colony. "The Regulation of Insider Trading in the Republic of the Philippines," 19 *Malaya Law Review*, (1977) 355, and generally B Rider and HL Ffrench, *The Regulation of Insider Trading*, (1979), Macmillan. Public confidence in the fairness – integrity – of the markets was seen as issues for security and stability, see also in this context, B Rider, "The Regulation of Insider Trading in the Republic of South Africa," 94 *South African Law Journal*, (1977) 437.

[19]   See for example, G Posner, *Warlords of Crime, Chinese Secret Societies*, (1988), Queen Anne Press. The relationship of organized crime to political authority in certain places such as the Shan states and Golden Triangle is highly complex, see for example, B Young, *Golden Triangle*, (1987), Joint Publishing Co. The legitimacy in folk perception of organized bandits who assume a 'political' mantel is long and well recorded and illustrated not just by the legends of Robin Hood, see S Nai'an and L Guanzhong, *Outlaws of the Marsh*, (3 vols, 1980), Foreign Language Press, Beijing, and in particular F L Davis, *Primitive Revolutionaries of China – a study of secret societies in the late Nineteenth Century*, (1971), Routledge. While today the relationship between the 14K triad and the Kuomintang in Taiwan is historical (see for example, "Step up crackdown on triads, says President Lien Chan," 23 September 1996, *Straits Times*), it has been a reality, see generally J Taylor, *The Generalissimo, Chiang Kai-Shek and the struggle for Modern China*,

the 1970s and 1980s. In the early years of this period, many inside and outside Hong Kong saw it as a very important asset for the United Kingdom. While the financial balance sheet was always a little ambiguous, it was clear that Britain saw Hong Kong as a vital factor in the character it had cast itself in on the world stage. During the Cold War it played, what some argued, a vitally important role in the Far East for the West.[20] Whether this was actually so may be left to others better placed to evaluate the wider political issues, but what was quite clear was that the USSR and increasingly the PRC recognized that it has key strategic significance and spared no resources in attempting to penetrate its very fabric.[21] While the USSR inserted agents and even financial institutions

---

(2011), Harvard University Press. Indeed, there was a perception within UK and Hong Kong government circles that the main 'triad threat' to Hong Kong emanated from Taipei rather than Beijing, or more precisely Guangzhou. This largely misconceived notion was perpetuated by the tendency of exposed triad bosses and corrupt officials making off to Taipei, usually on route to Vancouver. It is perhaps not surprising that organized crime will court 'cover' from governments and possibly vice versa, see for example, R McCarthy, "Japan's political thugs exposed," 26 September 1992, *The Independent*.

[20]   See generally, O Westad, *The Cold War – A World History*, (2017) Allen Lane. Hong Kong was not just a listening post in regard to China, but was seen a significant asset and, indeed, exemplar of western values in the region. In regard to its important SIGINT role see, for example, R Aldrich, *The Hidden Hand: Britain, America and Cold War Secret Intelligence*, (2001), John Murray, and in particular *GCHQ, The Uncensored story of Britain's most Secret Intelligence Agency*, (2010), Harper, Ch 8, specifically in regard to China. Hong Kong was seen as a significant asset for China in the development of its economic development, see generally B Hayton, *The South China Sea, the Struggle for Power in Asia*, (2014), Yale, perhaps less so in recent years, see generally, M Sheridan, *The Gate to China, A new history of the People's Republic of Hong Kong*, (2021), Collins.

[21]   While there were specific examples of direct and sponsored Soviet penetration of government and in particular the financial sector, perhaps the most disturbing issues were exposed as a result of financial misadventures. See in particular D Andelman, "Moscow Narodny Bank stirs Singapore trouble," 26 June 1976, *The New York Times* – "Specifically, under its shadowy Singapore-Chinese manager, Teo Poh Kong, the bank has managed to penetrate the intricate overseas Chinese business community whose complex familial and business connections run through all of Southeast Asia — from Hong Kong to Thailand, Malaysia, Singapore, Indonesia and beyond. And, in the process, it has acquired interests in land holdings, shipping and a number of potentially sensitive enterprises throughout the region." Interestingly, the initial allegations in regard to 'Soviet revisionists' were made in the *People's Daily* in China. Concern as to infiltration of the system, not least by China, has not diminished, see for example, C Hamilton and M Ohlberg, *Hidden Hand, Exposing how the Chinese Communist Party is reshaping the world*, (2020), Oneworld Publications, and C Moore, "China has a friend in Jesus," 10 June 2021, The *Spectator*, and C Parker *et al*, "Cambridge fellows tutor Beijing elite in art of leadership," 12 June 2021, *The Times*.

into the equation, the PRC, both at a national and a provincial level, attempted to use criminal organizations, including triads and smugglers.[22] British and American security and intelligence resources focused primarily on threats within and to the Crown Colony were limited, and without the Special Branch of the then Royal Hong Kong Police would have been wholly inadequate.[23] With a degree of supplementation from the military on the whole, attempts at disruption were contained, but those who wanted to see an official British continuation in Hong Kong increasingly found their arguments problematic and less convincing, even in Whitehall.[24] The extent to which the PRC sponsored activities within Hong Kong – effectively rendering the position of those who wished to see some form of continuation untenable and have facilitated

---

[22]   In particular the so-called Big Circle gang. Mainland Chinese often with criminal and state security affiliations were infiltrated into the Royal Hong Kong Police Force and to some degree the Royal Hong Kong Regiment. Corruption both in the facilitation of crime, but also as a form of entrapment became a very real security concern leading to the establishment of the ICAC, see R Lee (ed), *Corruption and its control in Hong Kong*, (1981), Chinese University Press, and in particular T Cheung and C Lau, "Profile of Syndicate Corruption in the Police Force," Ch 7, generally, F Welsh, A *History of Hong Kong*, (1993), Harper Collins at 475 *et seq*. The British Army garrison was required to intervene on at least one occasion against organized disobedience by the colonial police and was placed on alert on several other occasions. For a more recent analysis *vis a vis* China and India, see G Lee, *Police Corruption in Comparative Perspective*, (2020), Routledge.

[23]   This was a real concern within the colonial government of Hong Kong, see for example, *Report on the Hong Kong Triad Riots*, (1956), Governor of Hong Kong, Hong Kong Government Press. On the other hand, there was a reluctance to address the threat of money laundering, see "Banking chief rejects money-laundering claim," 5 August 1987, *South China Morning Post*. Towards the end of British rule in Hong Kong it was claimed that one of many triads, the Sun Yee On had over 40,000 members, see "Nine members of biggest HK triad charged," 3 December 1993, *Straits Times*. Concern about triad activity was not, in a colonial context, confined to Hong Kong, see for example, W Blythe, *The Impact of Chinese Secret Societies in Malaysia*, (1969), Oxford University Press; M Fong, *The Sociology of Secret Societies – A study of Chinese secret societies in Singapore and Peninsular Malaysia*, (1981), Oxford University Press, particularly Ch 3 and G Singh, *Malaysian Societies*, (1984), SGS. Concerns were evident in many Imperial possessions as to the risks presented by Chinese and other immigrants, see for example Report of the Royal Commission on Alleged Chinese Gambling and Immorality and Charges of Bribery Against Members of the Police Force, (1892), Government Printer, Sydney.

[24]   See generally, R Cottrell, *The End of Hong Kong: The Secret Diplomacy of Imperial Retreat*, (1993), John Murray, and D Bonavia, *Hong Kong 1997, The Final Settlement*, (1985), Columbus Books. The UK's colonial heritage remains controversial in Hong Kong, see B Macintyre, "Being a colony gave Hong Kong its freedoms," 18 June 2022, *The Times*.

the undermining of the agreed protections for Hong Kong residents after 1997 – may never be known.[25] Although less contentious and obvious, the situation in the Philippines[26] was also of concern, rendered more complicated by a resurgence of Japanese and Chinese criminal groups throughout the region.[27]

---

[25]   See C Dobson, "China's police chief met top triad bosses," 11 April 1993, *South China Morning Post*; "China's police chief willing to unite with patriotic triads" and "Triads meet top Chinese minister," 9 April 1993, *The Standard* (Hong Kong) and there are suspicions that Hong Kong gangs have operated against pro-democracy initiatives at least in sympathy with the Chinese Communist Party etc, see for example, L Lewis, "Hired thugs attack Hong Kong democracy protesters," 4 October 2014, *The Times*; M Sheridan, *The Gate to China, a new history of the People's Republic of China*, (2021), Collins, at 383, and possibly, J Ames, "Hong Kong threat sent to London team," 7 July 2022, *The Times*. See also generally S Twiston Davis, "Triads – Hong Kong's Legacy to the World," 19 November 1989, *Sunday Morning Post Magazine* (Hong Kong). On the threat of Chinese organized crime in the UK, see B Rider, "The Enterprise of Crime," 47 et seq, in B Rider and M Ashe (eds), *Organised Crime*, (1966), Sweet & Maxwell; P Tooler, "Triads – the Chinese Mafia," *Blitz*, 17 February 1989, 47 particularly at 49, and P Wilson and F Lafferty, "Chop Chop – the Triads in London," 11 February 1989, *ES Evening Standard Magazine*.

[26]   The history of organized crime in the Philippines is complex, bound up with politics, an almost feudal political system and regional and religious violence, mixed with an ambiguous heritage, see generally, P Bowring, *The Making of the Modern Philippines, Pieces of a Jigsaw State*, (2022), Bloomsbury.

[27]   See for example, K Chin, S Zhang and R Kelly, "Transnational Chinese Organised Crime," 4 *Transnational Organised Crime*, (1998) 127. See also D Kaplan and A Dubro, *Yakuza*, (2003), University of California Press, and B Rider (ed), *A Research Agenda for Organised Crime* (2023), Elgar. See B Rider, *Report to an ad hoc meeting of Ministers on international and national security in South East Asia with reference to the activities of certain organised crime and related subversive cells*, (1978), Government of the Philippines, Ministry of National Defence and Security, and B Rider, *Economic Destabilisation and Economic Warfare*, (1978), Report to the Office of the President and Co-ordinator General of National Security, Government of the Philippines. There has been debate as to the extent to which Chinese and Japanese criminals collaborated. There were, however, a number of instances particularly in regard to investment-related frauds and in particular commodity futures trading frauds in Hong Kong, where there was considerable cooperation. In more recent years there has been a high degree of cooperation in regard to the production and transportation of amphetamines, see for example, "China executes Japanese man for smuggling amphetamines," 25 July 2014, *South China Morning Post*, and "Japan nabs seven Chinese for smuggling 1 ton of amphetamines," 5 June 2019, *The Standard*. The Philippines government appealed for intelligence and other assistance in combating Japanese organized crime and in particular its involvement in illegal logging and mining on several occasions during the 1980s and 1990s.

Another example is that of South Africa and the so-called frontline states. Concern, internationally and particularly within Britain, about the apartheid policies of the South African government were made far more complex by the situation in Rhodesia/Zimbabwe. The Cold War in southern Africa was in many respects a hot war and the West had clear interests in not undermining its own investments and interests. On the other hand, there were clear limits as to how far the 'democracies' could go in tolerating – often turning a blind eye to – the abuse of human rights and worse in southern Africa.[28] The various embargoes against the Republic of South Africa led to the state using every means available to it to evade sanctions. It also unleashed attacks by agencies of the South African government against the economies around it, including Zimbabwe. While some attempts to undermine the integrity and efficacy of these economies involved state actors, many were in collaboration with criminals, both inside and outside the relevant economies.[29] This inevitably was a present and immediate danger to their stability and, thus, security. This 'war' – which has been rarely acknowledged, let alone documented and studied, in part because of the vested interests of the protagonists and their successors – exposes a dimension in development that is rarely perceived, outside the so-called 'war' on drugs.[30]

---

[28]   See *Mission to South Africa, The Commonwealth Report*, (1986), Commonwealth Secretariat, Chs 1 and 2. See also P Johnson and D Martin, *Apartheid Terrorism, The Destabilization Report – a report on the destabilization of the Frontline States*, submitted to the Commonwealth Committee of Foreign Ministers on Southern Africa, (1989), Commonwealth Secretariat.

[29]   The situation was complicated by the support (mostly unofficial and secret) that certain governments and their agencies afforded the South African regime. As most of this was offered through intermediaries, some of whom became very rich, it is difficult to substantiate the involvement of, for example, Israel and Taiwan. Agents of the South Africa Bureau of State Security were actively involved in sanctions busting. See also J Hanlon, *Who Calls the Shots in Mozambique*, (1991), Indiana University Press at 239 *et seq*, and see reported comments of the author, by M Chester, "SA infiltrated by mafia – expert," and J Soderlund, "How we came to fall among thieves," 23 February 1993, *The Star*, South Africa.

[30]   State agents in South Africa engaged in numerous attempts to destabilize the economies of Zimbabwe, Botswana and Malawi. This included forging currency, circulating forged currency and financial instruments, industrial sabotage, disruption of markets, kidnapping and threatening businesspeople and overseas suppliers, manipulation of markets and credit and trade-related fraud. A number of intergovernmental and national agencies gave assistance in fostering and supporting the transition of South Africa and in particular to capacity-building after the ANC came into government. This extended to rebuilding the security and law enforcement apparatus. Sadly much has been undermined by the persistence of corruption at all levels of government.

Financial integrity

From the early 1970s another threat – not just to the economies of the states involved, but internationally – was being industriously nurtured, primarily, albeit not exclusively, in the Caribbean and a little later in the Pacific. Small island nations increasingly felt marooned economically and to some degree politically. Trade blocs were increasingly able to make demands and expose the economic vulnerability of their cash crops. The solution for some was tourism, even on occasion with the support of those who in other parts of the world were themselves somewhat 'suspect'. Others, often on the advice of governments, including the UK, were persuaded to become offshore financial centres. Indeed, at the time development-conscious intergovernmental organizations such as the IMF and Commonwealth commended such a strategy.[31] Enough rushed into the offshore financial services market, often at the behest of those in the developed and highly taxed economies, to create effectively an offshore dimension to the world's economy.[32] This offered, in a variety of ways, anonymous financial facilities, the façade of legitimate but largely unregulated and unsupervised financial intermediaries, and increasingly tax-related incentives. Not only established banks and investors welcomed these discreet facilities, but also, of course, the crooks and those who worked with them.[33] At the time

---

[31]   Indeed, the Commonwealth Fund Technical Co-operation provided experts – as did the Overseas Development Agency and the Crown Agents (then and independent agency of the UK Government).

[32]   See generally, H McCann, *Offshore Finance*, (2006), Cambridge, and B Rider in *Review and Amendment of Labuan IOFC Legal Framework*, (2007), International Advisory Group, Government of Malaysia.

[33]   See R Ehrenfeld, *Evil Money*, (1992), Harper Business; N Shaxson, *Treasure Island – Tax Havens and the men who stole the world*, (2012), Vintage; R Blum, *Offshore Haven Banks, Trusts and Companies – the business of crime in the Euromarket*, (1984), Prager; D Chaikin (ed), *Money Laundering, Tax Evasion and Tax Havens*, (2009) University of Sydney, and in particular, J Sharman and R Gordon, Ch 6, "International Financial Centres, Tax Havens and Money Laundering Havens", D Masciandaro (ed), *Global Financial Crime, Terrorism, Money Laundering and Offshore Centres*, (2004) Ashgate, particularly B Rider, "The war on terror and crime and the Offshore Centres: The new perspective," at Ch 2. Of particular interest in regard to organized crime penetration see *Organised Crime and Banking*, Hearing, Committee on Banking and Financial Services, US House of Representatives, 140th Congress, 2nd Session (February 28, 1996) US Government. Issues related to bank secrecy and suspect wealth existed well before the development of these offshore centres, see for example, N Faith, *Safety in Numbers – the mysterious world of Swiss Banking*, (1982), Hamilton; B Rider and H L FFrench, *The Regulation of Insider Trading*, (1979), Macmillan at 420 et seq.; I Walter, *Secret Money*, (1985), George Allen and Unwin; D Brown, *The*

there were few who actually recognized the danger or the signs of danger.[34] Indeed many, in particular the Caribbean, saw these developments as wholly beneficial, increasing revenue, promoting education and affording a certain amount of political clout on the world stage.[35] The potential for corruption

---

Flight of International Capital – a contemporary history, (1987), Routledge, and K Hinterseer, *Criminal Finance – the political economy of money laundering in a comparative context*, (2002), Kluwer.

[34]   See comments of B Rider quoted in T Cozier, "Warning of Criminal states in Caribbean," 19 September 1986, *Financial Times*, and B Rider, *Keynote address, Conference on International Narco Trafficking and security of Caribbean states*, 19 – 21 January 1995, Institute of International Relations, University of the West Indies and Government of Trinidad and Tobago, published papers, and B Rider, "Too many spies?" 7 *Journal of Financial Crime*, 294. The Second Cambridge International Symposium on Economic Crime, held at Jesus College, Cambridge in July 1983 focused on practical problems facing investigators as a result of bank secrecy and offshore services, see also B Rider, The *Promotion of Cooperation in Combating International Economic Crime in The Commonwealth*, (1980), Report to Commonwealth Law Ministers, Commonwealth Secretariat; B Rider, *Economic Crime and the destabilization of small states*, (1985), Report of the Meeting of Law Officers of Small Commonwealth States, Commonwealth Secretariat and South Pacific Co-operation Council, Vanuatu; B Rider, "Commonwealth Initiative Against Commercial Crime," 6 *Commonwealth Judicial Journal*, (1986) 20; B Rider, "Combating international commercial crime – A Commonwealth perspective," *Lloyds Maritime and Commercial Law Quarterly*, (1985) 217, and also B Rider, "Policing the International Financial Markets: An English Perspective," XV1 *Brooklyn Journal of International Law*, (1990) 181. The extent that organized crime presents a distinct threat to national stability and security was underestimated in most countries until the early 1980s. The extent of at least the financial operations and implications of organized crime was not fully appreciated by organizations such as ICPO-Interpol until intelligence-related resources were freed up as a result of the 'ending' of the Cold War, see B Rider, *A Research Agenda for Organised Crime*, (2023), Elgar, Ch 1. There is, of course, always a danger of sensationalizing the issues and perhaps overstating the reach of organized crime, see C Sterling, *Crime without Frontiers, the worldwide expansion of organised crime and the Pax Mafiosa*, (1994), Little Brown and J Robinson, *The Merger – how organised crime is taking over the world*, (1999), Simon & Schuster, but also M Woodiwiss, *Gangster Capitalism – the US and the global rise of organised crime*, (2005), Constable, and R Naylor, *Wages of Crime, Black Markets, Illicit Finance and the Underworld Economy*, (2004, revised), Cornell.

[35]   See generally R Clarke, *Illicit Finance and the Law in the Commonwealth Caribbean; The Myth of Paradise*, (2022), Routledge. For a somewhat 'diplomatic' assessment see *Vulnerability, Small States in the Global Society, Report of a Commonwealth Consultative Group*, (1985) at 33 in regard to economic stability and security threats. More recently the so-called Pandora and Paradise Papers indicate the vast majority of those using offshore financial facilities do so for tax and other reasons, see generally *Pandora Papers*, International Consortium of Investigative Journalists, 19 October 2021; "Pandora Papers; biggest ever

of those involved in running these laundries and the almost inevitable slide into a criminal culture was less obvious, but nonetheless a reality.[36] Crime and highly organized crime has always existed in the Caribbean – largely as a result of geography and resources, but the offshore financial services boom created a new and vastly more complicated picture. Not least because, increasingly, other states became frustrated with the way in which these facilities were being employed to avoid and evade their own tax laws, hide illicit wealth and facilitate the laundering of the proceeds of crime,[37] thus promoting highly

---

leak of offshore data exposes financial secrets of rich and powerful," 3 October 2021, *The Guardian*; "Pandora papers: what has been revealed so far," 6 October 2021, *The Guardian*; "About the Pandora papers investigation," 9 October 2021, *Washington Post* and M Forsyth, "Paradise papers shines light on where the rich and elite keep their money," 5 November 2017, *New York Times*, and in particular S Bhuiyan, "The Pandora papers open up Pandora's box: integrity and crime," 22 February 2022, *Public Integrity*.

[36] See comments of the author reported by T Cozier, "Region at risk, organised crime a major threat to the Caribbean," 19 September 1986, *Weekend Nation*, Barbados (and also "Commercial Crime causing concern" 19 September 1986, *Barbados Advocate*), and in particular T Cozier, "Caribbean states becoming criminal," 19 September 1986, *The Financial Times*, and R Frail, "Organised crime targets Pacific," 12 August 1987, *The Sydney Morning Herald*, and see the UK governments warning in regard to Antigua and Barbuda, *HM Treasury News Release 66/99* 19 April 1999, and D Bohning, "Islands in the cocaine stream," 23 February 1997, *Miami Herald*, and D Adams, "Cocaine island in the sun," 27 December 1997, concerning St Kitts and Nevis. The report of *the Royal Commission of Inquiry into Drug Trafficking and Government Corruption* (1983) Government of the Bahamas and the earlier report of the Commission under Sir Ranulph Bacon (1966/67), Government of the Bahamas exposed wrongdoing at the highest levels of government in the Bahamas. For a recent example, note the allegations against the premier of the British Virgin Islands, H Tomlinson, "How Miami Vice snared premier," 30 April 2022, *The Times*. Some jurisdictions have been prepared to prostitute their sovereignty. See "Traffickers threaten tiny outposts," 23 February 1997, *The Herald* (US); M Sheehan, "Gangs launder billions in pacific island shack," 5 December 1999, *Sunday Times*, and generally J Robinson, *The Laundrymen*, (1994), Simon & Schuster, and in particular J Robinson, *The Sink*, (2003), Constable; N Kochan, *The Washing Machine*, (2005), Thomson; P Lilley, *Dirty Dealing*, (2nd ed, 2000), Kogan Page; R Dick, *The Bagman*, (1984), Kensal; M Naim, *Illicit*, (2005), Heinemann, and generally M Pickhardt and E Shinnick, *The Shadow Economy – corruption and governance*, (2008), Edward Elgar, particularly Ch 1.

[37] Identifying and interdicting wealth associated with criminal activity became a primary strategy in addressing criminal enterprises and is now the main response to crime and terror internationally, see historically B Rider and C Nakajima, *Anti- Money Laundering Guide (2 Vols)*, (1999), CCH, Ch 1; B Rider and M Ashe (eds), *Money Laundering Control*, (1996), Sweet & Maxwell; B Rider, "Wages of Sin – Taking the profit out of crime – A British perspective,"

organized criminal and subversive activity. The legal, administrative and corrupt barriers to cooperation resulted in some of these purveyors of offshore facilities becoming pariahs in the international financial system and suffering very real economic and political consequences.[38]

While there are those who argue, with a degree of plausibility, that the creation of a web of offshore facilities, particularly in the UK's dependent territories, was all part of a heinous post-colonial plot on the part of vested and privileged interests within the City of London,[39] the situation was and remains far more complex. Governments around the world, while initially at least seeing some

---

13 *Dickinson Journal of International Law*, (1995) 391; B Rider, "The Crusade against Money Laundering – Time to think," 1 *European Journal of Law Reform*, (1999) 501; B Rider, "Taking the Profit out of Crime," 1 *Financial Crime Review*, (2000) 2; B Rider, "The Limits of the Law: An Analysis of the Inter-relationship of the Criminal and Civil Law in the Control of Money Laundering," 2 *Journal of Money Laundering Control*, (1999) 209 (also published as an inaugural address by the University of the Free State, in 25 *Journal for Juridical Sciences*, (2000) 1 and in *The Practising Criminologist*, (1999) 25), and B Rider, "The Price of Probity," 7 *Journal of Financial Crime*, (1999) 1.

[38]   See generally D Thomas-James, *Offshore Financial Centres and the Law, suspect wealth in British Overseas Territories*, (2021), Routledge; R Murphy, *Dirty Secrets – how tax havens destroy the economy*, (2017), Verso, and N Shaxson, *Treasure Islands, Tax Havens and the men who stole the world*, (2012), Giffin. Of course, not all jurisdictions that deliberately created secrecy also embarked on becoming low- or no-tax jurisdictions, see R Antonie, *Confidentiality in Offshore Financial Law*, (2nd ed, 2014), Oxford University Press. All tax havens had secrecy and many in addition blocking laws – outlawing cooperation except in narrow circumstances, but mere offshore financial centre did not always enact additional secrecy laws, see D Campbell (ed), *International Bank Secrecy*, (1992), Sweet & Maxwell. For example, the City of London has always relied on the common law obligation of confidentiality, see *Tournier v National Provincial and Union Bank of England* (1928) 1 KB 461. Secrecy has been almost eliminated as a result of 9/11, numerous international initiatives against crime and corruption, and the concern of, in particular, leading western economies to address tax avoidance and fraud, see R Clarke, *supra* at 35.

[39]   See for example the documentary film *The Spyder's Web* – an investigation into the world of Britain's secrecy jurisdictions and the City of London, directed by M Oswald and also see also the observations of John Moscow, the lead prosecutor in the BCCI case in New York, "Firms told of cottage industry in laundering," 7 June 1999, *The Lawyer*. See also Ch 11 of N Shaxson, *supra* at note 38. The institutions of the City of London could do rather more to dispel such criticism, which has long been voiced, D Atkinson "Dirty money threat to City," 14 September 1999, *The Guardian*; Leading Article, "London Laundromat," 18 August 2018, *The Times*; A Persaud, "London the Money Laundering Capital of the World," 27 April 2017, *Prospect*; N Shaxson, "The City of London is hiding the world's stolen money," 11 October 2021, *The Times*, and in particular O Bullough, *Butler to the*

advantage to this discreet and efficient dimension to the international financial system, became concerned about the level of cooperation that they could harness in their own investigations into matters of high political and national interest.[40] While the Americans bribed, blustered and bullied some,[41] the British, French and occasionally the Dutch and Germans put in or recruited agents and informants.[42] In truth, none of these strategies provided, on a con-

---

World, how Britain became the servant of tycoons, tax dodgers, kleptocrats and criminals, (2022), Profile Books.

[40] The UK and in particular the then prime minister, Margaret Thatcher MP, woke up, perhaps not for the very first time, to the problems presented by nominees, bank secrecy and offshore issues in the investigation into certain transactions relating to Westland Helicopter in 1985, see B Rider, "Policing the City – combating fraud and other abuses in the corporate securities industry," 41 Current Legal Problems, (1988) 47 at n 67, see also R Jinman, "Margaret Thatcher lied to the House of Commons over the Westland affair," 17 October 2015, The Times. There have, of course, been many cases where investigators have, notwithstanding special powers, such as those under the Companies Act, been more or less frustrated, see for example, J Griffiths QC, Interim Report under section 172, Companies Act 1948, House of Fraser plc, (1984) HMSO and note the use of nominees etc in the notorious South Sea Bubble in the early eighteenth century, see M Balen, A very English Deceit, the South Sea Bubble and the world's first great financial scandal, (2002), Fourth Estate.

[41] The US Securities and Exchange Commission was quite robust in securing information in the face of bank secrecy and confidentiality laws, see for example D Szak, "International Cooperation in Insider Trading Cases," 40 Washington and Lee Law Review, (1983) 1149, and much earlier Staff Report on Evasion of the Federal Securities Laws by or through persons not within the territorial limits of the USA, (1958) Securities and Exchange Commission. See also T Clarke and J Tigue, Dirty Money, Swiss banks, the Mafia, Money Laundering and White Collar Crime, (1976), Millington Books, and "Hot on the heels of the mafia's middlemen," 11 December 1975, The Guardian. Other US agencies and in particular the Internal Revenue Service have been even more persuasive and have allegedly obtained information for payment. Indeed, it is often asserted that one of the incentives for the Swiss government in enacting a far-reaching mutual legal assistance treaty in the early 1970s was a very favourable trade deal with the US and see also the Swiss International Mutual Assistance in Criminal Matters Law (1982), and M Haraji and A Hirsch, "The Swiss Perspective on International Judicial Assistance," 9 Journal of International Business Law, (1987) 519, and B Rider, " Policing the International Financial Markets: An English Perspective," 16 Brooklyn Journal of International Law, (1990) 179.

[42] There have been prosecutions that have failed as a result of intelligence-related interventions, see for example, N Fielding, "MI6 agent wrecked £15m Cayman trial," 19 January 2003, Sunday Times; B Rider, "Who to trust!", 6 Journal of Money Laundering Control, (2003) 299 and other cases have not been commenced or have been discontinued as a result of the need to protect sources and intelligence assets. Not surprisingly, criminals have adopted similar tactics, see for example the comments of Sir Callum McCarthy, then chairman of the FSA, "there

sistent and continuing basis, the calibre of intelligence let alone evidence that the relevant legal systems required.

Indeed, the forcing – through both a stick and carrot approach – of typically small island states to adopt international standards,[43] whether in context appropriate and/or workable or not, based on the developed world's agenda against the evil of the day, on the basis that this facilitated their own domestic

---

is increasing evidence that organised crime groups are placing their own people in financial service firms so they can increase their knowledge of firms' systems and controls and thus learn to circumvent them ..." P Hosking and S Tendler, "Warning over mafia gangs infiltrating British banks," 16 November 2005, *The Times*. Similar concerns have been expressed in regard to infiltration of law and other professional firms, see R Mendick, "Police probe City firms' links to organised crime," 12 *The Lawyer* (24 November 1998) 46. See also B Rider, "Penetration of Banks – Myth or Reality," 15 *Journal of Financial Crime*, (2008) 5. This has long been recognized as an issue in the USA, see J Kim, "Experts: USA being infiltrated," 24 August 1999, *USA Today*. There may well come a point when infiltration results in control over the bank or other institution. The UK and USA expressed concern about organized criminals penetrating and running banks in Romania in the 1990s. The European Commission commissioned a special study on penetration of banks within the Union, see C Nakajima (ed), P Rutledge and B Rider (principal consultants), *Insider Fraud in the Retail Banking Sector*, (2009), European Commission – which remains classified! Potentially all infrastructure is at risk from organized crime, see for example, B Rider at 47 *et seq* in E Ellen (ed), *Ports at Risk*, (1993), ICC-IMB, and generally at 113, in D Trang (ed), *Corruption and Democracy, Institute for Constitutional and Legislative Policy*, (1994), Open Society Foundation, and at 34 *et seq*, *Combating the Financing of Terrorism*, Centre for International Security Policy, Switzerland and NATO, (2003), Government of Switzerland. It is also important to remember that there are parts of the world which remain very much under the direct control and influence of criminal organizations, see for example, "Speed Tribe, Inside the world of the Wa, Asia's deadliest drug cartel," Special Report, 16 December 2002, *Time*.

43   See for example, R Clarke, *supra* at n 35; D Thomas-James, *supra* at n 38; S Ali, *Money Laundering in the Caribbean*, (2003), Kluwer; D Jayasuriya, *Money Laundering, Financial Transactions Reporting and Terrorist Financing, Sri Lankan Legal Perspective*, (2007), Sridevi, and J Trehan, *Crime and Money Laundering – the Indian Perspective*, (2004), Oxford University Press. The UK government has in recent years taken a much more responsible approach to what goes on in its remaining overseas territories, see for example D Thomas-James, in B Rider (ed), *A Research Agenda for Organised Crime*, (2022), Elgar. None the less, there have been problems, see for example, S O'Neill, "Judge's death in paradise leaves six-year bribery trial on brink," 12 February 2021, *The Times*, in regard to the trial of the former premier of the Turks & Caicos Islands, albeit the trial did in fact continue. While Harrison J's untimely death at 84 was not suspicious, there have been cases, not least in Hong Kong, of judges dying in very mysterious circumstances effectively wrecking trials.

legal capabilities, was clearly not vouchsafed by their own record. The amount of suspect wealth actually placed beyond the reach of criminals and their organizations was and remains so small[44] as compared with what is 'guestimated' to be out there, that some argue that the real objective of those attacking the secrecy of some of these states was never to pursue ordinary criminals, but rather to facilitate the better collection of their revenue. Thus, concerns about international crime groups and terrorists were invoked, to trump even arguments based on national sovereignty. On this argument the anti-money laundering and corruption initiatives were in reality a 'trojan horse'.[45]

---

[44]   See B Rider, *A Research Agenda for Financial Crime*, (2022), Elgar. The UK National Audit Office estimated in the UK confiscation of criminal assets was no more than 26 pence in every £100 of criminal property and that in only 2 per cent of cases is the full amount of the confiscation order actually collected, *NAO Confiscation Orders*, 17 December 2013, and D Atkinson, "Dirty Money treat to the City," 14 September 1999, *The Guardian*. See also *Report of the House of Commons Committee of Public Accounts, Confiscation Orders*, 21 March 2014, SO. See also B Rider "Taking the Profit out of Crime" in B Rider and M Ashe (eds), *Money Laundering Control*, (1996), Sweet & Maxwell; B Rider, "Recovering the Proceeds of Corruption," 10 *Journal of Money Laundering Control*, (2007) 5 particularly 26 *et seq*, and A Kennedy, "An evaluation of the recovery of criminal proceeds in the UK" 10 *Journal of Money Laundering Control*, (2007) 33. Perhaps even more alarming is that notwithstanding over 350,000 suspicion-based reports to the authorities in the UK in 2015 only 7 bank accounts were actually blocked. See generally *UK National Risk Assessment of Money Laundering and Terrorist Finance*, (2015), UK Treasury and Home Office.

[45]   The more recent initiatives, not least by the UK, championed in particular by The Rt Hon Andrew Mitchell MP, to promote greater transparency and accountability of legal entities operating offshore, while in practical terms of limited effect, is nonetheless to be welcomed, see generally D Thomas-James, *supra* a n 43, and the Economic Crime (Transparency and Enforcement) Act 2022 creating a Register of Overseas Entities, also see "Crown dependencies face crackdown on secret companies," 1 March 2019, *The Financial Times*, and "Why British overseas territories fear transparency push," 3 March 2018, *Financial Times*. There are, of course, very real and strong arguments in favour of attempting to deprive criminals of their illicit benefits and in particular their ability to reinvest these in further criminal enterprises, see *supra* at n 37. There is also a strong moral argument, see generally *Recovering the Proceeds of Crime* (2000), Cabinet Office, *Proceeds of Crime, Consultation on Draft Legislation* (2001), Home Office, Cm 5066, *Proceeds of Crime, Home Affairs Committee, Report 5*, Session 2016/17, House of Commons, and in particular S Keene, *Threat Finance, disconnecting the lifeline of Organised Crime and Terrorism*, (2012), Gower, and J Drinkland, "US targets bin Laden cash," 25 September 2001, *USA Today*.

'Spies' and their tools

In part a better approach was to, in the context of much broader support, assist in the development of internal capabilities within the countries concerned. In part, as a result of the failure of domestic legal systems to adequately address economically motivated and organized crime throughout the developed world, there has been a tendency to adopt in the criminal justice system a strategy based on disruption of criminal organizations and networks.[46] This approach does not depend primarily on bringing the perpetrators of serious crime before the courts in the vain hope of securing a conviction – let alone seizing the ill-gotten gains of the criminal enterprise in question. Rather, it aims, through a raft of interventions, to increase the costs and risks to criminals of engaging in their illicit activities primarily in the jurisdiction concerned.

The adoption by the criminal justice system of essentially the tools of the spy has – theoretically and possibly practically – a number of advantages. It enables the state to act efficaciously and without regard to the normal constraints of legitimate jurisdiction against activity which threatens its national interests. On the other hand, it involves agencies and activities outside the traditional criminal justice system where accountability and certainly transparency may be limited. It does not appear to foster the values encompassed within the rule of law.[47] Nonetheless there is a debate to be had, well beyond the competence of this book, as to the extent it is justified or necessary for a state actor to take unto itself powers and capabilities to protect its proper interests,[48] including

---

[46]   See A Leong, *The Disruption of International Organised Crime*, (2007), Ashgate, particularly Ch 8; B Rider "Intelligent investigations: the use and misuse of intelligence – a personal perspective" 20 *Journal of Financial Crime*, (2013) 293; N Ridley, *Terrorist Financing – the failure of countermeasures*, (2012), Elgar, and B Rider "The Enterprise of Crime" in B Rider and M Ashe (eds), *Money Laundering Control*, (1996), Sweet & Maxwell. For a discussion of the sensitivity of, in particular, drug cartels to financial disruption see T Wainwright, *Narconomics – How to run a drug cartel*, (2017), Penguin. Of course, organized crime groups have adapted to address this threat, see generally, B Rider (ed), *A Research Agenda for Organised Crime*, (2023), Elgar.

[47]   See B Rider, "The price of effective international co-operation," 28 *Journal of Financial Crime*, (2021) 321 and B Rider. "Fraud – how serious are we?" 42 *The Company Lawyer*, (2021) 299.

[48]   See H Kennedy, *Legal Conundrums in the Brave New World*, (2004), Sweet & Maxwell, Ch 1; R Ashby Wilson (ed), *Human Rights in the 'War on Terror*, (2005), Cambridge University Press and A Ashworth, *Human Rights, Serious Crime and Criminal Procedure*, (2002), Sweet & Maxwell. See also J Murphy, *The United States and the Rule of Law in International Affairs*, (2004), Cambridge University Press.

the protection of its people, through perhaps novel mechanisms outside conventional international cooperation based, as it often is, on mutual interest.

It is also the case that circumspection is necessary in assuming that approaches to criminality that may be acceptable within established and well-resourced legal systems are viable and safe in societies without such traditions and institutions. We have already pointed out that there is, for example, the potential for tension between strategies based on intervention in fighting criminal enterprises and some aspects of the rule of law. In societies where there is real access to the courts with independent and competent judges, the tensions are arguably reduced and may be balanced by the public interest in controlling serious crime.[49] Where such protections are problematic, allowing agencies to effectively operate outside the traditional criminal justice system may well be a cause for real concern.[50]

---

[49]   How meaningful in practice access to the courts is and how independent the judiciary are is another issue. There is also the issue of judicial competence and integrity, see for example, L Lau, "No trust in Malaysian courts: judge," 15 January 2001, *The Strait's Times*, quoting Tan Sri Mohamed Dzaiddin, "this negative perception has held up development of the country when foreign investors are reluctant to invest because they perceive there is no level playing field in the courts." Furthermore, there has long been concern as to the seeming failure of the traditional criminal justice system, see R Rose, *In the Name of the Law – the collapse of Criminal Justice*, (1996), Jonathan Cape. Sir David Phillips, then Chief Constable of Kent, in a report to the Association of Chief Police Officers in 2000 stated "we have no real response to organised crime. We are losing the battle on crime and it can be said that we have lost it to organised crime," see J Clark, 24 September 2000, *Sunday Times*, and Special Report, "The Mafia: back from the dead," 2 December 2021, *The New European*. We have already noted the failure of the criminal justice system to protect the victims of fraud in the UK (and most other jurisdictions) and a declining trust in the ability and partiality of the police, see for example, G Seed, "Police corruption in the UK at Third World levels," 27 September 1998, *The Sunday Telegraph*, which is still an issue – see *An inspection of the Metropolitan Police Service's counter-corruption arrangements*, (22 March 2022) HMICFRS, which were branded 'not fit for purpose,' and the highly critical comments of Lord Agnew of Oulton on his resignations as the Treasury Minister with responsibility for combating fraud, 25 January 2022, *The Times*, and see D Byers, "Johnson has let UK become money-laundering haven," 26 January 2022, *The Times*.
[50]   See B Rider, "The price of effective international co-operation," 28 *Journal of Financial Crime*, (2021) 965. Particular concern arises where the interventions are by agents outside conventional law enforcement. While there is no assurance police officers will not abuse their positions, at least they tend to be more visible and accountable within an identified hierarchy, but see H de Quetteville, Special Feature, "The criminals among our crime-fighters," 3 November 2022, *The Daily*

Notwithstanding the justification for or efficacy of all this, the necessity for procedures for the collection of information which can be refined into intelligence and then institutions having the ability to deploy and use such, perhaps in aid of the conventional criminal justice system, is a reality. Numerous international and regional instruments recognize the importance of this and require countries to establish dedicated and expert financial intelligence units.[51] The importance of financial intelligence has long been recognized within the intelligence community and proved important during the Second World War in identifying enemy assets. Since then, with the development of financial sanctions for a wide range of political purposes, it has become all the more significant. The more emphasis that is placed on disrupting the flow of criminal and terrorist money and, in particular, in pursuing property associated with criminal activity, the more financial intelligence is required. Indeed, as we increasingly recognize the practical and evidential problems in linking property to a specific predicate crime and focus on unexplained wealth,[52] the

---

Telegraph. See also S Grey, "British spies take fight to the mafia," 17 November 1996, *The Sunday Times.*

[51] See for example, *The United Nations Convention against Corruption,* 2004. There is considerable variation in the location, mandate and operation of FIUs around the world, some are embedded in law enforcement agencies, such as in the UK, others are freestanding and some operate as part of the banking and fiscal regulatory system, see generally *Financial Intelligence Units – An Overview,* (2004), International Monetary Fund. Not all are seen as part of the broader fabric of law enforcement, see K Stroligo *et al, Financial Intelligence Units working with Law Enforcement Authorities and Prosecutors,* (2018), World Bank. Of course, in some cases there will be constitutional and other restrictions impacting on the ability of an FIU to work with the criminal justice system.

[52] Note, for example, the investigative provisions in relation to unexplained wealth introduced into UK law by the Criminal Finances Act 2017 (Proceeds of Crime Act 2002 s 362 *et seq*) as further amended, see F Hamilton, "New weapon in war on illicit wealth," 3 February 2018, *The Times.* It remains to be seen whether these provisions will make any difference in identifying criminal property, let alone interdicting it, see B Rider, "Explaining the Unexplained," 39 *The Company Lawyer,* (2018) 33. The experience in other jurisdictions such as Australia and Ireland is not encouraging, see "Special Report, Those Unexplained Wealth Orders," 15 March 2022, *Times 2,* and C Pooley, "Londongrad curbs will need robust enforcement," 1 March 2022, *Financial Times.* The English courts have shown a willingness to act robustly in cases involving foreign leaders who have amassed wealth in suspicious circumstances in the UK, see for example, E Midolo, "Mongolian leader barred from selling £111m London flat," 23 December 2020, *The Times,* in regard to a civil claim by the Mongolian government, see generally *ibid* at ns 107 and 108. International civil litigation, for a number of reasons, is well supported in the UK and, given the considerable fees charged by in particular City law firms, has been encouraged by the government and Corporation of the City of London, see for example, J Sharman, *Time for Change? The practicalities of*

more we need reliable financial intelligence. The extent to which countries are competent to collect, let alone analyse, relevant information and then deploy it effectively varies considerably. Even within the developed world, analytical resources are at a premium – particularly within government. The cost and resources required for the creation and operation of compliance systems within financial intermediaries able to supply raw information is a real burden for the most developed economies, particularly as this function has implications for regulatory and legal risk.[53] Given the opaque nature of the uses that this information is used for, there is a real debate as to the proportionality of the costs compared with the results that are achieved.[54] The burdens placed on those operating in the most developed economies are such that it is arguable

---

public-private collaboration against financial crime, (2022), Mischon de Reya LLP. Of course, it remains to be seen in many cases how much is left for the plaintiff after the lawyers, accountants, investigators and courts have taken their fees.

[53] The regulatory and legal risks to financial institutions for compliance failures are sometimes draconian and arguably disproportionate, see for example, "Standard Chartered fined $1.1bn after money laundering and sanctions failings," 20 April 2019, *The Guardian*. There are many examples where regulators have imposed extremely large financial penalties amounting to billions of pounds on financial institutions. The indirect costs and risks resulting from the need to implement compliance procedures is not always appreciated, see B Rider, *A new approach, Inaugural Conference, NACO,* UK Association of Compliance Officers, 23 October 1990. The imposition of compliance procedures is not just a result of specific legal and regulatory requirements, but might also be necessary to constitute a defence to allegations of, for example, complicity in bribery, see for example, section 7, UK Bribery Act 2010 and Part 3, Criminal Finances Act 2017 in regard to facilitating tax fraud. Furthermore, compliance obligations might well have legal implications in terms of the civil law, see for example, *Agip (Africa) Ltd v Jackson* [1991] Ch 547 and *Shah v HSBC Private Bank* (UK) Ltd [2012] EWHC 1283 (QB).

[54] We have already noted that the amount of suspect wealth actually interdicted as a result of these various mechanisms is minimal. If the primary justification for this approach is to deprive criminals of their ill-gotten gains or cut terrorist funding, then by any analysis the 'costs' are wholly disproportionate to these outcomes in any jurisdiction, including the USA. Punishing companies for compliance failures largely depends upon fines (see *supra* at n 53), which arguably harm those who have little control over those actually responsible in senior management, see B Rider, "Facilitators beware," 38 *The Company Lawyer*, (2017) 37, and B Rider, "Exposing the modesty of companies," 34 *The Company Lawyer*, (2013) 263. There is also a danger that in some cases, institutions may because of their importance in the economy be essentially beyond reach, see C Blackhurst, *Too Big to Jail, inside HSBC, the Mexican drug cartels and the biggest banking scandal of the century*, (2022), Macmillan. It is also debatable whether criminalizing banks and other financial institutions for 'mere' failures of compliance is compatible with promoting investor confidence.

that financial institutions from developing countries, lacking the resources and ability to pass on costs, are effectively disadvantaged and perhaps denied access. While the evidence may be debated, there are indications that intermediaries and in particular banks in the developed world have withdrawn or at least reduced their exposure to markets where compliance is less reliable and more problematic. The fear of disinvestment and the creation of legal, regulatory and cost barriers is real and well documented, and is discussed in this book.[55]

A diversity of approach?

Consequently, it remains to be seen whether the primary strategies of developed nations in addressing what seems to be an ever-expanding catalogue of concerns ranging from organized crime to oligarchs[56] is viable within developing countries and might serve to fragment the international financial system. While there are examples in some developing jurisdictions of considerable

---

[55]   See discussion in Chapter 8 of this book.

[56]   While there has long been concern about the extent to which wealth under the control of Russian oligarchs impacts adversely on the UK economy, it took the Russian invasion of the Ukraine to 'justify' legal intervention, see C Pooley, *supra* at n 52; P Lashmar, "Invasion of the rouble barons – how the Moscow mafiya gangs took a grip on London," 12 September 1999, *The Independent on Sunday* and Leading article, "Rotten Roubles, dirty Russian money is a threat to national security," 21 May 2018, *The Times*; T Burgis, *Kleptopia, How Dirty Money is conquering the world*, (2020), Collins; J Heathershaw *et al*, *The UK Kleptocracy problem – how servicing post-Soviet elites weakens the rule of law*, Chatham House, Royal Institute for International Affairs, December 2021. See also the 'racy' accounts in B Browder, *Freezing Order*, (2022), Simon & Schuster, and in particular, C Belton, *Putin's People*, (2020), Collins, Chs 11 and 13. While there has also been concern expressed about the significance of foreign purchasers of prestige UK property, in circumstances where there are reasonable suspicions as to the source of funds, there has been less appetite in government to intervene, see M Savage, "UK must not be a haven for dirty money," 28 July 2015, *The Times*, and P Aldrick, "Lack of hard evidence of money laundering doesn't mean City is clean," and "Study funds London's property market awash with laundered money," 22 June 2016, *The Times*. Concerns about China have tended to focus more on state-sponsored interventions and influence than financial penetration, see *supra* at n 21 and for example, L Brown, "China spying at blistering pace, warns head of MI5," and editorial comment, "China crisis" 7 July 2022, *The Times*, and C Parker, "China's secret police stations in the UK must be probed, says MPs," 27 October 2022, *The Times*.

experience and competence in developing and utilizing financial intelligence,[57] the vast majority do not have the competence and resources. Lending or even attempting to build capacity, given the political sensitivities, cannot be a panacea. Furthermore, it must also be remembered that in some developing countries, the holding and transfer of wealth may not be susceptible to the same kind of surveillance and monitoring that is feasible in a conventional Western banking system. Informal and unconventional mechanisms might well, in the circumstances, be far more viable, efficient and socially acceptable than traditional banking. Indeed, they may facilitate a significant and beneficial economic activity, such as the transfer of earnings by nationals working overseas.[58] Failure to appreciate the role and utility of such mechanisms in a society can be detrimental.[59] The assumption that methods of transferring and holding wealth that do not comport with Western notions of transparency and accountability are essentially suspect, has been damaging. For example, a senior analyst at Europol castigated Islamic financial institutions as money laundering facilities because of their traditional secrecy and accounting practices. This coloured attitudes to Islamic finance within a number of agencies and institutions, including MI5. Obviously, there are aspects of, for example,

---

[57] For example, the Directorate of Revenue Intelligence in India. Those policing agencies with a more military orientation have found it easier to accommodate intelligence, albeit not always appropriately or in a manner that has produced satisfactory results. The Royal Malaysian Police Force invested in the development of financial intelligence during the 1980s, but found it difficult to deploy and utilize given the almost inevitable political barriers and sensitivities. See and B Rider, "We need new weapons to beat these crimes," 21 September 1984, *Financial Weekly* and comments of the author in "Economic Crimes linked to terrorism," 9 March 1985, *The Times of India*.

[58] There are developing countries, such as the Philippines, where remittances from nationals working overseas contribute significantly to the domestic economy, see I Naar, "Cash remittances from overseas workers remain a lifeline for many in the Philippines," World (UAE), 16 June 2022, the amount remitted annually is estimate at over US$31 billion from over 1.7 million overseas workers, see Philippines Statistics Authority, 7 March 2022. There are also substantial remittances from those engaged in illicit activity. For example, it has been estimated that there are over 90,000 Filipinos involved in the sex trade in Japan. In addition to conventional mechanisms for remitting money there are numerous informal arrangements (see *ibid* n 60) some under the control of organized crime groups. The Philippine authorities and in particular the Bureau of Taxation has traditionally turned a blind eye to much of this, notwithstanding there have been instances of exploitation, fraud and loan sharking.

[59] See B Rider, "The Financial World at Risk – the dangers of organised crime, money laundering and corruption," 8 *Managerial Auditing Journal*, (1993) 3, and B Rider, "Anti-money laundering laws vital for Sri Lanka," 22 February 2002, *Daily News* (Sri Lanka).

the hawala that can be utilized by those who wish to be discreet in their financial dealings, but a sense of proportion and context is necessary.[60] The approach of many governments and their agencies, as well as intergovernmental initiatives, is not always helpful in this regard. We have already noted the dangers of transplanting rules that have been developed in one environment to another.[61] The same is equally true in regard to, for example, the obligations placed upon those who mind other people's wealth to 'know their customers' and conduct due diligence. Processes that are suited to residents of a developed, well-ordered metropolitan society may be wholly unworkable in the context of a developing rural economy.[62]

International cooperation – a level playing field?

Another very real issue in addressing the risks presented by economically motivated crime is the ability of law enforcement and judicial authorities to obtain meaningful cooperation from their counterparts in other countries. This is sufficiently problematic to constitute a real hurdle between developed jurisdictions, let alone those where the legal system is underdeveloped and under-resourced.[63] Competition for resources is always a problem within law enforcement, and understandably priority will often be given to promoting

---

[60]   See B Rider, "Fei Ch'ien laundries – the pursuit of flying money," 1 *Journal of International Planning*, (No 2) (1992) 77, continued (No 3); G Posner, *Warlords of Crime – Chinese Secret Societies*, (1988), Queen Anne Press at 221 *et seq*; Z Alwi, "Big threat from dadah money," 8 January 1992, *Business Times*, Malaysia, and in particular, C Blackhurst, "Dirty Money – secrets of the banks underground," (June 1984) *Business*, and reported comments of the author at 86. the problem of cash entering these networks, remains a problem, see J Simpson, "Woman took suitcases of dirty cash to Dubai," 29 July 2022, *The Times*.

[61]   See *supra* at note 15.

[62]   A practical issue in some developing countries, particularly in townships and rural economies, is the ability to specify with accuracy residential addresses. There is also the problem of establishing personal identity. Indeed, some of these issues are not confined to the developing world but have manifested themselves as issues in providing wider access to banking facilities in developed economies, for example to homeless or migrant workers.

[63]   Of course, the smaller the jurisdiction involved, the greater are likely to be the resource issues, the more so in the case of those who have deliberately promoted themselves as financial centres. Mention has already been made of the need for states to address a comprehensive range of legal needs and responsibilities regardless of their size, see *supra* at note 11.

and protecting the interests of those who fund the system and its agencies.[64] While there is a clear benefit to all in adequate policing of serious crime, no matter where it occurs and impacts, political realities augur in favour of priority being accorded to threats which attract most concern at home. It is also the case that some threats are more visible than others and dictate a higher priority. The physical harm that certain crimes engender inevitably mandates reactions within the justice system, perhaps to the detriment of addressing more insidious threats, such as corruption and fraud.[65] Many developing countries do not have adequate resources to protect their societies from even the most obvious threats and can therefore justify scant assistance to external concerns and requests. Indeed, prioritizing the concerns of agencies in the developed world over and above ensuring adequate policing at home is properly a matter for criticism.[66] The dilemma facing agencies in developing countries is often exacerbated by the terms upon which aid and training is offered.[67]

---

[64]   Criticism has been made of the use of resources to assist in the detection of crime in other jurisdictions. For example, senior officers in the Metropolitan Police were criticized for the resources which were used in exposing money laundering in the Caribbean in Operation Cougar in the mid-1980s. It was said that this was no concern of London ratepayers!

[65]   We have assumed in this chapter that corruption and the like are detrimental to society and the economy as an almost *a priori* precept, see for example, "Dirty money in the UK is harming more than our reputation," 7 December 2021, *Financial Times*, and Leader Comment, "Rotten Roubles, dirty Russian money is a threat to national security," 21 May 2018, *The Times*. On the other hand, it is appreciated that even in terms of development there is a debate to be had as to the balance of harm, see generally, R Fishman and M Golden, *Corruption, what everyone needs to know*, (2017), Oxford University Press, Ch 4 in particular. See also B Rider, "Policing Corruption and Economic Crime – How can we do better," 10 *Frontiers of Law in China*, (2015) 625, and B Rider, *Corruption, Economic Crime and Development*, (2017), Institute of African Studies, Russian Academy of Sciences.

[66]   Prioritizing the concerns of other governments, in this context, has been politically controversial in, for example, Jamaica, St Vincent, Samoa and Fiji. See for example, comment of the author, reported in "Drug crime fears here," 25 August 1986, *Fiji Sun*. See also comments of the author reported in C Batchelor, "The growing difficulty of catching international fraudster," 12 July 1984, *Financial Times*.

[67]   A justification sometimes made for providing training to foreign officers is that they will be more inclined to understand and prioritize the importance of responding to requests for assistance. Indeed, within law enforcement, trained overseas officers are often perceived as 'assets' of the agency extending assistance. On the other hand, there are also issues in seconding officers to overseas agencies, B Rider, *Commercial Crime and Financial Supervision* (1983) in Report for Meeting of Law Officers of Small Commonwealth Jurisdictions, Commonwealth Secretariat, Isle of Man; B Rider, *Economic Crime and the destabilization of small*

The Commonwealth 'experiment'

Returning to the era of the district officer, it is arguable that a facility – albeit far from perfect – existed, at least for the passing of information reinforced by some degree of commonality of approach. While the 'old boys' network had many weaknesses, there was a perception that it functioned rather more effectively, than, for example, the early forms of Interpol.[68] Indeed, in the late 1970s, investment was forthcoming from several Commonwealth governments to see whether some kind of network based on common heritage and values could be created to assist in particular the more vulnerable societies in addressing the threats posed by corruption and economic crime.[69] While

---

states (1985), Report of the Meeting of Law Officers of Small Commonwealth States, Commonwealth Secretariat and South Pacific Co-operation Council, Vanuatu, and B Rider, *Report on Economic Crime and the Risks to Small States* (1986), Commonwealth Secretariat (basis of Commonwealth initiative to protect economic stability of small states). See also comments of the author reported by C Tam, "Labuan plan carries risks, expert warns," 27 September 1990, *Business Times*, Malaysia.

[68]   See generally, F Bressler, *Interpol*, (1992), Sinclair, Pt 1. Commonwealth Law Ministers at their meeting in Winnipeg, Canada in 197, specifically stated that police force to police force cooperation in fighting economic crime did not work. There was concern as to the ability and willingness of ICPO-Interpol to recognize and address the priorities of developing countries, see B Rider, *The Promotion of Cooperation in Combating International Economic Crime in The Commonwealth* (1980), Report to Commonwealth Law Ministers; B Rider, *The role of ICPO-Interpol in promoting international cooperation in combating serious international crime* (1980), Report to Commonwealth Law Ministers, and D. Chaikin, *Mutual Assistance in Criminal Matters* (1983), Report to Commonwealth Law Ministers Meeting. In many respects ICPO-Interpol was overly focused on the issues of concern to European police forces reflecting its institutional history and funding. It also had a relatively narrow interpretation of its constitutional mandate to address ordinary crime.

[69]   The Legal Division of the Commonwealth Secretariat with the assistance of the Foreign and Commonwealth Office prepared a preliminary study in 1978 canvassing the establishment of a facility for co-operation alongside that of ICPO-Interpol and the Customs Co-operation Council. The Government of Hong Kong was a prime mover in this initiative, in part because of the security concerns discussed above, see B Rider, *Report on Commercial Crime in Hong Kong with recommendations for the establishment of a Commercial Crime Unit within the Legal Department of the Hong Kong Government and the creation of a specialised unit within the Royal Hong Kong Police Force* (1980), Submitted to the Attorney General of Hong Kong. The Commonwealth initiative supported and gave assistance in the establishment and development of special intelligence, investigative and prosecutorial agencies in a number of countries including Zambia, Zimbabwe, Ghana, South Africa, Mozambique, Malawi, Kenya,

essentially a Commonwealth initiative, it was by no means confined to the Commonwealth and enjoyed a measure of support from the US federal and state agencies as well as certain jurisdictions, such as the Philippines and Indonesia, which were surrounded by Commonwealth interests. The initiative was sanctioned at the highest levels in government and specifically endorsed by Commonwealth law ministers at three meetings.[70] While initially focused on fraud-related conduct, it was soon extended to corruption, money laundering and organized crime.[71]

Officials in this service were primarily based within the Commonwealth Secretariat, which afforded them individually and collectively diplomatic status[72] within all Commonwealth jurisdictions. While the core group of

---

Tanzania, Singapore, Malaysia, Australia, New Zealand, Fiji, Trinidad and Tobago, Sri Lanka and Malta. It also assisted in the development of similar agencies in a number of non-Commonwealth jurisdictions including the Philippines, Indonesia, Thailand, the Sudan, Turkey and Taiwan. Not all fared well, see for example, *Attorney-General of Hong Kong v. Reid* [1994] 11 All ER 1. Arguably elitism, in some instances, bred arrogance and corruption! Specialized units operating within the intelligence community, but supporting traditional policing and other agencies were not entirely new. The UK government established, for example, in Zambia in the late 1970s a Special Team on Economy and Trade (SITET), staffed in part by UK officers.

[70] See *Minutes of Commonwealth Law Ministers Meetings, Winnipeg 1977, Barbados 1979, Sri Lanka 19983 and Zimbabwe 1986*, Commonwealth Secretariat. There was also endorsement from Commonwealth Heads of Government, Finance Ministers and Home Affairs Ministers and at numerous regional meetings, see generally, "Commonwealth drive against dirty money," *Commonwealth Currents*, April 1982, 5, and B Rider, "Commonwealth Initiative against Commercial Crime," *Commonwealth Currents*, December 1983, 20. See also C Gunn, "Nations will crackdown on Mafia fraud," 18 March 1983, *Financial Weekly*, referring to the unit identifying £8 bn worth of fraud in its first year of operations and international ministerial support for the extension and expansion of its mandate, supported by the UK government and additional resources. See also B Rider, "We need new weapons to beat these crimes," 21 September 1984, *Financial Weekly*, and comments of the author, reported in A Khan, "Commonwealth Fights White Collar Crime," 6 December 1981, *National Weekend Magazine* (Kenya); 18 November 1981, *Times of Zambia*; 20 November 1981, *Daily News*, (Tanzania); 9 December 1981, *Otago Daily Times*, (New Zealand); 11 December 1981, *Tonga Chronicle*; 28 November 1981, *The Borneo Bulletin*; 9 December 1981, *Advocate – News*, (Barbados); 5 December 1981, *Umtali Post*, (Zimbabwe).

[71] B Rider, *Memorandum on Organised Crime* (1986), submitted to the Commonwealth Law Ministers, Meeting in Harare, Zimbabwe, *Memoranda*, Commonwealth Secretariat.

[72] Commonwealth Secretariat Act 1966, replicated in many Commonwealth jurisdictions. On the importance of diplomatic immunity for the unit see C Gunn, "International fraud crackdown," 15 January 1987, *London Daily News*.

experts was small, it was supplemented through secondments from police, security, intelligence, fiscal and prosecutorial agencies. Well before it became vogue, its mandate was essentially to develop intelligence and then intervene to disrupt criminal activity and minimize harm. While its staff operated internationally, primarily action was taken through designated liaison officers, appointed by law and finance ministers. As has already been pointed out, this was not confined to Commonwealth jurisdictions. For example, a senior Assistant Director in the US Federal Bureau of Investigation was designated at the federal level in the US. The network was not confined to those jurisdictions with a common law heritage. Of particular significance was the involvement of a number of European countries, including Switzerland,[73] Italy and the Netherlands. This initiative was supported by the ICPO-Interpol General Secretariat[74] and the Commonwealth unit fed intelligence and information into the Interpol network and promoted and facilitated its role in many developing countries.[75] Although essentially an intelligence facility, this ini-

---

[73]   Co-operation with Switzerland was at the time of crucial significance given the perception (in some measure unfounded) that a high percentage of dubious wealth ended up there. The unit developed a close relationship with the Swiss Federal Office of Police Matters in Berne and with police agencies in the cantons, particularly Geneva and Zurich. The unit assisted Swiss examining magistrates in pursuing their inquiries in a number of Commonwealth jurisdictions. It was with US law enforcement agencies that the unit had the closet working relationship, see for example, "Harare man wanted for $28m fraud," 20 August 1988, *The Herald* (Zimbabwe), and see C Batchelor, "The tough battle against crooks with a telex machine," 10 September 1985, *Financial Times*.

[74]   The head of the unit was designated an observer to ICPO-Interpol and the Secretary General of ICPO-Interpol issued a formal notice requesting all Interpol bureaus to cooperate with the unit, *Notice No 26/D3/RELCO/930*, 9 September 1982. There were similar arrangements with other organizations including the Customs Co-operation Council (particularly under *the Nairobi Convention on Mutual Administrative Assistance for the Prevention, Investigation and Repression of Customs Offences*, 9 June 1977), International Association of Airport and Seaport Police, (see for example, *Year Book, International Association of Airport and Seaport Police*, (1982), Cornhill Publications at 81 *et seq*) and the ICC-International Maritime Bureau. Where relevant, observer status was also extended by UN bodies and other inter-governmental organizations.

[75]   The unit was particularly supportive of the General Secretariat of ICPO-Interpol's early initiatives in regard to suspect wealth in the Caribbean and Africa. It put in place technical advisers to assist governments and their agencies and facilitated training. It also provided expert assistance in regard to financial frauds, see for example, C Wolman, "Shares sting that netted £100m," 31 January 1987, *The Financial Times*, and in particular commodity related frauds, see D Chaikin, "Something's stirring in the commodities jungle," 21 September 1984, *Financial Weekly*. Perhaps most significantly, it provided the senior management of the General Secretariat with access to ministers and an intergovernmental platform.

tiative brought in other resources, including expert technical assistance and training.[76] Indeed, it even provided assistance in the design and drafting of legislation and institutional responses.[77]

Throughout the decade that this initiative continued, thousands of interventions occurred in many countries. Very few attracted publicity[78] and many involved those in positions of power and influence. For example, a senior minister in one African country who had fallen under the 'spell' of a highly sophisticated advance fee fraudster with political connections in the UK was

---

Governments often regarded Interpol as essentially a 'club' for police forces, which constitutionally it was.

[76] This was supported by UNDP, the Commonwealth Fund for Technical Assistance and various national development funds including some outside the Commonwealth, such as the Swedish International Development Agency (particularly in regard to Mozambique) and US Aid. The Commonwealth initiative also involved the establishment of an international panel of vetted experts available to assist governments.

[77] The Legal Division of the Commonwealth Secretariat developed accession kits to facilitate in particular smaller and less well-resourced jurisdictions acceding and implementing international obligations and standards as well as model legislation and best practice, see for example, Commonwealth Secretariat, *Combating Money Laundering and Terrorist Financing*, (2005), Commonwealth Secretariat. It also provided technical assistance and drafting a role that was later strengthened by the Sir William Dale Centre for Legislative Studies within the Institute of Advanced Legal Studies, London, see B Rider, *Law at the Centre*, (1999), Kluwer, Ch 4. There was also considerable collaboration with other agencies such as the IMF, UNCTAD (see for example, *Maritime Fraud and Piracy*, Report of UNCTAD Secretariat, GE 85-57017, 23 October 1985 at Ch 4) and the WHO, see for example, B Rider, XXXV No 4, October 1983 UN Bulletin on Narcotics, 63, and B Rider, *Memorandum to the WHO Working Party on National Drug Initiatives* (1986), pp.40, in *Guidelines for National Drug Initiatives* (1987) WHO. The unit also provided technical and legal assistance to non-Commonwealth countries, including Indonesia, Thailand, Colombia and Taiwan.

[78] References to some of the cases handled by the Commonwealth Commercial Crime Unit (initially referred to as the Commonwealth Fraud Liaison Service) are referred to in the *Annual Reports* of the Commonwealth Secretary-General, see for example, *Annual Report 1983*, at 46 and *Annual Report 1987* at 64. See also C Batchelor, "The tough battle against crooks with a telex machine," 10 September 1985, *The Financial Times*; M Bose and C Gunn, *Fraud*, (1989), Unwin at 22, 189–93, 213 and 231; B Rider, C Abrams and M Ashe, *Guide to Financial Services Regulation*, (3rd ed, 1997), CCH at 429 *et seq*, and C Blackhurst, "Dirty Money – secrets of the bank underground," (June 1984) *Business*, 86 particularly at 90, and D Francis, *Contrepreneurs*, (1988) Macmillan. See also the Review of Legal Activities of the Commonwealth Secretariat, LMM (83) 2, published in 1983 Meeting of Commonwealth Law Ministers, Sri Lanka, February 1983, *Memoranda, Commonwealth Secretariat* at para 17 *et seq*.

provided with compelling information indicating this individual's relationship with criminals in the UK and USA and several frauds in other countries. The timely deployment of this information, which probably would not have stood up in court,[79] allowed the government concerned to retrieve a large deposit that it had made and cancel a project which may well have resulted in the collapse of that administration.[80] In another case, involving a small country in the Pacific, officers of the unit 'faced down' in front of the country's prime minister members of a yakuza organization that had all but 'captured' a significant slice of that country's economy.[81] This yakuza group was also involved

---

[79]   See reference to the author and such cases, C Batchelor, "Third World falls prey to bogus moneylenders," 8 May 1984, *The Financial Times*, and B Rider, "When crime knows no boundaries," 24 September 1986, *The Royal Gazette*, Bermuda, and *Bermuda Sun*. Information is not, of course, intelligence and neither are necessarily evidence, let alone admissible evidence. While information may properly inform a decision and intervention – for a variety of reasons, it might not qualify as evidence fit for a judicial determination. Of course, the reliability of information will depend on many factors, see, for example, B Rider, "Intelligent Investigations, the use and misuse of intelligence – a personal perspective," 20 *Journal of Financial Crime*, (2013) 293 and "Unit of Intelligence," *Commonwealth Currents*, April 1985.

[80]   Given that the fraudster had duped the minister into encouraging the country's president to befriend him, the termination of the project did not receive public attention. Indeed, coyness on the part of the victims of fraud is often a barrier to the fraudsters being properly exposed.

[81]   The primary export of the country in question was hardwood timber and the company controlled by a senior member of a yakuza group had acquired – with the government's support, an exclusive licence, see Reuter, "Yakuza make an investment in Western Business World," 9 January 1987, *Standard* (Hong Kong), and comments of the author in K Stafford, "Japanese gangs spread tentacles," 12 January 1987, Business Times (Malaysia), and G Posner, "Chasing the Triad Dragon," 5 March 1989, *Observer Magazine*, 30 at 39. See also in regard to another case involving an island state in the Pacific that lost one of its two hospitals as a result of fraud and organised crime, K Stafford, "White-collar crime on the rise world-wide," 13 January 1987, *The Star* (Malaysia), quoting the author "there is compelling evidence that some national economies, primarily in the Third World, are coming under attack from organised crime groups … and their political institutions have been significantly weakened and corrupted," and also the author's comments reported in A Hogg, "Gang bosses buying up Third World States," 12 May 1985, *The Sunday Times,* and see similarly, C Gunn, "Crime endangers or economies," 23 March 1984, and "Organised crime business threat," 21 March 1984, *Daily Telegraph*, referring to the authors address to the ICC and UNCTAD (specifically in regard to related UNCTAD initiatives, see "UNCTAD convinced of need for anti-fraud convention," *International Cargo Crime Prevention*, June 1985, 4), also J Conlon, "Top Don warns of threat from Chinese triads," 23 October 1991, *Cambridge Evening News*, and also "Commonwealth confronts the kings of crime," *Commonwealth Currents*, April 1985 7. Of course, these risks are

in an international commodity fraud which inveigled into its 'Ponzi type' scheme a number of ministers, senior politicians and officials throughout South East Asia. These well-connected and in some cases 'protected' gangsters were pursued at an intelligence level to Singapore, Malaysia, the Philippines, Hong Kong, Taiwan and then Australia and New Zealand. They were finally put out of business by the unit, working with the Australian and New Zealand authorities, in assisting an Australian TV network putting together and running a documentary chronicling their criminal activity.[82] While essentially a gigantic financial fraud, those at its core were also engaged in other forms of serious crime, including human trafficking[83] and prostitution. They did not hesitate to employ extreme violence against anyone who stood in their way.[84]

---

not confined to developing countries, see R. Ford, "Criminal gangs are running swathes of Britain says Theresa May," 12 June 2014, *The Times*, and generally, B Rider (ed), *A Research Agenda for Organised Crime*, (2023), Elgar, Ch 1.

[82]   See *Annual Report of the Commonwealth Secretary-General 1987*, at 65, and *Four Corners Documentary Report, Far East Fraud* (1987), and also on 24 October 1988, Australia.

[83]   The unit disrupted a number of trafficking operations in Singapore, Malaysia, Thailand, the Philippines and South Africa. Perhaps one of the most disturbing cases involved trafficking in children for unofficial adoption and possibly sexual abuse, see F Meigh, *The Jack Preger Story*, (1988), Tabb House. In many of these cases corrupt government officials were complicit. See G Ritchie, *Report of Human Trafficking and Sexual Exploitation*, (1983), Commonwealth Secretariat. A further complication in tracing in particular the 'stolen' children from Bangladesh to 'homes' in certain developed countries (such as the UK, Switzerland and France) was whether it was not better for them to live in a secure developed country irrespective of their family and cultural heritage. There was unconfirmed information that at least one of the 'stolen children' was killed on camera in the USA in a so-called 'snuff movie'. There is also evidence that children and others, particularly from developing countries, have been exploited and worse by organized criminals, working with medical practitioners, in the illicit human organ trade.

[84]   A female witness was abducted in New Zealand and was never found. On the unit's role in regard to triads see generally, S Triston Davis, Triads, *Sunday Morning Post Magazine*, Hong Kong, 19 November 1989, and D Connett, "Lone Voice amid Chinese Whispers," 17 June 1990, *The Independent*. While the unit did not court publicity, on occasion the media were helpful in exposing misconduct and in particular unrecognized threats. For example, until the late 1980s many in Japan were reluctant to accept the threat that yakuza organizations presented to other societies. The unit collaborated with Granada TV's World in Action team in a series of documentary programmes on organised crime to draw attention to the threat. The audaciousness of these groups was illustrated in the program on the yakuza commencing with a murder – filmed by yakuza gangsters see "Full of Eastern menace," 24 November 1987, *The Times*. Obviously, this occasioned controversy and diplomatic concern, not least from Japan.

In evidence to the Senate investigation in the USA into the BCCI affair,[85] the Office of the District Attorney of Manhattan claimed that it was intelligence from this service that alerted the authorities in New York to the extent of criminality within the BCCI.[86] The extent to which similar intelligence had been provided to other agencies, including the Bank of England – which at that time was responsible for supervision of the UK's banking system – was disputed by the UK government. Indeed, allegations were made in litigation before the English courts that the UK authorities had gone to considerable lengths to

---

[85]   See Senator J Kelly, *BCCI Affair, Report to the Committee on Foreign Relations, US Senate*, December 1992, 102d Congress, 2d Sess, Senate Print 102-140, and·see also S Bowers, "Out, damned BCCI," 5 November 2005, *The Guardian*. In regard to the BCCI see M Potts, N Kochan and R Whittington, *Dirty Money, the inside story on the BCCI – The World's sleaziest bank*, (1992), National Press, especially Chs 9,10 and 11; P Truell and L Gurwin, *BCCI – the inside story of the world's most corrupt financial empire*, (1992), Bloomsbury; J Ring Adams and D Frantz, *A full service Bank – how the BCCI stole billions around the world*, (1991), Simon & Schuster; N Kochan and B Whittington, *Bankrupt – the BCCI Fraud*, (1991), Rowland, particularly at 113 *et seq.*

[86]   See Senate Report *supra* at note 85, *BCCI's Reputation, Contributing to Initiation of Investigation* "During the July 4th weekend of 1989, several members of District Attorney Morgenthau's staff attended an international conference on money laundering in Cambridge, England. At the conference, they learned that BCCI had an international reputation for capital flight, tax fraud, and money laundering that far exceeded the conduct charged in the Florida indictment." The conference had been organized by the Commonwealth unit, which had previously also briefed officials in the Bank of England and law enforcement agencies in the UK see also Channel 4, *The Bandung File*, 17 January 1989, and T Day, "Officials warned of BCCI fraud in 1989," 28 July 1991, *Mail on Sunday*. This was relevant to the claims against the liquidator and Bank of England, brought by depositors and others who lost their money on the collapse of the BCCI, see "Bank of England faces £1 billion claim over money laundering scam," Insight, 25 August 2002, *Sunday Times*. In the claim against the Bank of England an important issue was exactly what the bank knew. The government, Bank of England claimed they had no relevant knowledge and this was more or less accepted by the courts (see *Three Rivers District Council et al,* [2006] EWHC 816, and R Miller, "Judge blasts BCCI legal team," 13 April 2006, *Daily Telegraph*, and Lord Bingham. It was also revealed in a document disclosed during the litigation that a former intelligence officer, employed by the financial regulator circulated information for the purpose of discrediting officers in the unit. In a letter to the author from Lord Neill of Bladen QC, Chair of the Committee of Standards in Public Life, observed, "you are plainly a BCCI casualty. As you know, there were others in the USA, who, being diligent seekers after the truth concerning BCCI, became targets for attack and suffered career blight or worse..." 21 February 2002. See also BBC Panorama documentary on the BCCI and spies, 29 July 1991.

protect the BCCI.[87] Of course, many – probably most – of these cases involved powerful individuals, who innocently or otherwise had been inveigled into the fraud. Indeed, the classical *modus operandi* of many of these confidence tricksters is to trade on the reputation and confidence in those who they inveigle into the fraud at an earlier stage. While many became themselves corrupt and part of the problem – promoting the fraud to others and/or frustrating investigation – a good many through their gullibility or wishful thinking actually believe in the fantasy.[88] The complexity – often deliberately created by the fraudster – can easily obscure the real facts and inevitably many factors and interests came into play.[89] In many of the so-called advance fee frauds, by the time the true facts are known, the crooks have been introduced to the president, senior ministers or given official positions – including diplomatic immunity.[90] The system has in effect invested in the fraudster and his or her

---

[87]   There were allegations (unsubstantiated) of government connivance – at different levels, although the heavily redacted official report of Lord Bingham in the main did not confirm this, see Bingham LJ, *Inquiry into the Supervision of the BCCI* (1992) HMSO. The report did, however, confirm that discussion did take place at the conference in Cambridge in regard to the BCCI, see 2.134 and also ITV News (Anglia) comments on the BCCI and Commonwealth Conference 23 October 1991, and see J Pope's letter, 24 February 1994, *The Times*, and that of Shridath Ramphal, 17 February 1994.

[88]   See *supra* at note 80. Some politicians took the view that the 'suggestion' that money that was being offered as investment, even by known criminals, could (indeed, should) be cleansed by being used to build hospitals, schools, roads and even government buildings in the developing world. The inability of US agencies to adequately address the drug problem in the US was not, for example, a reason to impede development of vital services and infrastructure, according to this view – which was not necessarily confined to politicians in developing countries! Indeed, the premier of an Australian state publicly expressed similar sentiments. Another practical difficulty, in terms of intervention was that in many cases it was unclear whether the promised investment actually existed or was part of an advanced fee fraud.

[89]   Politicians and even governments have been prepared to go along with projects even when they know or suspect that the money in question is tainted or even non-existent, see *supra* at n 80. Indeed, there is always the convenient argument that spending it on worthy projects 'cleanses' it! While not entirely convincing, there are examples, for instance the UK and US, where donation of suspect wealth to a charity has been accepted as rehabilitating it.

[90]   In the case of Dr Akah-Blay Miezah, an outstanding con-man, the Ghanian Government seemingly provided him with a diplomatic passport (Diplomatic Passport, Republic of Ghana No 0033899 issued by the Ministry of Foreign Affairs, 4 December 1986) and letters – for example, allegedly from G Koramteng-Addow, Attorney-General, 24 December 1975, F Beecham, Secretary, Supreme Military Council, 17 May 1976, Dr K Botchway, Minister of Finance, 12 February 1987, 24 April 1988 (attested by a English solicitor), 4 January 1989 and Capt Kojo Tsikata,

delusion. Consequently, it takes a very brave individual in that system to 'blow the whistle'. In many of the schemes that were essentially based on those who had been duped bringing in and sponsoring other victims, the early victims' only hope of recovering their own investment or reputation was to maintain the pyramid. Thus, they were effectively turned into aiders and abettors of the fraudster. The genius of such a fraud is that even victims appreciating the truth of the situation have a vested interest in the fantasy continuing. There is an institutionalized virtue in turning a blind eye to what is occurring.[91]

Deputy Head of State, 24 February 1990) (all or some of which may have been forged – but were not at the time denied), asserting that he was working with the then Minister of Finance. See T Shipman, "Fatman and the Nkrumah millions," 25 March 1987, *London Daily News*. Indeed, there were allegations that the then Ghanaian government operated almost a profit-sharing relationship with him. While never substantiated, there are still those who consider him a patriot, see *GhanaWeb, Sports News*, Thursday 11 August 2022, and the Namibian, News International, 14 January 2019. Some of those involved in the scams were in fact successfully prosecuted, with the aid of the Commonwealth unit in the USA, see for example, "Ghana Man accused of 14 year international swindle", 20 March 1986, *AP News*, and *US v R Ellis and J Bishop*, US District Court (eastern Pennsylvania), 14 April 1992. Blay Miezah and his associates were are able to inveigle into their fraud very senior people including former members of the US government and senior politicians in several other western countries. The fraud became so significant that whether the Oman Ghana Fund actually existed or not it had serious political implications. There were concerns that the 'saga' could contribute to Ghana's destabilisation and there was direct involvement from intelligence agencies which also muddied the waters.

91   It is surprising how far otherwise experienced and competent investors are prepared to suspend common sense remaining in and, indeed, furthering such schemes, even in the face of reality. See for example, F Ng, "Pyramid concern," 23 January 1992, *The Malay Mail*; J Oppenheimer, *Madoff with the Money*, (2009), John Wiley, and E Arvedlund, *Too Good to be True, the rise and fall of Bernie Madoff*, (2009), Portfolio, and generally, C Kindleberger, *Manias, Panics and Crashes*, (1996), John Wiley, and C Mackay, *Extraordinary Popular Delusions and the Madness of Crowds*, (1980), Harmony. The mania that gripped Albania in the 1990s did considerable harm to the economy, see "Troops mobilized to quell protests at Albanian fraud," 27 January 1997, *The Times*, and T Judah, "Mafia pick up the pieces in Albania,"16 March 1997, *Sunday Telegraph*, and also in Russia, C Freeland, "Russia's MMM fund president arrested in raid," 5 August 1994, and more recently see A Jonsson, *Why Iceland*, (2009), McGraw Hill – mention has already been made, albeit in another context, of the South Sea Bubble, see *supra* at note 40. Such schemes are often fuelled by dubious securities issued occasionally by those in government, for example the US $25 million each bearer bonds allegedly issued by the Indonesian Government, 27 October 1985, used as the 'basis' for an international fraudulent investment scheme.

Return to reality

The Commonwealth initiative was before its time. It was misunderstood and not appreciated by many within traditional law enforcement agencies.[92] Indeed, there was in some quarters a perception that it represented, at least in terms of approach, unwelcome competition.[93] The criticism of traditional responses to the threats posed, particularly to the more fragile developing economies, by economic crime from which the programme was born did not help. ICPO-Interpol was itself going through a period of self-doubt exacerbated by rivalry, at many levels, between what might be described as continental attitudes to policing and in particular policing priorities – typified by the domination of a French police culture, and increasing involvement from the English-speaking world and especially the US. While individuals with influence within the General Secretariat of Interpol who for personal and professional reasons wished to see more support from the US and in particular agencies such as the Federal Bureau of Investigation and Secret Service, found the Commonwealth a useful ally – particularly as its officials had access to ministers and purse strings, which police officers, no matter how senior, had, they were reluctant to take on board the concerns of the developing world. When senior officers from countries such as India were brought in, they were often marginalized if not patronised.[94] The personal attachment of many

---

[92] See generally B Rider, "Disrupting the disrupters," 7 *Journal of Money Laundering Control*, (2004) 119, and B Rider "The control of money laundering – a bridge too far," 5 *European Financial Services Law*, (1998) 27.

[93] There were those who claimed that it muddied the waters and undermined the traditional criminal justice system – albeit as Lord Roskill pointed out in his report on fraud, "the public no longer believes that (the criminal justice) system is capable of brining the perpetrators of serious fraud effectively and efficiently to book ..." he added that the overwhelming evidence he and his committee had seen proved that the public were correct, *Fraud Trials Committee Report*, (1986), HMSO, and see B Rider, *A Research Agenda for Financial Crime*, (2022), Elgar, Ch 1, and comments of the author in C Wolman, "City regulators fail to stop fraud," 23 November 1987, *Financial Times*.

[94] A good example, was the case of Inspector General Jyoti Trehan, see generally J Trehan, *Crime and Money Laundering, the Indian Perspective*, (2003), Kluwer. Notwithstanding this very experienced and senior officer's position in the All India Police Service and Central Bureau of Investigation on secondment to the General Secretariat, he was allocated a junior position in the general studies division. There were other examples of what, at the time, was considered discrimination. Insofar as ICPO-Interpol was essentially an association of traditional police agencies, see F Bressler, *supra* at n 68, there was not always scope for sensitizing the organisation to political issues. For example, the initial support within Interpol for Taiwan over and the People's Republic of China. There was

in the General Secretariat to the 'generosity' of police agencies in Taiwan complicated relations with China. In the result, the Commonwealth initiative became less attractive to those who by then had managed to take the reins of the organization away from the French.

Many within the intelligence community distrusted what they saw as essentially a law enforcement orientation to the operation of the unit. For example, it was said that there was disquiet in certain circles that the unit was drawing too much attention to the criminal activities of people in the BCCI at a time when western intelligence agencies had assets within the BCCI.[95] The disruption by the unit, working with US and Swiss police of an arms-trafficking operation, also resulted in embarrassment. The exposure of money laundering facilities – of interest to, in particular, the CIA – was another problem. The interception of an arms shipment to an island the Pacific was yet another. It was also the case that some of those of interest to the unit were well placed to complain and even assert that the unit was undermining national sovereignty.[96] Perhaps the main strength of the unit – the fact that it sat within an intergovernmental organization[97] – turned out to be its Achilles' heel. When the time to 'clip its wings' came, those who supported its activities had no direct way of influencing the outcome.[98] There was no ministerial structure with political accounta-

---

95   also a reluctance to involve agencies concerned with aspects of law enforcement, such as anti-corruption authorities, but which were not conventional police forces. This was also a serious issue in the development of financial intelligence and to some degree remains a problematic issue, see *supra* at n 51. Things have improved, see F Madsen, *Interpol – Transnational Organised Crime*, (2009), Routledge, but perhaps not as much as they should, see M Bennetts, "Interpol is failing victims of Kremlin war crimes," 13 October 2022, *The Times*, and in particular the Times editorial "Undue Influence, Interpol is increasingly being used to target political opponents by repressive regimes," 14 October 2022, *The Times*.
      See *supra* at note 85 Senator J Kelly's report, at Ch 11, BCCI, CIA and Foreign Intelligence.

96   See *ibid* at note 114.

97   An informal 'ministerial' committee was established to 'support' the unit under the chairmanship of the Attorney-General of Bermuda, with the Attorney Generals of Singapore, Malaysia, Hong Kong, South Africa and Cyprus. Within the Secretariat the unit usually reported to one of the Deputy Secretary-Generals.

98   It has been claimed that elements within the US intelligence community in London were the prime movers given the unit's involvement in compromising their interests, see *supra* at notes 85, 86 and 87. There were matters in regard to which, for example, the London station of the CIA appeared to have different perspectives than for instance the US Justice Department and certainly law enforcement officials further down the 'food chain' such as *supra* at 90 and *ibid* at n 114. The situation was also complicated by 'rivalries' and personal jealousies within the Commonwealth Secretariat itself, see for example, Prufrock,

bility. In the result the mandate to address cases let alone intervene was quietly shelved and the initiative largely forgotten.

"Colleges of Crime," 11 August 1991, *The Sunday Times*. There was also a feeling that some senior officials had been 'wrong footed' by certain of the unit's investigations and the publicity that they had attracted (see for example, A Jack, "Sir Sonny had a special loan," 16 February 1994, *Financial Times*, and letter from Shridath Rampal, "basis of contacts between Sir Sonny Ramphal and BCCI," 17 February 1994, *Financial Times*). A similar strategy involving further unfounded allegations against members of the unit were circulated by a former MI5 officer, working for Mohamed Al Fayed in his campaign to discredit an investigation by the Trade and Industry Select Committee, see *First Report of the Select Committee on Standards and Privileges*, Session 1997–98, Appendix 33, sub-appendix 4, *Fayed's attempts to intimidate members of the Select Committee on Trade and Industry, witnesses and a Special Adviser* (1990), Published by order of the House of Commons, see also *Letter* from B Rider, 11 February 1997, to the Committee in Appendix 86. See also T Bower, *Fayed the Unauthorized Biography*, (2001), Pan, 263 et seq, C Wolman, "Harrods bosses may face smear charges," 18 August 1991, *The Mail on Sunday*, and letter from the Solicitor General to Sir Kenneth Warren MP, Chairman of the Select Committee on Trade and Industry, 19 February 1992 stating that while a prosecution could not be brought on the admissible evidence, "what occurred was disgraceful." It has become increasingly common for those under investigation for misconduct to attack the integrity of those confronting them. For example, the Bureau of Investigation and Intelligence established in the Philippines with technical assistance from the US and UK, because it proved effective in highlighting corruption, was disbanded after its budget was slashed and unproved allegations made against its senior management. Attempts to discredit individuals including senior Interpol officers have occurred including the planting of illegal drugs (in Israel, Albania and Nigeria) and firearms (France and Italy). Indeed, a senior member of the Commonwealth unit was arrested in New Zealand on entirely false claims that he had flown from London with an unauthorized firearm. The last French Secretary-General of Interpol allegedly was subject to a dirty tricks campaign. Of course, some allegations are justified, albeit there might be other agendas than the mere pursuit of justice, see for example the arrest and conviction for bribery in China of Vice Minister Meng Hingwei who had been elected President of Interpol at the 85th General Assembly in Bali, 2016, see C Bodeen, "Ex Interpol President went missing for months indicted on bribery charges in China," 10 May 2019, *The Independent*, and "Meng Hongwei confesses to bribery in China trial," 20 June 2019, *The Guardian*, and also in regard to another senior officer, D Tang, "Xi's purge on corruption snares his loyal enforcer," 26 August 2021, The *Times*. Nonetheless, false and distorted information has become a very effective and cheap weapon in the hands of the unscrupulous – official and unofficial – see for a recent example, C Wheeler, "Dirty dossiers on S&M and affairs as rivals for leadership turn to dark arts," 10 July 2022, *The Sunday Times*. Sadly the media is not always sufficiently well informed, robust or for that matter independent.

As we have indicated, in many ways this initiative was and remains before its time. There was not a wide understanding of the importance of addressing the wealth behind crime and terror, and law enforcement had not really discovered the virtues of disruption as a strategy.[99] Nonetheless, the answer for many fragile economies must surely involve supranational protection delivered at an early stage before harm occurs and confidence in leadership is lost. While many have advocated developing international criminal law,[100] for the developing world this provides few answers. It is too limited, too slow and relatively inaccessible. As Commonwealth law ministers recognized in 1977[101] at their meeting in Winnipeg, police force to police force cooperation does not work, and for so many reasons Interpol is of limited relevance. Multi-agency interventions orientated to prevention and loss minimization are what is required, if vulnerable and potentially unstable societies are to be given any hope of meaningful protection.

---

[99]   Regulators did understand the need to act prudentially and proactively, see B Rider, *Commercial Crime and Financial Supervision*, (1983), in Report for Meeting of Law Officers of Small Commonwealth Jurisdictions, Commonwealth Secretariat, Isle of Man. However, while the unit worked closely with agencies in the US at state and federal level and securities and corporate commissions in Australia and Canada, at the time there was still a debate in the UK as to whether we needed an official regulator, see for example, B Rider and E Hew, "The Regulation of Corporation and Securities Laws in Britain – the beginning of the real debate," 19 *Malaya Law Review*, (1977) 144; B Rider (ed), *The Regulation of the British Securities Industry*, (1979), Oyez; B Rider, *Insider Trading*, (1983), Jordans, Ch 3, and B Rider, D Chaikin and C Abrams, *Guide to the Financial Services Act 1986*, (1987), CCH, particularly Chs 1 and 2. Things have moved on, see B Rider, S Bazley, K Alexander and J Bryant, *Market Abuse and Insider Trading*, (4th ed, 2022), Bloomsbury, Chs 3 and 6.

[100]   See R Durrieu, *Rethinking Money Laundering and Financing of Terrorism in International Law*, (2013) Nijhoff; G Stessens, *Money Laundering – A New International Enforcement Model*, (2000), Cambridge University Press, and see M Wolf, "World needs an Anti-Corruption Court," 147 *Daedalus*, (2018) 147. There have, of course, been very significant developments in international and humanitarian law in holding individuals personally accountable, see for example, P Sands, *From Nuremberg to the Hague, the future of international criminal justice*, (2003), Cambridge University Press, and R Burbach, *The Pinochet Affair*, (2003), Zed, however, it remains to be seen how viable the development of meaningful direct personal liability for corruption, fraud and misappropriation, at the international as opposed to the transnational level is. Perhaps the most likely developments will be in the obligation of the state to protect and in relation to the environment, see generally, A Bellamy, *The Responsibility to Protect*, (2009), Cambridge University Press. Of course, international law plays a significant role in supporting domestic law see N Boister, *An Introduction to Transnational Criminal Law*, (2012), Oxford University Press.

[101]   See *supra* at note 70.

It is difficult to conceive where in the firmament of international and regional agencies such a facility is tenable.[102] While there have been attempts to facilitate and support intelligence initiatives against organized crime[103] in the IMF, these have been limited by the very mandate of the organization.[104] Of particular interest is the potentially important initiative of the World Bank and its family of assisting states to pursue stolen assets. The Star programme, as it is called, while not entirely novel, as the Commonwealth attempted to use the civil law to

---

[102]   It is important to note that the work of the Commonwealth Secretariat in the wider area of criminal justice continues, particularly in regard to the dissemination of legal information, the promotion and operation of Commonwealth schemes, such as for the rendition of fugitives and in promoting human rights.
   The appointment in 1990 of Professor Bill Gilmore, Professor International Criminal Law at the University of Edinburgh to head what was left of the initiative was helpful in emphasizing its more academic and non-interventionalist role. See W Gilmore, *Dirty Money*, (1995), Council of Europe. The important contribution of the unit in networking and profiling issues in regard to economic crime was continued, to some degree, by the Centre for International Documentation on Organised and Economic Crime (CIDOEC) established in 1988 in Cambridge and through the annual Cambridge international symposia on economic crime, see www.crimesymposium.org. Much of the training, research and legislative studies role was taken up by the Institute of Advanced Legal Studies, see B Rider (ed), *Law at the Centre*, (1999), Kluwer, Chs 4, 8 and 18, but see also R Rose, *Commonwealth Legislative Drafting Manual*, (2017), Commonwealth Secretariat.

[103]   Specifically in regard to the fostering of financial intelligence agencies in, for example, the Pacific.

[104]   Over the last two decades the World Bank, IMF and other intergovernmental organizations have become far more engaged in addressing the threats presented by corruption and economic crime. World Bank President James Wolfowitz emphasised the importance of intergovernmental action in 2005 and committed the World Bank to taking a stand, see H Marquette, "The World Bank's fight against Corruption," 13 *Brown Journal of World Affairs*, (2007) 27. There was a time when such issues were considered to be properly within the domestic competence of governments and that it was inappropriate for international organizations to become involved. Of course, there remain profound issues of sensitivity given that many issues might be described as involving 'crimes of the powerful'. Furthermore, international bodies have had their own scandals to contend with.

pursue fraudsters and the like,[105] points in a direction that is at least hopeful.[106] The results of the Star programme have been limited, but it does not stand alone, and similar initiatives have been undertaken by governments alone or in collaboration. Commonwealth law ministers were encouraged to endorse and facilitate the use of all weapons within the legal armoury in promoting and protecting integrity in 1980.[107] The Commonwealth initiative against economic crime, as has been mentioned, involved technical and other assistance, including investigative assistance, in identifying and pursuing bribes and misappropriated property. Indeed, this approach has even been advocated for China as

---

[105]   See for example, L Sealy, *The Enforcement of Civil Liability in regard to Commercial Crime and Corporate Abuse* (LMM (83) 17, Paper to Commonwealth Law Ministers Meeting, Sri Lanka 1983, Commonwealth Secretariat. See also for the potential for civil liability in cases of misconduct, B Rider,
"Amiable Lunatics and the Rule in Foss v. Harbottle," *Cambridge Law Journal*, (1978) 270; B. Rider, *Insider Trading*, (1983), Jordans, at 311 *et seq*, and B Rider and M Ashe, *The Fiduciary, the Insider and the Conflict*, (1995), Sweet & Maxwell, Ch 12. Note the significant developments in the common law facilitating civil recovery of stolen assets, discussed in B Rider, S Bazley, R Alexander and J Bryant, *Market Abuse and Insider Dealing*, (4th ed, 2022), Bloomsbury, Chs 2, 6, 8 and 15; B Rider, "Blunting the sword of justice," 19 *Journal of Financial Crime*, 324 and B Rider, "A simple approach to justice," 21 *Journal of Financial Crime*, (2014) 379. Of course, there are always problems with empowering victims, see L De Koker, B Rider and J Henning, *Victims of Economic Crime*, (1999), University of the Free Stat, particularly Ch 11.

[106]   See B Rider, "Corruption should not pay," 7 *Journal of Financial Crime*, (1999) 7, B Rider, "The crusade against money laundering," in *Politica Criminal Derechos Humanos Y sistemas Juridicos en el Siglo XX1* (2001) Depalma, also published as an occasional paper by the CALI (Argentine Centre for International Affairs) and B Rider, "Probing Probity – A Discourse on the Darkside of Development," in, S. Schlemmer-Schulte and K.Y. Tung (eds), *Liber Amicorium, Ibrahim Shihata*, (2001), Kluwer. See also S Ali, *Taking the Profit Out of Crime,* National Integrity Action, (2014), Government of Jamaica.

[107]   There has been some interest in the development of enforcement mechanism outside the traditional criminal law, such as civil enforcement and civil offences, see B Rider, "Civilising the Criminal Law – The use of civil and Administrative Proceedings to Enforce Financial Services Law," 3, *Journal of Financial Crime*, (1995) 11; B Rider, Civil Sanctions," 5 *Journal of Financial Crime*, (1997) 110, and B Rider, "Civilising the Law – the use of civil proceedings to enforce financial services law in the United Kingdom," in D Feldman and F Meisel (eds), *Corporate and Commercial Law: Modern Developments*, (1996), Lloyds of London Press, but see also B Rider, "Presumption of Innocence," 4 *Journal of Money Laundering Control*, (2001) 208. Another important development has been the use of deferred prosecution agreements see generally B Rider, 'New and Not so new strategies in fighting financial crime" 3 *Journal of Law, Governance and Society*, (2018) 1, and see B Rider, "Corruption – the sharp end of governance," in A Ali, *Risky Business – perspectives on corporate misconduct*, (2010), Caribbean Law.

part of its campaign against corruption.[108] While government agencies can if they so choose greatly assist in rendering viable asset recovery litigation, there are limits. Notwithstanding the importance attached to asset recovery as a tool in fighting corruption in the United Nations Convention against Corruption (UNCAC), there are practical and legal limits.[109] The fostering of asset recovery actions by private actors possibly with third party funding is an important development, but no silver bullet.

In attempting to deliver protection and in particular capacity to the developing world, there is the obvious problem that in addressing sophisticated criminals and in particular fraud, most developed jurisdictions have fared poorly. With Britain described as the fraud capital of the world, not to mention others dubbing the City of London as the world's pre-eminent money laundering centre,[110] how qualified is the UK to offer, at the official or private level, expertise to the developing world? It is not surprising that some take the view that physicians should first heal themselves! It is sadly the case that over the

---

[108]   See B Rider, H Yan and Li Hong Xing, *The Prevention and Control of International Financial Crime*, (2020), People's Bank of China (published in Chinese); B Rider, "Policing Corruption and economic crime – how can we do it better? 10 *Frontiers of Law in China*, (2015) 625; B Rider, "When Chinese Whispers become shouts," 20 *Journal of Financial Crime*, (2013) 136; B Rider, *Old Weapons for New Battles – the Role of Stewardship in the Development of the Common Law in its fight against Corruption and Self-Dealing* (pp. 33 to 71) in Centre of Anti-Corruption Studies (2009) ICAC, Hong Kong, and B Rider, *Organized Economic Crime* (In Chinese), (1999), Peking University Law Journal, 1–12. Specialised training was provided to judges and prosecutors on asset tracing and recovery by the Institute of Advanced Legal Studies in the mid-1990s and direct technical and legal assistance was provided in several cases involving serious corruption.

[109]   See for example the discussion in B Rider, "Protecting our economies and re-enforcing integrity in the financial system – an analysis of new and alternative strategies," in C Yen (ed), *Yearbook of the Taiwanese Society of International Law* (2016), TSIL, and in particular, K Stephenson *et al*, *Barriers to Asset Recovery – an analysis of the key barriers and recommendations for action*, (2011), Stolen Asset Recovery Initiative, World Bank, and M Ashe and B Rider (eds), *International Tracing of Assets* (2 vols) (1997), FT Law and Tax. For the emphasis that is being placed on investigating (occasionally interdicting) unexplained wealth see, B Rider, "Unexplained Wealth," 26 *Journal of Financial Crime*, (2019) 2, and "What price integrity,"10 *Journal of Financial Crime*, (2002) 103 and see *supra* at n 52.

[110]   See for example the comments of Sir Ivan Lawrence QC, former chair of the Home Affairs Committee, House of Commons in the Foreword, B Rider (ed), *Research Agenda for Financial Crime*, (2022), Elgar, and B Rider, "Fraud – how serious are we?" 42 *The Company Lawyer*, (2021) 299, and "Business as usual?" 42 *The Company Lawyer*, 1; "See no evil, hear no evil and certainly speak no evil," 34 *The Company Lawyer*, (2013) 163; "A Serious Fraud," 31 *The Company Lawyer*, (2010) 381.

years the level of practical and relevant expertise that has been made available overseas through UK development agencies has not always been effective or, for that matter, competent. The perception, if not necessarily the reality, is that retired police officers, sometimes with minimal and dated experience, are most available, notwithstanding their ignorance of the local context. Analytical expertise is very limited within UK agencies and in practice is rarely shared. Attitudes have changed more recently and the concern to 'justify' development aid at least in part with the UK's security priorities has arguably improved the level and competence of technical assistance, as has subcontracting programmes to external providers.[111]

The benefits that serving personnel and their agencies can obtain through limited periods of secondment and collaborative programmes, in terms of capabilities, understanding and cooperation, should not be underestimated.[112] However, there have always been practical issues within organizations in releasing serving personnel for overseas assignments. That there is a parochial attitude in many agencies, militating against meaningful assistance and even cooperation, has been long been a hurdle. Resources are always limited and obviously organizations have their own priorities which, even if extending to providing international assistance and support, are often trumped by more proximate and immediate concerns. For the key skills required in addressing the issues that we are discussing, there is not only real competition within government service, but also with the private sector. The more that financial institutions are placed in the front line in addressing the policing of money laundering, terror-related finance, economic sanctions and economic crime, the more they require expertise in their compliance structures. This expertise is primarily sourced from the public sector. In the result, there is a persistent drain of relevant expertise from government to banks and, as we expand the responsibility of all commercial actors to 'police' corruption, to the business world. Developing countries are faced with the additional problem of having to try and meet the relevant international standards for compliance in their own financial and commercial institutions, while also attempting to provide and sustain this expertise within their agencies for both domestic and international purposes. It is hardly surprising that few succeed in either respect. Indeed, multinational financial institutions value contextual expertise and often compound the situation by recruiting such expertise, as exists, in the

---

[111]   See generally I Kerusauskaite, *Anti-corruption in International Development*, (2018), Routledge, and N Kochan and R Goodyear, *Corruption*, (2011) Palgrave.
[112]   See, however, *supra* at note 67 and the subsequent commercialization of these relationships might not be as positive.

developing world. Similar compliance-related skills are also not just required in the context of traditional crime and terror, but are increasingly required in relation to establishing good governance, corporate social responsibility and environmental protection.[113]

What is clearly required, if our current strategies are to be sustained, is far more training and retention of expertise within the general public sector and particularly in developing countries. This has been recognized to a limited extent by the United Nations and organizations such as the Egmont Group of Financial Intelligence Units. However, international attempts to provide and foster relevant training in areas such as fraud and corruption interdiction have not fared well and have suffered many of the practical issues associated more broadly with international technical assistance. This in part reflects whether in fact sufficient expertise exists and is susceptible to sharing and whether those involved are truly competent and committed. Intelligence and in particular analytical training is a difficult and potentially costly process, even within developed countries.

Would many of these issues be at least partly resolved by the sharing of more information and intelligence and of supranational handling of such? Agencies are rightfully cautious about sharing information, let alone information that has been developed into intelligence. Even if there are legal gateways enabling this, there will be concerns about sources being compromised and potential liability. The use of information for purposes other than which it has been provided is a perennial concern, as is the compromising of investigations and other interventions. For example, in one case involving corruption, money laundering and illegal arms trafficking information provided to a Commonwealth country in the Caribbean, at the highest level, by US and UK agencies was handed immediately to individuals in regard to whom Interpol had already issued a number of Red Notices. As a result of this disclosure, an undercover US agent was exposed, another badly injured and officials, including the then Secretary-General of Interpol and an examining magistrate,

---

[113]   There is similar concern in regard to the need for compliance in the context of Islamic financial services, see generally B Rider and C Nakajima, "Corporate Governance and Supervision – Basle Pillar 2," in S Archer and R Karim (eds), *Islamic Finance – The Regulatory Challenge*, (2007), Wiley; B Rider, Ch 3 in *Strategies for the development of Islamic Capital Markets*, (2011) IFSB and Asian Development Bank; B Rider, *Islamic Financial Law – Back to Basics in The Changing Landscape of Islamic Finance*, (2010), Islamic Financial Services Board, and in particular, B Rider, "Corporate Governance in Financial Institutions offering Islamic Financial Services," in C Nethercott and D Esienberg (eds), *Islamic Finance – Law and Practice* (2nd ed, 2020), Oxford University Press.

threatened with defamation suits. Indeed, aspects of this matter resulted in lit-igation before the House of Lords in the UK and European Court of Justice.[114] In another case involving allegations of organized criminal activity in the UK, a request for information communicated to the appropriate police agency in China was in the hands of those suspected in London – within 20 minutes of it being sent. There are, of course, many other examples, involving the falsi-fication of information and its use to frustrate rather than facilitate effective action. Where there is a greater likelihood of those to whom the information relates being able to corrupt or simply frustrate appropriate interventions, caution and circumspection are all the more important. Whether the creation of a facility, rather like that established by the Commonwealth, is a preferred way of protecting developing countries – at least to some degree – is worthy of discussion, but in reality some way off.

We have already mentioned the importance of countries having the legal capacity through their own laws and institutions to protect themselves. Technical assistance in this process is important, but again something which requires regard to the total environment within which the law and its proce-dures is required to operate. Legislative drafting and processing of legislation is time-consuming and requires a level of expertise which is not widely available in developing countries. Resources for the creation of legislation, let alone its proper implementation, are limited even in the most developed jurisdic-tions. As we have already noted, smaller and less developed states still have much the same needs in terms of substantive law than their much bigger and well-endowed neighbours. While to some extent these needs can be addressed

---

[114]   *Owens Bank v Fulvio Braco*, House of Lords [1992] 2 AC 443, Court of Appeal, [1992] 2 WLR 127 and 15 April 1991, *The Times*, and Sir Peter Pain, High Court, 8 January 1991, *The Times*. See also EUECJC-129/92, 20 January 1994, [1994] 1 All ER 336. See in particular, C Wolman, "Storm hits offshore bank," 4 August 1991, *The Mail on Sunday*, referring to the author. There were aspects of this matter related to the collapse of the Bank Ambrosiano, see P Willan, *The Last Supper, the Mafia, the Masons and the killing of Roberto Calvi*, (2007), Robinson; D Yallop, *In God's Name, an investigation into the murder of Pope John Paul 1*, (1984), Pan; L Gurvin, The *Calvi Affair*, (1984), Pan; C Raw, *The Money Changers*, (1992), Harvill; P Willan, *Puppet Masters – the political use of terrorism in Italy*, (1991), Constable, Ch 3; J Cornwall, *A Thief in the night*, (1989), Viking; L di Fonzo, *St Peter's Banker – Michele Sindona*, (1983); R Cornwell, *God's Banker, the life and death of Roberto Calvi*, (1984) Unwin. and R Holt, *The Vatican Connection*, (1982), Holt, and in particular reports in *The Mail on Sunday*, 27 May 2012 and see Obituaries: Flavio Carboni, 10 Feburary 2022, *The Times* and also T Kington, "Top food critic masterminded Italy's deadliest terror attack," 6 February 2021, *The Times*. See also C Sterling, *The Mafia – the long reach of the international Sicilian Mafia*, (1990), Hamish Hamilton at Ch 12 in regard to Sidona.

by borrowing specific laws and by the use of templates, implementation and administration are rather different issues.

There are, of course, many other areas of importance to the sustainable development of states than those referred to here. We have tended to focus on what many would see as the dark side. On the other hand, it is activity in the shadows that has the potential to do most damage to the stability and, thus, the security of developing countries. The preamble to the United Nations Convention against Corruption emphasizes this, and while there is limited academic testament, anecdotal evidence from around the world manifestly supports this view.[115] Indeed, even simply in terms of providing countries with a plausible excuse for reducing aid, perceived levels of corruption and self-dealing are often called in aid. Whether in societies where most survive at subsistence, these issues weigh heavily in the balance, can be debated. Indeed, there is an argument that integrity is itself a luxury. However, what is clear is that in countries where corruption is endemic and crime and exploitation are the order of the day, notwithstanding the tendency of criminals to monopolization, there is profound waste – at least of human aspiration. There is a need for caution in trusting our Western tools often based on transparency, as perhaps only in some relatively privileged societies does transparency actually facilitate accountability.[116] Merely appraising the weak and the disadvantaged of the depths of their exploitation, without empowering them to do anything about it is scant contribution to their fate.[117] Obviously, however, there are limits as to the legitimacy of external intervention, even perhaps from an armchair.

---

[115]   See generally, B Rider (ed), *Corruption, the enemy within,* (1997), Kluwer, Ch 16; B Rider, *Corruption, the Third World perspective,* (3 November 1987), Third International Anti-Corruption Conference, Published Papers, Government of Hong Kong. We have already noted that many of these concerns are not limited to under-developed economies. Consider, for example, the impact of the front-page headlines – G Odling, "Thousands of corrupt police on our streets," 2 November 2022, *Daily Mail.* Referring to the UK.

[116]   See B Rider, *Corruption, Economic Crime and Development,* Published Paper, Three Is initiative, US Department of State and Asian Development Bank, Manila (2012), and B Rider, "Too much sunlight can damage your health," 17 *Journal of Money Laundering Control,* (2014) 126, and B Rider, "The price of sunlight," 1 *International Journal of Disclosure and Governance,* (2004) 208. A good example is the Philippines where journalists are often able to expose corruption, but nothing much seems to happen.

[117]   To the extent that this occasional frustration and a sense of hopelessness may serve to undermine stability. Indeed, one of the reasons that international collaboration in fighting corruption, in some places may be inhibited – is that there may be those who have a vested interest in perpetuating a ruling elite in which it has made an investment, or at least sees as a relatively predictable partner. See for

What we hope is that those in the academy will become more mindful of their capacity and thus, arguably, responsibility to engage rather more in the analysis and discussion of the issues canvassed here. Development studies is a vital tool for facilitating the sustainable development with justice, for so many. This present discussion, albeit focused, perhaps too much so, will hopefully contribute to providing a platform for much more thought, engagement and hopefully empowerment. As Sir Shridath Ramphal[118] used to and still emphasizes, in this highly interdependent world, there is, in terms of consequences for us all, no divide between the developed and the developing; we all sail in the same ship.

---

example, R Spencer, "Ethical foreign policy has tied us in knots, autocratic allies have made Britain look foolish in its claimto put human rights front and centre," 6 July 2022, *The Times*, see also E Lucas, "Criminal regimes are biggest threat to West- democratic countries are in a fight for survival against kleptocracies, the merchants of sleaze," 24 May 2021, *The Times*. We have already touched upon similar issues in the context of the BCCI, see *supra* at notes 86 and 87. While there is much to be gained by international and in particular supranational initiatives, the world is clearly not interested, see for example, S Froomkin, "World agency needed to fight growing white-collar crime threat," 15 January 1987, *The Royal Gazette*, Bermuda.

[118]   See Shridath Ramphal, "Wither our world – a reflection by Shirdath Ramphal," 28 September 2022, *The Cleaner*. This philosophy was very much at the centre of his stewardship of the Commonwealth Secretariat for many years as its Secretary-General. On the notion of interdependence in the law see M Saloman, *Global Responsibility for Human Rights*, (2007), Oxford University Press, Ch 2.

2　Stability, security and sustainable development

Ingrida Kerusauskaite

Illicit financial flows, serious organized crime, corruption, tax evasion and other economic crimes are more salient today than ever. With Russia's invasion of Ukraine, many jurisdictions have stepped up their game against economic crime more broadly. The UK introduced a new Economic Crime Bill to enhance measures to combat ill-gotten Russian money being invested in the country, including establishing a register of foreign owners of property in the country and facilitating the use of unexplained wealth orders by the authorities, and is taking steps to reform Companies House.[1]

The Biden administration has made significant progress in setting out a Strategy on Countering Corruption and curbing illicit finance domestically, bilaterally and multilaterally with accompanying investments and focus on mainstreaming a focus on anti-corruption in development work.[2] This includes the creation of a taskforce to support the implementation of the strategy and mainstream corruption considerations across the US Agency for International Development (USAID) policy and programming. Accordingly, USAID's FY 2023 budget highlights fighting transnational corruption and advancing corruption as the first key aim of the budget.[3] Furthermore, the administration has designated corruption as a core national security priority.[4]

---

[1]　'Government Takes Landmark Steps to Further Clamp down on Dirty Money', *GOV.UK* <https://www.gov.uk/government/news/government-takes-landmark-steps-to-further-clamp-down-on-dirty-money> [accessed 21 June 2022].

[2]　'Fact Sheet: U.S. Strategy on Countering Corruption', *The White House*, 2021 <https://www.whitehouse.gov/briefing-room/statements-releases/2021/12/06/fact-sheet-u-s-strategy-on-countering-corruption/> [accessed 21 June 2022].

[3]　USAID, 'Budget | U.S. Agency for International Development', 2022 <https://www.usaid.gov/cj> [accessed 8 November 2022].

[4]　The White House, 'FACT SHEET: Establishing the Fight Against Corruption as a Core U.S. National Security Interest', *The White House*, 2021 <https://www.whitehouse.gov/briefing-room/statements-releases/2021/06/03/fact-sheet

Positive developments have occurred on enforcement of anti-corruption laws as far as they relate to developing countries. For example, Glencore pled guilty in the US, the UK and Brazil to charges of corruption and bribery to secure access to crude oil in various African countries.[5] Together with ongoing investigations in the Netherlands and Switzerland, it expects to pay up to $1.5 billion in fines – or 50% of its projected profits in the first half of 2022.[6]

While these moves are welcome, the pace, extent, focus and funding of the efforts to tackle economic crime in many cases need more work. Many also argue that action to fight Russian dirty money is too little too late,[7] and question the proportionality of fines as well as the adequacy of mechanisms to repatriate funds to the countries whose resources have been looted.

This chapter discusses the economic crime-related security, stability and sustainable development issues, recommending areas of further research which would be of particular interest to both practitioners as well as the academic community. The first section of this chapter gives an overview of some of the security challenges we are faced with today. These include the economic crime-related repercussions of health crises, most recently Covid-19, conflicts and wars, environmental (in)security and ensuing irregular migration flows. The second section considers the challenges of combatting economic crime, particularly in fragile and development contexts; looking at measuring economic crime, tailoring approaches and prioritizing resources. The third section highlights a proposed focus on prevention, from focusing on alternatives to crime, to understanding and working with social norms that influence the acceptance of and engagement in economic crime and working with values-based in addition to rules-based approaches.

-establishing-the-fight-against-corruption-as-a-core-u-s-national-security -interest/> [accessed 14 August 2022].

5 The firm's activities in Nigeria, Cameroon, Equatorial Guinea, Ivory Coast and South Sudan were investigated by the UK; and in Nigeria, the Democratic Republic of Congo and Venezuela – by the US.

6 Timmins, 'Mining Firm Glencore Pleads Guilty to UK Bribery Charges', *BBC News*, 21 June 2022, section Business <https://www.bbc.com/news/business -61857005> [accessed 23 June 2022].

7 See for example: Emma Haslett, "No One in Government Cared until the War': How the UK Left It Too Late to Fight Financial Crime – New Statesman', *The New Statesman*, 15 March 2022 <https://www.newstatesman.com/the-business -interview/2022/03/no-one-in-government-cared-until-the-war-how-the-uk-left -it-too-late-to-fight-financial-crime> [accessed 21 June 2022].

Economic crime in times of crises

Global shocks: health and conflict

The Covid-19 pandemic took the world largely unprepared. As a result, emergency protection and procurement measures needed to be put in place at record speed. Some research and investigations have been undertaken to understand the levels of transparency, adequacy of the design of emergency processes and scale of leakages in national health and other procurement systems; however, this is only an emerging topic.[8]

There is a need to thoroughly assess the unintended consequences of the emergency measures taken during Covid-19, and design more preparedness systems should another disaster strike. One notable effect of emergency measures put in place in the context of Covid-19 was the shrinking democratic space alongside a reduction of civil and political liberties in many countries; however, some of these are still in place two years later.[9] In fragile and conflict-affected states, Covid-19 has contributed to reshaping state and non-state political positions. As put by the International Institute for Democracy and Electoral Assistance (IDEA), '[b]oth state and non-state actors have used the pandemic to bolster or legitimate claims to power, and in some cases insurgent groups have been able to opportunistically divide the limited attention and resources of the state to gain the upper hand in the conflict'.[10] International IDEA's annual report on the Global State of Democracy notes that countries have been

---

[8]   See for example: National Audit Office, *Investigation into the Management of PPE Contracts – National Audit Office (NAO) Report* (National Audit Office, 30 March 2022)   <https://www.nao.org.uk/report/investigation-into-the-management-of-ppe-contracts/> [accessed 14 August 2022]; National Audit Office, *Investigation into Government Procurement during the COVID-19 Pandemic – National Audit Office (NAO) Report*, 26 November 2020 <https://www.nao.org.uk/report/government-procurement-during-the-covid-19-pandemic/> [accessed 14 August 2022]; Transparency International UK, 'For Whose Benefit? Transparency in the Development and Procurement of COVID-19 Vaccines', *Transparency International UK* <https://www.transparency.org.uk/publications/whose-benefit-transparency-development-and-procurement-covid-19-vaccines> [accessed 14 August 2022].

[9]   Felix S. Bethke and Jonas Wolff, 'COVID-19 and Shrinking Civic Spaces: Patterns and Consequences', *Zeitschrift Für Friedens- Und Konfliktforschung*, 9.2 (2020), 363–74 <https://doi.org/10.1007/s42597-020-00038-w>.

[10]   Erin Houlihan and William Underwood, *Emergency Law Responses and the Covid-19 Pandemic (Global State of Democracy Thematic Paper 2021)* (International Institute for Democracy and Electoral Assistance, 2021) <https://doi.org/10.31752/idea.2021.84>.

consistently moving towards increased authoritarianism for the last five years, and in the last year this represented a three-fold difference in the number of countries increasingly authoritarian rather than vice versa.[11]

A number of non-governmental agencies interviewed by the author as part of a research project on the regulation of private cross-border philanthropic flows into developing countries talked of the shifts in funding to major crises, such as addressing the impact of Covid-19. While the need for Covid-19-related support was clear, a range of organizations interviewed have noted that the overall pot of funding available for development work had not increased, but was rather redirected. This has had the effect of inhibiting progress towards issues that require long-term sustained investment, such as shifting norms around corruption or setting up effective structures to combat economic crime. A sustainable approach is needed to ensure both immediate crisis needs as well as long-term development goals are met, and more research into frameworks of how this could be operationalized would be beneficial.

Ongoing conflicts in various regions (including Syria, Yemen, Ethiopia) and Russia's invasion of Ukraine have demonstrated that we have merely seen a proliferation of tactics used to create instability rather than a complete change of the nature of warfare. Nevertheless, newer forms of warfare and destabilization have become increasingly common, particularly cybercrime attacks and malign foreign interference in elections. This raises new risks and challenges for governments, civil society and businesses to ensure that they are continuously reviewing and adapting their risk management structures to counteract emerging threats.

The urgent need to support Ukraine in defending their country from Russia's invasion, as well as to establish support structures for the millions of refugees, has led to a remarkable show of generosity by countries and individuals. This resulted in significant flows of funding to Ukraine, also making it easier for fraudsters to set up credible requests for funding under false pretences.[12] As the conflict becomes more protracted, there is a need to ensure that the funding goes where it is intended, in collaboration with the very strong Ukrainian anti-corruption community. Research would also be beneficial to identify where leakages have occurred and consider whether and what changes are

---

[11]   International IDEA, *The Global State of Democracy*, 2022 <https://www.idea.int/our-work/what-we-do/global-state-democracy> [accessed 21 August 2022].

[12]   Jarrett & Lam CIFAS, 'Fraud Focus – Ukraine Donation Scams and Exploitation of Rising Energy Bills | Cifas', 2022 <https://www.cifas.org.uk/newsroom/fraud-focus-14-march> [accessed 14 August 2022].

needed to countries' and organizations' preparedness mechanisms to provide emergency assistance structures in geographies that have not traditionally required as much support.

In the context of conflict, we have also seen the importance of a carefully thought through approach where financial crime considerations are incorporated from the outset of interventions rather than as an afterthought. This has been demonstrated by negative consequences resulting from the relative neglect of considerations of financial crime in stabilization interventions, for example in Iraq.[13]

To help prepare for any forthcoming crises, more research is needed on holistic preparatory systems and structures to increase countries' resilience to shocks – health, environmental, political and financial – to highlight safeguards that may need to be put in place should these shocks occur, as well as on frameworks to more effectively integrate financial crime considerations in emergency responses.

Irregular migration

The increasing climate disasters, conflict and insecurity have resulted in the numbers of people who were forced to flee their homes consistently rising in the last two decades. The number of people forcibly displaced has hit another record in 2021, with 89.3 million people being displaced by the end of the year. With the addition of displaced Ukrainians, in mid-2022 there were more than

---

[13]   Jennifer Schoeberlein, *Overview of Corruption and Anti-Corruption in Iraq*, U4 Helpdesk (CMI and Transparency International, 11 December 2020), p. 4 <https://knowledgehub.transparency.org/assets/uploads/helpdesk/Overview -of-corruption-and-anti-corruption-in-Iraq_2021_PR_final.pdf> [accessed 29 August 2022]. Schoeberlein (2002:4) argues that: 'In focusing on a military rather than a diplomatic solution, in the years that followed, the US and its alliance poured significant support, both financial and logistical, into the Iraqi military while turning a blind eye to the regime's corruption, sectarianism, nepotism and the security forces' human rights violations (Chayes 2014 and Chayes & Wehrey 2014). According to Chayes and Wehrey (2014) the resulting instability, lack of regime legitimacy and citizen frustrations have contributed to Iraqi government failure and internal strife. They have also contributed to the advance of ISIS after 2014, both because widespread corruption had weakened the Iraqi military, and because corruption, nepotism, a lack of rule of law and a side-lining of large parts of the Sunni population, have increased frustrations with the regime, making citizens more receptive to the cause of the militias.'

100 million people forcibly displaced.[14] Figure 2.1 summarizes the change in total numbers of displaced persons, showing the great increases in the numbers of forcibly displaced people evident during the last 20 years.

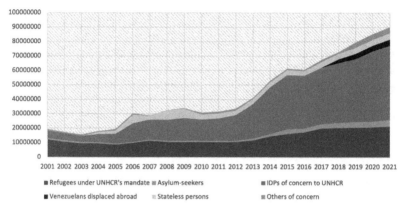

Source: author's compilation from UNHCR data (https://www.unhcr.org/refugee-statistics/download/?url=s1y5zA [accessed 10 July 2022])

Figure 2.1   People forced to flee worldwide, 2001–2021

The highest numbers of people fleeing are hosted by developing countries – the 2021 UNHCR Global Trends report highlights that 83% of the world's refugees and Venezuelans displaced abroad are hosted in low- and middle-income countries, and 72% in countries neighbouring their countries of origin.[15]

An interesting development to note is also the categories in which people are placed. The Global Trends report distinguishes 'Venezuelans displaced abroad' rather than incorporating these figures into the existing categories of asylum seekers or population of concern to UNHCR. The data on Venezuelans displaced abroad is available on a dedicated website managed by the Regional Interagency Coordination Platform for Refugees and Migrants of Venezuela,[16] jointly led by UNHCR and IOM. Reportedly, such a designation was compromised upon by the two UN agencies for them to be able to jointly respond to people fleeing a political and economic crisis, as well as widespread human

14   UNHCR, *Global Trends* (UNHCR) <https://www.unhcr.org/globaltrends.html> [accessed 22 June 2022].
15   UNHCR, *Global Trends*, p. 2.
16   R4V, 'Home | R4V', 2022 <https://www.r4v.info/en> [accessed 22 June 2022].

rights abuses, without having one of the agencies lead the response. Additional research would be beneficial to establish the effects on migrants that different categorizations, such as this novel category, have, including on their access to services and protection.

In 2022, European countries led the continent's largest effort since the Second World War to accept Ukrainians displaced by Russia's invasion. As of 6 July 2022, UNHCR had recorded more than 5.65 million refugees from Ukraine in Europe, with more than 3.6 million having registered for temporary protection or similar national protection schemes across Europe.[17] UNHCR also estimates that some 7 million people have been displaced internally within Ukraine; and in total one third of Ukrainians have been forced out of their homes.[18] The response to Ukrainian refugees across Europe differed from previous refugee crises, as a very large number of individuals welcomed refugees into their homes. For example, in April 2022, *Wall Street Journal* quoted the Vice President of Warsaw saying that of 300,000 refugees at the time in Warsaw, only 10,000 were staying in temporary housing set up by the city.[19]

There have been calls to emulate the exemplary compassion shown for Ukrainian refugees to those fleeing other conflicts, persecution and human rights abuses (see for example Deng 2022[20]). Indeed, further research would be particularly useful to learn lessons from what worked and what did not work in the response to Ukrainian refugees and why, and apply these lessons in future conflicts.

The response to the Ukrainian refugee population stands in stark contrast to how groups of people seeking refuge via Belarus were received by its EU neighbours only months before Ukraine was invaded. For example, in June 2021, the Government of Belarus started facilitating asylum seekers mostly from Iraq but also from a range of other countries including Syria, Afghanistan, Yemen

---

[17]   UNHCR, 'Situation Ukraine Refugee Situation', 2022 <https://data.unhcr.org/en/situations/ukraine> [accessed 10 July 2022].

[18]   'Internally Displaced Persons (IDP)', *UNHCR Ukraine*, 2022 <https://www.unhcr.org/ua/en/internally-displaced-persons> [accessed 10 July 2022].

[19]   Ian Lovett Journal Natalia Ojewska and Eric Sylvers | Photographs by Dawid Zielinski for The Wall Street, 'Flood of Refugees From Ukraine Mostly Are Finding Shelter in Private Homes', *Wall Street Journal*, 4 April 2022, section World   <https://www.wsj.com/articles/flood-of-refugees-from-ukraine-mostly-are-finding-shelter-in-private-homes-11649064600> [accessed 10 July 2022].

[20]   Nhial Deng, 'Treat All Refugees with the Same Compassion', 2022 <https://www.aljazeera.com/opinions/2022/5/24/treat-all-refugees-with-the-same-compassion> [accessed 10 July 2022].

and Iran, to fly into Belarus legally, before being transported to the country's border with Poland, Lithuania or Latvia and forcefully being pushed across. Direct asylum seeker flows of such magnitude were novel for the three EU countries. For example, Lithuania had 81 irregular border crossings in 2020, 46 in 2019 and 104 in 2018;[21] whereas in June 2021 it detained 470 irregular migrants, which rose to 2,600 in July 2021.[22] Poland, Lithuania and Latvia initially responded to the irregular migrant flows by detaining those that had crossed the border in temporary facilities, before adopting the approach of pushing people back to Belarus, sometimes violently,[23] without an examination of the individuals' claims for asylum. This was accompanied by deploying troops at the border and building walls on the border with Belarus to make crossings more difficult.[24]

The argument put forward by the Polish, Lithuanian and EU authorities was that the migrants are part of Belarus's declared hybrid warfare against the EU countries, aiming to destabilize the EU. It is argued that this is partly in response to the European countries' support to Lukashenko's political opponents and sanctions imposed on the country following a forced landing of a Ryanair plane while crossing Belarusian air space,[25] with Putin also being behind the operation. Polish officials argued that the numbers of migrants pushed across the border increased in retaliation for providing asylum to Belarusian athlete Tsimanouskaya;[26] and that the people are not genuine refu-

---

[21]   Lithuanian Official Statistics Portal, 'Nelegalių migrantų krizė - Lietuvą užklumpa nebe pirmą kartą', 2021 <https://osp.stat.gov.lt/en/straipsnis-nelegaliu-migrantu -krize-lietuva-uzklumpa-nebe-pirma-karta> [accessed 10 July 2022].

[22]   Thebault Reis and Dixon Robyn, 'Why Are so Many Migrants Coming to One of Europe's Smallest Countries? Blame Belarus, Officials Say.', *Washington Post*, 1 August 2021 <https://www.washingtonpost.com/world/2021/08/01/lithuania -belarus-migrants/> [accessed 10 July 2022].

[23]   HRW, *Violence and Pushbacks at Poland-Belarus Border* (Human Rights Watch, 7 June 2022) <https://www.hrw.org/news/2022/06/07/violence-and-pushbacks -poland-belarus-border> [accessed 23 June 2022].

[24]   BBC, 'Poland Blocks Hundreds of Migrants at Belarus Border', *BBC News*, 8 November 2021, section Europe <https://www.bbc.com/news/world-europe -59206685> [accessed 23 June 2022].

[25]   Euronews, 'Belarus Border Chaos a 'Hybrid Attack Not a Migration Crisis': VDL', *Euronews*, 10 November 2021, section news_news <https://www.euronews .com/2021/11/10/dozens-of-migrants-detained-in-poland-after-breaking-across -belarus-border> [accessed 10 July 2022].

[26]   Reuters, 'Poland Says Belarus Lets Migrants Cross Border in 'hybrid War' with EU', *Reuters*, 5 August 2021, section Europe <https://www.reuters.com/world/ europe/poland-says-belarus-lets-migrants-cross-border-hybrid-war-with-eu -2021-08-05/> [accessed 10 July 2022].

gees. Migrants, many from Iraq, Syria and Afghanistan, themselves therefore become 'living weapons' (as explicitly named by the deputy interior minister of Poland)[27] in this 'hybrid warfare' approach, often being left with no humanitarian support in particularly precarious situations.[28]

This, however, stands in contrast with the non-refoulement principle, below, enshrined in Article 33 of the 1951 Convention relating to the Status of Refugees (Poland, Lithuania and Latvia have all acceded to the Convention[29]), Article 14 of the Universal Declaration of Human Rights[30] ('Everyone has the right to seek and to enjoy in other countries asylum from persecution'):

> 1. No Contracting State shall expel or return ('refouler') a refugee in any manner whatsoever to the frontiers of territories where his [or her] life or freedom would be threatened on account of his [or her] race, religion, nationality, membership of a particular social group or political opinion (Article 33 of the Refugee Convention).[31]

It is worth noting that Article 42 of the convention explicitly does not permit countries to make reservations to Article 33. The exception included in Article 33 of the 1951 Refugee Convention only relates to those individuals who have been convicted of having committed a serious crime and therefore which constitute a danger to the community of the receiving country.[32] This does not cover individuals (especially children) whose mere presence in a country is understood as a threat to the country's stability and security.

The Universal Declaration of Human Rights, in Article 14, similarly only adds limitation to the right to seek asylum from persecution only for those who have

---

27   Reuters.

28   This includes being stranded in the forest or border zone between the two countries in freezing conditions, see for example: BBC.

29   UNHCR, 'States Parties, Including Reservations and Declarations, to the 1951 Refugee Convention', 2019 <https://www.unhcr.org/protection/convention/5d9ed32b4/states-parties-including-reservations-declarations-1951-refugee-convention.html> [accessed 8 July 2022].

30   UN, 'Universal Declaration of Human Rights' (UN, 1948) <https://www.un.org/en/about-us/universal-declaration-of-human-rights> [accessed 8 July 2022].

31   UNHCR, 'Convention and Protocol Relating to the Status of Refugees', 1951 <https://www.unhcr.org/protection/basic/3b66c2aa10/convention-protocol-relating-status-refugees.html> [accessed 8 July 2022].

32   '2. The benefit of the present provision may not, however, be claimed by a refugee whom there are reasonable grounds for regarding as a danger to the security of the country in which he is, or who, having been convicted by a final judgment of a particularly serious crime, constitutes a danger to the community of that country.' Article 33, UNHCR, 'Convention and Protocol Relating to the Status of Refugees'.

engaged in non-political crimes: 'This right may not be invoked in the case of prosecutions genuinely arising from non-political crimes or from acts contrary to the purposes and principles of the United Nations.'[33] In a clarification note, UNHCR has specified that the principle applies to those who have not yet formally granted refugee status if their cases have not yet been fully reviewed, as well as those who have already received it:

> Given that a person is a refugee within the meaning of the 1951 Convention as soon as he or she fulfills the criteria contained in the refugee definition, refugee status determination is declaratory in nature: a person does not become a refugee because of recognition, but is recognized because he or she is a refugee. It follows that the principle of non-refoulement applies not only to recognized refugees, but also to those who have not had their status formally declared. The principle of non-refoulement is of particular relevance to asylum-seekers. As such persons may be refugees, it is an established principle of international refugee law that they should not be returned or expelled pending a final determination of their status.[34]

Human rights groups have repeatedly voiced concerns about the treatment of the migrants at the Belarus/EU borders, documenting human rights abuses, including violence, rape, extortion and death, noting that these pushbacks are unlawful and that '[i]t's unacceptable that an EU country is forcing people, many fleeing war and oppression, back into what can only be described as hellish conditions in Belarus'.[35] Many irregular migrants also found themselves in freezing temperatures between the two borders, unable to enter either country.[36] In addition, some EU nationals who chose to help people stranded by the Polish–Belarus border by providing them food or shelter have reportedly risked criminal prosecution, particularly as journalists and non-governmental organizations, and other non-residents, were prohibited from entering the border area when a state of emergency was declared over the 'migrant crisis'. Human Rights Watch and Polish Grupa Granica argue that four volunteers were simply providing humanitarian aid by helping a family with seven chil-

---

[33]   UN.

[34]   UNHCR, 'Advisory Opinion on the Extraterritorial Application of Non-Refoulement Obligations under the 1951 Convention Relating to the Status of Refugees and Its 1967 Protocol' (UNHCR, 2007), pp. 2–3 <https://www.unhcr .org/4d9486929.pdf> [accessed 8 July 2022].

[35]   HRW.

[36]   Jacopo Barigazzi, 'European Defense Leaders Warn: Belarus Migrant Crisis Could Morph into Military Crisis', POLITICO, 10 November 2021 <https:// www.politico.eu/article/poland-belarus-border-migrants-military-crisis-defence -leaders-europe/> [accessed 10 July 2022].

dren in the forest when they were charged with 'organizing illegal migration', punishable by up to eight years in prison.[37]

The Belarus/EU border example is only one of the recent refugee management approaches which attracted similar controversies in relation to human rights violations. Frontex, the European Border and Coast Guard Agency, was notably involved in the Greek authorities pushing back at least 957 asylum seekers in the Aegean Sea in 2020–21.[38] The Italian government has blocked male migrants from disembarking a rescue ship in November 2022 as part of a 'crack down on migrants travelling across the Mediterranean', when only children and people with medical issues were allowed to disembark the rescue ships.[39] The BBC notes that SOS Humanity has called such an action illegal, as 'Rejecting the 35 people seeking protection aboard Humanity 1 from territorial waters is a form of collective refusal and is therefore illegal.'[40]

There is a clear need for more research, and dissemination of it to policymakers, on the effectiveness and the unintended consequences of interventions designed to curb irregular migration and their compatibility with existing international legal frameworks designed to protect and meet the needs of people fleeing persecution, famine or other risks. The need for such data has been publicly discussed, for example when the UK government's Home Secretary at the time, Priti Patel, acknowledged that the controversial policies to process asylum applications in Rwanda attempted by her department were not based on evidence of effectiveness or evidence-based modelling, arguing that it would be 'imprudent' to delay action until such data is available.[41] The

---

[37]   HRW.

[38]   Giorgos Christides and Steffen Lüdke, 'Frontex Involved in Illegal Pushbacks of Hundreds of Refugees', *Der Spiegel*, 28 April 2022, section International <https://www.spiegel.de/international/europe/frontex-involved-in-illegal-pushbacks-of -hundreds-of-refugees-a-9fe90845-efb1-4d91-a231-48efcafa53a0> [accessed 17 July 2022].

[39]   Binley, 'Standoff as Italy Stops Male Migrants from Disembarking Rescue Ships', *BBC News*, 6 November 2022, section Europe <https://www.bbc.com/news/world -europe-63533769> [accessed 8 November 2022].

[40]   Binley.

[41]   Ione Wells, 'Patel Warned of Uncertainty over Rwanda Plan's Deterrent Effect', *BBC News*, 17 April 2022, section UK Politics <https://www.bbc.com/news/uk -politics-61133983> [accessed 21 June 2022].

UK Home Affairs Committee recommended against such policy announce-
ments,[42] noting that:

> There is a worrying trend in Home Office policy announcements being made
> before detailed policy has been worked through, tested and even agreed between
> Government Departments, as exemplified by early announcement both of military
> control of channel operations and the Migration and Economic Development
> Partnership with Rwanda. We recommend that the Home Office seek to delay
> announcing new policy initiatives on channel crossings until sufficient detailed
> planning has been done to substantiate the chances of their success against the
> underlying strategic goals.

More research on holistic assessments of the risks of interventions would
be useful, as one-dimensional approaches can have significant unintended
consequences, for example increasing border controls without addressing
the drivers of irregular migration can contribute to the professionalization
and consolidation of organized crime groups. This has been observed on the
Iran–Turkey border, where increased measures and patrols have led migrants
to undertake more dangerous journeys through the mountains, which require
more expertise, funding and networks. The journeys became facilitated by
more organized groups that may engage in a range of crimes and cross-border
smuggling (including drugs and weapons) in 2015, taking over from previously
looser migrant smuggling networks.[43] Furthermore, as noted by the UK Home
Affairs Committee,[44] 'The provision of safe and legal routes to the UK should
be a key part of the Government's strategy to counter the criminal trade, and
this has not yet received the attention it deserves.'

Additionally, research into the financing of migrant journeys could be
expanded to provide more detail on where people legitimately fleeing persecution from repressive regimes might start to engage with actors involved
in criminal activity, and to facilitate a 'follow the money' approach to tackle
organized crime groups involved in irregular migration.

---

[42]   UK Home Affairs Committee, 'Channel Crossings, Migration and Asylum –
        Home Affairs Committee', 2022, p. 19 <https://publications.parliament.uk/pa/
        cm5803/cmselect/cmhaff/199/report.html> [accessed 8 November 2022].
[43]   Tinti Peter and Tuesday Reitano, *Migrant, Refugee, Smuggler, Saviour* (Oxford
        University Press, 2018), pp. 262, 266–67.
[44]   UK Home Affairs Committee, p. 41.

Environmental security

Environment security is a challenge both at state and individual levels. This section considers environmental security at the level of individuals who, due to droughts, wildfires, crop failures and other disasters, are increasingly forced to move, sometimes across borders. However, people fleeing natural disasters do not fall under the 'refugee' definition discussed above, which requires there to be an element of persecution.

The Internal Displacement Monitoring Centre estimates that, in 2021 alone, 23.7 million people were displaced within their countries due to various disasters (see Table 2.1), in addition to the 14.4 million people displaced internally due to conflict and violence.[45] Fortunately, in 2021 most displacements due to disasters were temporary, but 5.9 million people were still displaced at the end of the year.[46]

Table 2.1   Breakdown of types of disaster that caused internal population displacement in 2021

Type of disaster	Total number of people displaced	Sub-type	Number of people displaced
Geophysical	1.4m	Earthquakes	671,000
		Volcanic eruptions	663,000
		Landslides	44,000
Weather-related	22.3m	Storms	11,500,000
		Floods	10,100,00
		Wildfires	451,000
		Droughts	240,000
		Landslides	37,000
		Extreme temperatures	20,000

Source: IDMC data (IDMC).

[45]   IDMC, *IDMC | GRID 2022 | 2022 Global Report on Internal Displacement* (IDMC, 2022) <https://www.internal-displacement.org/global-report/grid2022/> [accessed 22 June 2022].
[46]   UNHCR, *Global Trends*, p. 27.

UNHCR Global Trends report[47] notes that the number of people displaced by slow-onset events such as droughts, changes in sea and precipitation levels is predicted to rise significantly, by 2050 reaching 200 million to 1 billion according to different estimates. Furthermore, in 2021, 91% of internal conflict displacements and 78% of new refugees and asylum seekers originated from countries that are highly vulnerable to the impacts of climate change.[48]

The explicit consideration of corruption in the context of environment, social and governance (ESG) factors needs more attention from researchers and practitioners. Transparency International UK released a report outlining how corruption and lack of business integrity more broadly can jeopardize impact investors' positive impact on the environment.[49] The report also shows that corruption is considered by most impact investors from the compliance perspective – conducting due diligence prior to funding disbursement and reactively revisiting the information if issues arise. More proactive management of corruption and business integrity risks in the context of achieving development impact, however, is often deprioritized. Transparency International UK is now working on setting out guidance for impact investors, who are often pioneer investors in complex environments, and their investees on incorporating considerations of corruption in the context of development (including environmental) impact. This is a topic that will require additional research and work to develop and gather wide support for standards on considering business integrity in the context of ESG and impact investing.

This section gave only a brief overview of how different types of crises can affect economic crime and vice versa. Preparedness for climate-, health- and security-related crises emerges as a key theme that requires focus in the future. At the same time, approaches need to be found to ensure that issues requiring more structural change, such as those relating to economic crime, are continued to be addressed alongside supporting emergencies when these arise.

---

[47]   UNHCR, *Global Trends*, p. 10.
[48]   UNHCR, *Global Trends*, p. 11.
[49]   Tilly Prior, *Values Added* (Transparency International UK, 2022) <https://www
.transparency.org.uk/values-rules-based-anti-corruption-compliance-guide-for
-companies> [accessed 21 June 2022].

Challenges

Measuring corruption and economic crime

An understanding of the levels of corruption and economic crime is needed to more accurately target interventions. It is also needed to assess whether interventions, safeguards and policies are having the desired effect, and the various risks in a given geography and sector.

Measuring the levels of corruption, money laundering and economic crime in general is challenging. Taking corruption as an example, the first difficulty is defining exactly what we mean by corruption in a particular context. This is due to the varying ways in which corruption can manifest in different sectors and contexts and the sometimes grey lines that exist between actions that may or may not be considered as 'corrupt' – such as certain types of 'revolving door' arrangements between the public and private sectors, deliberate bankruptcy or jurisdiction shopping to avoid tax.[50] Furthermore, corruption often occurs between two consenting parties where both have gains to be made and both might face consequences if their corrupt arrangement was made public; victims may not be aware of having been wronged; potential whistleblowers might be reluctant to report corruption due to fear of retaliation; and controls and investigations do not pick up all incidences of corruption. Therefore imperfect proxies need to be used to measure the extent of the phenomenon.

A range of measurements has been established over time, based on perception surveys, experience-based surveys and official statistics. The UNODC Manual on Corruption Surveys[51] categorizes measures of corruption into direct and indirect measures. Direct measures measure actual experiences, rather than perceptions, of corruption. This includes official data (such as reported cases of corruption from the police, prosecutors, courts and anti-corruption agencies; conviction figures; electoral scrutiny findings) and experience-based sample surveys, which collect data on the experience of representative samples of a given population. Official statistics, however, might be an indicator of the

---

[50]   Ingrida Kerusauskaite, *Anti-Corruption in International Development*, 1st edition (Routledge, 2019), pp. 12–37.
[51]   UNODC, Centre of Excellence in Statistical Information on Government, Crime, Victimization and Justice, and UNDP, *Manual on Corruption Surveys: Methodological Guidelines on the Measurement of Bribery and Other Forms of Corruption through Sample Surveys*, 2018, pp. 20–29 <https://www.unodc.org/documents/data-and-analysis/Crime-statistics/CorruptionManual_2018_web.pdf> [accessed 21 June 2022].

effectiveness of the criminal and anti-corruption authorities rather than the actual incidences of corruption and ultimately measure the crime that has come to the authorities' attention rather than the full extent of the crime. Experience-based sample surveys might suffer from non-disclosure bias where participants do not want to admit having engaged in corruption themselves.

Indirect measures are used often, as actual occurrences of corruption are difficult to measure. These can be based on expert assessments (where selected experts are asked to assess corruption trends and patterns in a given country or countries) and are sometimes composite measurements combining different types of statistical data into one indicator of corruption.[52] Indices such as the Corruption Perception Index (CPI) can raise awareness of issues of corruption, and in some cases give a push to some countries to do better on anti-corruption, not wanting to be ranked low or lower than certain other countries. Overall, however, composite indices generally do not give a targeted view of where improvements should be directed, nor do they necessarily accurately reflect the actual improvements or worsening of corruption in a particular country. It also matters who is consulted to formulate indexes. National and international experts' opinions might be based on different data points and personal experience; and experts' and households' perceptions of the pervasiveness of corruption in a given country can differ, as demonstrated by Razafindrakoto and Roubaud (2010).[53]

Undue influence, fraud and corruption have also been identified in global rankings and indices. Most notably, the World Bank Doing Business Index, which has been used an indicator of the administrative burden placed on businesses resulting in a higher risk of corruption and economic crime, was discontinued in 2021 after 'improper changes to the data for China (*Doing Business 2018*) and Saudi Arabia, the United Arab Emirates, and Azerbaijan (*Doing Business 2020*) were effected'.[54] The investigation report identified

---

[52]   UNODC, Centre of Excellence in Statistical Information on Government, Crime, Victimization and Justice, and UNDP.

[53]   Mireille Razafindrakoto and François Roubaud, 'Are International Databases on Corruption Reliable? A Comparison of Expert Opinion Surveys and Household Surveys in Sub-Saharan Africa', *World Development*, 38.8 (2010), 1057–69 <https://doi.org/10.1016/j.worlddev.2010.02.004>.

[54]   Ronald C. Machen and others, *Investigation of Data Irregularities in Doing Business 2018 and Doing Business 2020; Investigation Findings and Report to the Board of Executive Directors* (Wilmer Cutler Pickering Hale and Dorr LLP, 15 September 2021), p. 1 <https://thedocs.worldbank.org/en/doc/84a922cc9273 b7b120d49ad3b9e9d3f9-0090012021/original/DB-Investigation-Findings

undue influence[55] by the Bank's senior leadership to improve China's rankings against the backdrop of 'sensitive negotiations over [the Bank's] ongoing capital increase campaign' and concerns that key countries might reject the proposed financial contributions.[56] China's rankings were changed for political reasons, as the points awarded for multiple specific Chinese laws were increased to meet China's requests to maintain their rankings, after the Banks's staff had explored various other options to change the methodology to improve China's position.[57] The investigation report notes that the then CEO Georgieva explained that 'the bank was in "very deep trouble" if the [capital increase] campaign missed its goals'.[58]

Similarly, in 2019 the Bank's employees were instructed by the DEC Director Djankov to 'alter the data such that Jordan fell from its first-place position in the Top Improvers list', to be replaced by Saudi Arabia.[59] Potential motivations for such actions included the desire for the Bank to demonstrate the effectiveness of its lucrative consultancy services designed to improve countries' Doing Business scores.[60] Some have argued that discontinuing the index is akin to throwing the baby out with the bathwater, as more stricter methodological approaches with controls on changing methodologies to suit a particular country as well as separation of the Bank's evaluation teams from the political engagement and 'business development' side of the organization could have enabled the organization to continue incentivizing countries to review their business environment-related regulations while controlling for political influence risks.

Mungiu-Pippidi and Fazekas (2022)[61] overview the diverse methods to measure corruption that have emerged in recent years in addition to the dominant use

---

-and-Report-to-the-Board-of-Executive-Directors-September-15-2021.pdf> [accessed 21 June 2022].

[55] Also referred to as '"judgement calls" to push the data in a certain direction to accommodate geopolitical considerations' Machen and others, p. 6.

[56] Machen and others, p. 1.

[57] These were later dropped due to political reasons of incorporating Hong Kong in the ranking or where changes in the methodology would have also improved other countries' scores in the index (Machen and others, pp. 4–5).

[58] Machen and others, p. 2.

[59] Machen and others, p. 7.

[60] Machen and others, p. 11.

[61] Alina Mungiu-Pippidi and Mihály Fazekas, 'How to Define and Measure Corruption', in *A Research Agenda for Studies of Corruption*, ed. by Alina Mungiu-Pippidi and Paul M. Heywood (Edward Elgar, 2020), pp. 7–26 <https://www.elgaronline.com/view/edcoll/9781789904994/9781789904994.00008.xml> [accessed 21 June 2022].

of expert and population surveys to measure corruption. This includes picking up on the traces left by the crime in areas such as financial records, public tenders and company ownership. The authors also offer a guide as to which indicators (e.g., percentage of public contracts won by bidders connected to public officials or politicians, public employment and politicization of the civil service, use of audit data) might be best suited to measure corrupt phenomena in different circumstances.

Efforts are ongoing by a range of academics and organizations, such as the International Anti-Corruption Academy, to 'design a robust, relevant and useful approach to measuring corruption'.[62] Sector-specific initiatives such as the Maritime Anti-Corruption Network (MACN), Extractive Industries Transparency Initiative (EITI) and the Infrastructure Transparency Initiative (CoST) are very welcome and now established initiatives which would benefit from being emulated for a broader range of sectors.

The context of technological innovation has been very useful in facilitating the identification of corruption red flags using big data analysis (see for example Fazekas' work on public procurement red flags[63]). Technology has also helped uncover economic crimes. For example, in the early stages of MPESA use in Kenya, police discovered networks of corruption by investigating traffic officers' mobile payment (MPESA) records.[64] Police noticed that junior traffic department police officer's financial activity on MPESA exceeded their legitimate earnings, and also that they were regularly transferring fixed amounts to their superiors. This suggested they were given a regular target to make from traffic bribes; and anything they made above that they could keep. In Afghanistan, a trial to pay police officers' salaries using MPESA resulted in police officers getting 30% more pay, as that amount had been skimmed by their superiors when their salaries were paid in cash.[65] The trial also identified

---

[62]   IACA, 'Global Programme on Measuring Corruption – Global Programme on Measuring Corruption' <https://www.iaca.int/measuring-corruption/> [accessed 10 November 2022].

[63]   Mihály Fazekas and Gábor Kocsis, 'Uncovering High-Level Corruption: Cross-National Objective Corruption Risk Indicators Using Public Procurement Data', *British Journal of Political Science*, 50.1 (2020), 155–64 <https://doi.org/10.1017/S0007123417000461>.

[64]   John Aglionby, 'Corruption in Kenya Evolves for a Digital Age', *Financial Times*, 30 August 2016 <https://www.ft.com/content/1a734368-6911-11e6-ae5b-a7cc5dd5a28c> [accessed 21 June 2022].

[65]   Tim Harford, 'Money via Mobile: The M-Pesa Revolution', *BBC News*, 13 February 2017, section Business <https://www.bbc.com/news/business-38667475> [accessed 21 June 2022].

that a tenth of police officers were ghost workers – i.e., salaries were being paid for non-existent workers.

In the medium term, however, technological innovations and digitization efforts have been hampered by those who adapt to new ways of tracing funds. In the context of Kenya, this has meant that corrupt traffic officers quickly went back to demanding bribes in cash rather than MPESA. Others have hampered the digitization of records to maintain the possibility for facilitation payments or, even more creatively, in one case using technology to demand bribes from service users before granting them access to services. One interviewee described how when registering a car using a country's new online system, she was contacted multiple times by the people who had digitized the system demanding a bribe so they put the 'submit' button back on the system to allow the processing of a car registration request.

A more global and concerted effort would be beneficial to establish more targeted measures of corruption and other types of financial crime, leveraging emerging technologies, for the range of contexts the crimes occur in and to track our progress towards mitigating these.

One size does not fit all

In addition to the variations between the priorities and mechanisms in different sectors and geographies, there is a stark difference in the way humanitarian and development industries operate. The former is often seen as a shorter-term rapid response, which we could call a 'band-aid' or tourniquet approach. Development would then be the planned surgery with pre- and after-care for the patient. This distinction, however, blurs in many contexts, such as protracted crises where large populations' residency status is in flux. Lines between shorter-term humanitarian support and development support are difficult to draw in contexts such as supporting Palestinians who have lived in refugee camps for multiple generations; or the good practice of interventions supporting refugees alongside host populations to reduce tensions between the two groups.

The acknowledgement of the broader environment is important in the context of fighting financial crime for a range of reasons, of which this chapter will discuss two. First, the suitability of financial crime controls in contexts for which they were not designed should be considered. Many of the systems and controls required by donors are set up for environments that are not only politically relatively stable and secure, but also have certain processes and norms established in society that would make it rather difficult to circumvent these. This does not always manifest in practice, including in stable countries. As a simple example, in a country I worked in, with my expenses being reimbursed on the basis of receipts provided, I was repeatedly asked by waiters whether I would like my wine to be charged as a salad or a main course, as they had understood from me crossing out alcohol from receipts during previous visits that alcohol was not reimbursable. Others have been asked, 'How much would you like the receipt to be for?' You could easily get VAT receipts for items you did not purchase. Similarly, people working in more fragile contexts, such as Iraq and Somalia, talk of the 'show' that is sometimes put on for formal compliance purposes, on a much larger organizational scale. Compliance can be seen as a tick-boxing exercise which masks the real dealings. It is key to understand the local systems and players, build trust and take a tailored approach to mitigating against corruption.

Second, the timelines and predictability of funding can be challenging. Tackling long-standing development issues, particularly those relating to governance and the social norms that influence people's acceptance of certain behaviours and actions, takes a very long time. Engrained behaviours and acceptability of those is difficult to change, and fluctuations in funding for initiatives that try to do so make their success even more challenging. It takes time to build trust with the stakeholders, who need to be on board for any change to be meaningful. This often means that those currently in power, and usually those that would lose out of a tightening of rules or enhanced oversight and implementation of regulations, would need to be the very people pushing through the reforms internally.

Among other topics, additional research would be useful to understand what makes people comply with regulations to curb economic crime *in different contexts*. Targeted social norms research would be useful to understand the entry points that hold most promise in different regions, sectors and organizations. Often a higher, country-level overview is too generic to be useful.[66]

Prioritization

Economic crime has a demonstrable impact on all societies, regardless of the level of wealth. The link between not only the predicate crimes such as

---

[66]   See a more detailed discussion: Mushtaq Khan, Pallavi Roy, and Antonio Andreoni, *Anti-Corruption in Adverse Contexts: Strategies for Improving Implementation* (Anti-Corruption Evidence SOAS Consortium, September 2019) <https://ace.soas.ac.uk/publication/anti-corruption-in-adverse-contexts -strategies-for-improving-implementation/> [accessed 21 June 2022].

corruption, tax crime, smuggling and fraud as well as negative development outcomes has been established,[67] but also negative effects of illicit financial flows themselves.

These include negative effects on the economy as whole, with less tax revenue being collected. It also creates the potential for a vicious circle where people do not see the benefits of their tax payments in public services and question why they should be paying if they get nothing in return. As such, tax evasion can further reduce the financing available and therefore the quality of public services, including healthcare, education and, with it, trust in government. Depending on the industry corruption occurs in, this might also be harmful to people's health, for example because of sale of substandard food or medicine products. Negative consequences of illicit financial flows could be seen on the environment, as bribes can be used for circumventing pollution and safe waste disposal regulations, or environmental regulations designed to prevent damage to natural landscapes and habitats. This can in turn lead to health consequences for populations living in affected areas.

There are also risks related to violence and political stability, formation and strengthening of organized crime groups, and modern slavery exploitation as a result of illicit finance. Negative effects on gender dynamics can also be observed as the task to manage illicit financial flows can hold women from elected office, as such political systems tend to rely more on informal selection processes which benefit men who are already in the political system, and typically have greater social and financial capital.

Despite the very apparent harms that economic crime causes, many countries have a range of competing challenges to address, sometimes with very limited resources. Small island states in particular have voiced concerns about the level of resources that is mandated by international standards for anti-money laundering and terrorism finance prevention, and the high costs of non-compliance (in particular, relating to de-risking and loss of correspondent banking relationships). Small states are particularly concerned with climate and natural disaster prevention, as this disproportionately affects them. For example, Caribbean small states are subject to seven times more frequent disasters which inflict six times more damage compared with other larger states.[68] As

---

67   See for example Kerusauskaite, pp. 63–71.
68   Sònia Muñoz and İnci Ötker, 'Building Resilience to Natural Disasters in the Caribbean Requires Greater Preparedness', *IMF* <https://www.imf.org/en/News/Articles/2018/12/07/NA120718-Building-Resilience-to-Natural-Disasters-in-Caribbean-Requires-Greater-Preparedness> [accessed 23 July 2022].

an example, Dominica incurred damage amounting to 226% of the country's economy by Hurricane Maria in 2017.[69] Heightened exposure to disasters also has negative macro-economic effects, including lower investment, lower GDP per capita and higher poverty; therefore mitigation is particularly important.

Additional research could be beneficial on more effective implementation of risk-based approaches as well as international collaboration mechanisms, in particular considering how countries that have more advanced systems are more significantly exposed to financial crime risks, or those that have more resources could more effectively support others (e.g., through the creation of targeted regional collaboration hubs).

Focus on prevention

Focusing on alternatives to crime

Interesting work is being done in the donor space on countering serious and organized crime (SOC), where the focus is on positive activities and alternatives to SOC. Projects are emerging that focus on (1) understanding the underlying issues that lead young people in specific areas/municipalities to join SOC, (2) tailoring interventions to address these issues (such as lack of decent job opportunities, discrimination, lack of inter-generational understanding), with the interventions being monitored and adapted,[70] (3) innovative communications campaigns, based on social-norms research, and (4) establishing models for multi-agency collaboration to identify and support those at risk of getting involved in SOC at an early stage. This means that a project working with young people might not even mention that it is a 'SOC prevent' project.

This marks a shift away from a focus on 'don't do crime' in an environment where the alternative options might be perceived as scarce, instead focusing on increasing the knowledge and confidence in other, positive, options available. Some research on the effectiveness of such an approach is ongoing, and additional data on the effectiveness of more innovative prevention interventions could offer data on a broader range of approaches to reducing crime.

---

[69]   Muñoz and Ötker.
[70]   Progressing approaches include gathering diverse groups of well-performing and 'at-risk' children for activities to avoid stigmatizing particular 'at-risk' groups.

One of the projects referred to above is relatively unusual in fully incorporating an academic team amongst the project operations team. This does come with challenges in how different institutions are set up and their differing goals (e.g., interventions vs publications as primary institutional focus), but an understanding of the different organizations' working approaches, goals and restrictions (such as data use and intellectual property) can lead to fruitful collaborations.

An increased focus across the board on fully incorporating academic teams in development projects would be useful. This would enable a research team to get a full overview of the discussions and deliberations at a project implementation level, in addition to benefiting from the rigorous approach to data collection which can guide implementation. This would also help mitigate the real difficulties of conducting research on initiatives that do not label themselves as 'anti-crime' initiatives[71] as an outsider organization. This could be beneficial to assess the effectiveness of indirect approaches to combatting economic crime, including corruption, where interventions are often delivered under a different label, such as business environment improvement or public sector efficiency.

Furthermore, although the collective action theory (which argues that individuals do not make decisions about whether to engage in corruption in isolation from their environment) has dominated the anti-corruption scholarship for the last several decades, many frameworks to combat corruption appear to be based on the principal–agent theory – designed for transactional rather than systemic corruption.[72] Additional research would be beneficial to outline which frameworks would be particularly useful to adapt to combat systemic corruption, which is often present in particularly fragile environments.

The importance of social norms

Recent work to understand the social norms that underpin behaviour and design compliance programmes and activities accordingly has generated interesting results in the context of corruption. Social norms work has been previously mostly considered in healthcare and tax interventions. Social norms are defined as 'the mutual expectations held by members of a group about the

---

[71] Anti-corruption programmes can be called 'business environment reform' programmes, 'transparency' or 'accountability' work, 'social service provision improvement', etc. Similarly, programmes designed to prevent serious organized crime might not have the name in the title.

[72] Kerusauskaite, pp. 56–58.

right way to behave in a particular situation'.[73] These are enforced by social rewards and sanctions (for example, social recognition or exclusion) and can be more influential than personal attitudes when it comes to decisions around how to act, particularly when certain people are around.

It is interesting to observe what happens when official rules and norms do not align, and often the norms win. This is particularly when there is a more convenient way of doing or not doing things which will not attract significant consequences. A simple, non-financial crime example might be people's willingness to walk across a red traffic light when there are no cars (or police officers in countries where you can get a fine for jaywalking) around. Social norms research in Uganda showed that where corruption becomes normalized behaviour, being not corrupt can subject police officers to ridicule and suspicion by other officers, and peer pressure to conform with established corrupt practices or face consequences such as transfer to remote and undesirable posts.[74]

Recent research on social norms and communications has shown that communications approaches that essentially say 'don't do bad things' – whether it be corruption or tax evasion – do not deliver the desired results. They can also have the opposite to the desired effect as poorly crafted and untargeted 'anti-corruption' messages might make people think there is so much corruption around that it would be futile to go against the flow and fight back against corruption.[75] Research has also suggested that people can be more likely to engage in bribery when they believe (1) that others engage in bribery frequently and (2) that this situation leaves them with few other options regarding engaging in bribery themselves, even where bribery remains considered as socially inappropriate.[76]

---

[73]   Cheyanne Scharbatke-Church and Diana Chigas, *Understanding Social Norms: A Reference Guide for Policy and Practice* (The Fletcher School, Tufts University, September 2019), p. 9 <https://www.corruptionjusticeandlegitimacy.org/_files/ugd/0379c5_f6f60113cb70443daf96b83b4cf47f27.pdf> [accessed 21 June 2021].

[74]   Scharbatke-Church and Chigas.

[75]   Nic Cheeseman and Caryn Peiffer, *The Unintended Consequences of Anti-corruption Messaging in Nigeria: Why Pessimists Are Always Disappointed* (Anti-Corruption Evidence SOAS Consortium, June 2020) <https://ace.soas.ac.uk/publication/unintended-consequences-of-anti-corruption-messaging-in-nigeria/> [accessed 21 June 2022].

[76]   See for example: Nils Kobis, Ivan Soraperra, and Marleen Troost, *Social Norms of Corruption in the Field – Posters Can Help to Reduce Bribery in South Africa*, 2018, p. 19. <https://www.researchgate.net/publication/330142689> [accessed 21 June 2022].

While more research is being conducted on social norms and corruption, it is still a relatively little explored area. Understanding what kind of messaging works for which audiences in what contexts and for how long combined with what interventions could be beneficial for more effective anti-corruption work.

Values-based approaches

In 2020, the Albanian tax administration conducted research on the types of messages that are more effective to tackle tax evasion.[77] At the start of the pandemic, the tax administration sent out two types of letters to businesses suspected of under-declaring monthly payroll payments. Both contained nudges designed to tackle under-declaration of worker salaries in monthly payroll submissions to the tax authorities. The first type emphasized 'the public goods nature of truthful payroll declarations': that under-declaring wages deprives employees of pension payments, health and unemployment benefits, and reduces the quality of public services enjoyed by all. The second type of letters focused on the potential threat of enforcement actions if caught committing tax fraud. The tax authority found that firms receiving the first type of the letter submitted significantly larger payroll declarations compared with the control group, while those receiving the second had no statistically significant impact.

Transparency International has been advocating for a shift towards values-based, in addition to the rules-based, approaches to control of financial crime. A recent Transparency International UK report, *Values Added*,[78] urges businesses to adopt a four-step approach – understanding the company's existing values, defining the values a company would like to have, embedding these, and measuring the impact of these changes on the tolerance and prevalence of corruption, with the aim to 'encourage self-policing and intrinsic motivation rather than mere compliance with rules and legal requirements'. This, however, is not a new debate, as values have been espoused by companies for decades, and discussed widely following the collapse of Enron, which famously had 'integrity' as one of the company values. Values are discussed

---

[77]   Delina Ibrahimaj Shijaku Christoph Ungerer, Jonathan Karver, and Hilda, 'How Should Governments Communicate with Taxpayers during the COVID-19 Pandemic?', *Brookings*, 2020 <https://www.brookings.edu/blog/future-development/2020/09/14/how-should-governments-communicate-with-taxpayers-during-the-covid-19-pandemic/> [accessed 21 June 2022].

[78]   Prior, p. 5.

in the context of corporate wrongdoing, such as Glencore's recent case and Volkswagen's emissions scandal.[79]

Additional research would be beneficial to understand the effectiveness of values-based approaches to countering economic crime across a broader range of sectors and geographies.

Conclusion

Some of the challenges are clear, but not necessarily the most effective ways to address them. This chapter has recommended research topics for the various issues discussed, which could inform evidence-based interventions to combat corruption and financial crime which negatively affects stability, security and economic development.

There is a need for greater collaboration across the private, public and third sectors. This can not only help build trust but also help better understand, measure and counter economic crime, drawing on different stakeholders' thematic expertise, data and ability to implement change.

It is also useful to share what has not worked and why, alongside sharing what has worked. It is much harder to admit failure, but mistakes or attempts to address complex issues such as economic crime in varying contexts could help others build better approaches. Some donor programmes are now structured to be agile and take problem-driven, iterative and adaptive approaches.[80] This requires programmes to continuously evaluate whether their interventions are working, what the unintended effects of these are, and invest more where the results seem promising while cutting their losses early where the interventions do not look likely to succeed. The more that research could be undertaken alongside a range of policy, prevention and enforcement-oriented interventions, following rigorous methodologies and couched in sound theoretical frameworks, the closer we might get to building a stronger evidence base to

---

[79]   Hotten, 'Volkswagen: The Scandal Explained', *BBC News*, 22 September 2015, section Business <https://www.bbc.com/news/business-34324772> [accessed 10 November 2022].

[80]   Jamie Pett 'Navigating Adaptive Approaches for Development Programmes: A Guide for the Uncertain', *ODI: Think Change*, 2020 <https://odi.org/en/publications/navigating-adaptive-approaches-for-development-programmes-a -guide-for-the-uncertain/> [accessed 21 June 2022].

guide more effective approaches to combatting economic crime in the contexts of stability, security and sustainable development.

Finally, more research would be useful to outline the way politics continues to influence economic crime trends and controls. Many interventions seek to harness political will to make positive changes and act at the right moment; and could benefit from insights as to how organizations have succeeded at doing so. Understanding political influences could also be useful at improving controls for integrity, as discussed with the World Bank's Doing Business Index, and to better guide interventions in the context of particularly politically sensitive topics such as corruption and irregular migration.

3   Economic crime in developing and transition economies

Dayanath Jayasuriya

Economic crime in developing and transition economies is not an entirely unknown phenomenon. However, what is new is that more and more such economies are becoming vulnerable to economic crimes that used to typically occur in developed countries. With globalization, perpetrators of economic crime find it easier to transcend national frontiers and zero in on countries that are less susceptible to detection. As Barry Rider observed: 'Economic crime does impact on the security and stability of all states, but its implications can, in different ways, be more serious for developing, transition and specially small states.'[1] Access to the internet is a key tool in the hands of criminals who have been able to hack even sensitive defence information in the United States of America, a country that pioneered the development of databases seemingly beyond third party interference. In October 2018, the BBC reported that 'some of the most cutting-edge weapons in the US's military arsenal can be "easily hacked" using "basic tools" … The Government Accountability Office (GAO) found "mission-critical" cyber-vulnerabilities in nearly all weapons systems tested between 2012 and 2017.'[2] In the early days, China and Russia were two countries implicated for hacking, but since countries across southeast Asia and the Middle East have come online over the last decade, they have been tempting targets for hackers.[3] The category of 'economic crime' eludes easy description and its exact conceptualization remains a challenge. In 1981, for example, the Committee of Ministers of the Council of Europe identified 16 offences as economic crimes (recommendation No. R (81)): cartel offences; fraudulent practices and abuse of the economic situation by multinational companies; fraudulent procurement or abuse of state or international organ-

---

[1]   Rider, B. (ed) 'Introduction' in *Research Handbook on International Financial Crime*, Edward Elgar, 2015, p. xxxix.

[2]   BBC, https://www.bbc.com/news/technology-45823180 (accessed on 20 August 2022).

[3]   New York Times, 'Hackers Find 'Ideal Testing Ground' for Attacks: Developing Countries' https://www.nytimes.com › 2017/07/02 (accessed on 20 August 2022).

izations' grants; computer crime; bogus firms; faking of company balance sheets and book-keeping offences; fraud concerning the economic situation and corporate capital of companies; violation by a company of standards of security and health concerning employees; fraud to the detriment of creditors; consumer fraud; unfair competition, including payment of bribes and misleading advertising; fiscal offences and evasion of social costs by enterprises; customs offences; offences concerning money and currency regulations; stock exchange and bank offences; and offences against the environment.

A complete inventory of economic crimes in or emanating from developing and transition countries does not exist; however, various reports issued from time to time list the following crimes: corruption; counterfeit currency and similar transactions; cultural heritage crime; drug trafficking; environmental crime; financial crime; firearms trafficking; human/people trafficking; illicit goods smuggling; maritime crime; terrorism; vehicle crime and war crimes; sale of children, child prostitution and pornography; illegal trade in endangered species of wild fauna and flora; art and cultural property; toxic waste dumping; and forced labour.

Over time, the seriousness or gravity of an economic crime will vary from country to country and from region to region. For instance, in the African region the Lome Declaration of 2000 reiterated that cross-border criminality, illicit proliferation circulation and trafficking of small arms and light weapons, drug trafficking, corruption and terrorism constitute serious threats to security and stability, and hamper the harmonious economic and social development of the continent.

Global Financial Integrity (GFI) is a Washington, DC-based think tank that focuses on illicit financial flows, corruption, illicit trade, and money laundering. Through high-calibre analyses and fact-based advocacy, GFI works with partners to increase transparency in the global financial and trade system, and address the harms inflicted by trade mis-invoicing, transnational crime, tax evasion, and kleptocracy.

It has focused on illicit financial flows (IFFs), namely illegal movements of money or capital from one country to another. GFI classifies this movement as an illicit flow when funds are illegally earned, transferred, and/or utilized across an international border. Some examples of illicit financial flows include:

- A drug cartel using trade-based money laundering techniques to mix legal money from the sale of used cars with illegal money from drug sales;

- An importer using trade mis-invoicing to evade customs duties, value-added tax, or income taxes;
- A corrupt public official using an anonymous shell company to transfer dirty money to a bank account in the United States;
- A human trafficker carrying a briefcase of cash across the border and depositing it in a foreign bank; or
- A member of a terrorist organization wiring money from one region to an operative in another.

GFI estimates that the annual value of trade-related IFFs in and out of developing countries has amounted to, on average, about 20% of the value of their total trade with advanced economies.

The impact of illicit financial flows is a loss of what are often desperately needed resources to fund public initiatives or critical investments. This represents hundreds of millions of dollars in lost or foregone tax revenues that could have otherwise been collected and used for supporting sustainable economic growth, creating jobs, reducing inequality, poverty, and addressing climate change, among other things. With billions of dollars estimated to be illicitly leaving developing countries every year, GFI estimates that this drain of public resources undermines the efforts of countries to mobilize more domestic resources in order to meet the internationally agreed Sustainable Development Goals (SDGs) by the target date of 2030.

The problem of illicit financial inflows is also a serious issue. Common reasons for illicit inflows are tax evasion and for financing the illegal activities of international criminal networks engaged in human trafficking and smuggling of arms, drugs and valuable minerals. Both illicit outflows and inflows result in the same problem: taxes not being paid to governments.

According to GFI:

> Illicit financial outflows from developing countries ultimately end up in banks in developed countries like the United States and United Kingdom, as well as in tax havens like Switzerland, British Virgin Islands, or Singapore. This does not happen by accident. Many countries and their institutions actively facilitate—and reap enormous profits from—the theft of massive amounts of money from developing countries. GFI believes developed countries have a responsibility alongside developing countries to curtail the flow of illicit money.[4]

---

[4]   Global Financial Integrity, https://gfintegrity.org/issue/illicit-financial-flows (accessed on 25 August 2022). See also, May, Channing, Transnational Crime and the Developing World, Global Financial Integrity, March 2017.

GFI has proposed that the most effective way to limit illicit financial flows is to increase financial transparency and recommends governments enact policies to:

- Detect and deter cross-border tax evasion;
- Eliminate anonymous shell companies;
- Strengthen anti-money laundering laws and practices;
- Work to curtail trade mis-invoicing; and
- Improve transparency of multinational corporations.

The new resolution on 'Promoting reconciliation, accountability and human rights in Sri Lanka' that was presented at the 51st regular session of the Human Rights Council in October 2022 was adopted with 20 voting in favour, while 7 voted against the resolution and 20 abstained from voting.[5] What is of significance for the purposes of this chapter is that 'economic crime' received particular attention in the context of the country having declared bankruptcy due to mass-scale economic crimes that had gone largely undetected or not prosecuted. The resolution called upon 'the Government of Sri Lanka to address the ongoing economic crisis, including by investigating, and where warranted, prosecuting corruption, including where committed by public and former public officials, and stands ready to assist and support independent, impartial and transparent efforts in this regard'.[6]

Particular issues and problems in developing and transition economies

Many developing countries have taken ages to review the legislation enacted during the colonial period. Recent changes elsewhere are not taken into account when legislative amendments or new laws are enacted. The drafting and approval process tends to be very long, as competing interests have to be taken into account. Lawmakers in some countries are keen to maintain their status quo and are unhappy with any changes that provide for greater transparency and accountability.

Law enforcement agencies generally have limited trained staff. Salaries tend to be very low and working conditions are appalling, to say the least. Where

---

[5]   UNOHR on 'Promoting reconciliation, accountability and human rights in Sri Lanka' A/HRC/51/5.
[6]   Ibid.

through bilateral or multilateral agencies staff members are sent abroad for training, many of them stay behind because of higher wages and better living conditions.

Where parliamentary oversight committees exist, it is rarely that the members of such committees would risk questioning powerful ministers because of the possibility of retaliation. Recommendations of such committees and reports and findings of the auditor-general, for instance, gather dust with no effective follow-up action being taken.

Even though attempts are made to improve international cooperation, delays tend to stifle action. Interpol 'red notices' to arrest fugitive criminals serve little or no purpose, as exemplified by the case when the Sri Lankan authorities arranged for a red notice for the apprehension of a former governor of the Central Bank who is a Singaporean national and seen widely in public in Singapore. The 'red notice' remained without execution for several years.

The involvement of diplomatic personnel in facilitating economic crimes has resulted in camouflaging the illegal movement of contraband. Very recently, media reported[7] the story of a Bentley Mulsanne V8 – a flagship car of the British motor company worth upwards of £240,000, making it the brand's largest and most expensive handcrafted saloon – having been stolen from London and discovered almost 5,000 miles away in Pakistan. A search and tip-off initiated by the UK National Crime Agency led Karachi authorities to a bungalow in the city. The vehicle had apparently been taken to Pakistan on the fake documents of a European diplomat, and was found with forged registration plates, one of which was handmade. The authorities managed to identify the car not only by its chassis number but also due to the failure to remove or switch off the tracing tracker in the Bentley, which helped authorities pinpoint its exact location. Police have launched an investigation into the forged import documents and a loss of $1.3 million (£1.12 million) in taxes to the exchequer.

In an interesting development, a US court sentenced Sri Lanka's former ambassador to Washington to a US$5,000 fine and two years' probation, in a case that may have reverberations in Colombo and capitals around the world. Colombo's former ambassador to the United States, had pled guilty to diverting and attempting to embezzle US$332,027 from the government

---

7   Yousuf, Muhammad, 'Stolen Bentley from London found in Karachi, Pakistan', Sky News, 8 September 2022.

of Sri Lanka, as it purchased a new embassy building in Washington in 2013. According to Judge Tanya S. Chutkan, 'Even though this was not millions of dollars, it represents a serious theft from the people, and by a person that they entrusted to represent their interests in the capital of the most powerful country in the world … What you have done is a serious betrayal.'[8] The case is unusual and the ruling is significant, demonstrating the limits of diplomatic immunity.

A stimulus to action has been the mounting pressure to achieve the Sustainable Development Goals (SDGs). The United Nations' New York Summit held in 2015 led to the adoption of 17 SDGs, aimed at making the world a fairer, better and safer place by 2030.

SDG 16 focuses on promoting peaceful and inclusive societies for sustainable development, providing access to justice for all and building effective, account-able, and inclusive institutions at all levels. It has the following targets:

- Significantly reduce all forms of violence and related death rates everywhere;
- End abuse, exploitation, trafficking, and all forms of violence against and torture of children;
- Promote the rule of law at the national and international levels and ensure equal access to justice for all;
- By 2030, significantly reduce illicit financial and arms flows, strengthen the recovery and return of stolen assets, and combat all forms of organised crime;
- Substantially reduce corruption and bribery in all their forms;
- Develop effective, accountable, and transparent institutions at all levels;
- Ensure responsive, inclusive, participatory, and representative decision-making at all levels;
- Broaden and strengthen the participation of developing countries in the institutions of global governance;
- By 2030, provide legal identity for all, including birth registration;
- Ensure public access to information and protect fundamental freedoms, in accordance with national legislation and international agreements.

At the Eleventh United Nations Congress on Crime Prevention and Criminal Justice held in Bangkok in 2005, consideration was given to 'Economic and

---

8   United States v. Wickramasuriya (1:18-cr-00120) District Court, District of Columbia.

financial crimes: challenges to sustainable development', and the following recommendations were formulated:

(a) Establishment of mechanisms at the national, regional and international level to improve data collection on economic and financial crimes, with particular emphasis on those areas where advances in technology are providing new opportunities for criminal activity;

(b) Consideration of ways in which the global legal framework to counter economic and financial crimes can be improved. If the concept of economic and financial crimes is regarded as too broad, it may help to identify specific areas (such as fraud on the Internet) where steps can be made towards a more effective global response;

(c) Provision of effective technical assistance to developing countries to improve the capacity of their law enforcement and prosecutorial agencies and judicial sectors to confront the problem, given in particular advances in technology and resulting new opportunities for economic and financial crime;

(d) Agreement on measures to improve the cooperation between government and the private sector in preventing economic and financial crime, as well as working together to identify new vulnerabilities to organized crime;

(e) Identification of effective measures to curb money-laundering in countries where participation in the 'formal' financial system is low, including in the areas of research, training, skills development, technical assistance programmes and regional and international cooperation.

The experts were concerned about the staggering amounts of assets stolen by politically exposed persons, often using those assets for financing political campaigns and acquiring luxury goods, such as yachts, private jets, premium real estate and jewellery. The experts highlighted such large-scale corruption as depriving states of the resources required to provide vital public services, such as healthcare, education, housing, food or basic infrastructure. Preventing and combating large-scale corruption would thus contribute to domestic resource mobilization for the achievement of the SDGs.

It is important to note that economic problems can give rise to new financial crimes that existed at a low-key level. Sri Lanka offers an interesting example, where, after decade of corruption, bribery and mismanagement of state funds, the country recently declared bankruptcy after defaulting on the payment of bonds.[9] In October 2022, ex-President Maithripala Sirisena stated that Sri Lanka's latest currency collapse is driving girls into the sex trade in a phenomenon which was difficult to imagine, given their family backgrounds.[10] Inflation

---

[9]   Jayasuriya, Dayanath 'Sri Lanka, one-time Asia's role model becomes a bankrupt nation', The Round Table, June 2022, 111(3):457–458.

[10] The Island [Sri Lanka], 1 October 2022, p.1. See also, 'Economic Crisis Hits Sex Industry- Charges of Women and Men Go Up', Daily Mirror [Sri Lanka], 11 October 2022, p. 1

topped 70% after two years of money printing to keep rates down. He added that due to current economic conditions, social problems were worsening. Sri Lanka's rupee collapsed from 182 to 360 to the US dollar after two years of money printing to suppress rates to stimulate the economy.

This chapter will focus on selected economic crimes that seem to pose the greatest threat to developing and transition economies and indeed to the economy of the rest of the world. As countries tighten control systems, share intelligence information and develop robust software, criminals swiftly shift the focus of their attention to other areas that are not closely monitored.

Credit card and related scams

While credit card fraud is not new, the problem has escalated to an alarming extent due to the development of sophisticated technology and the availability of new channels to move proceeds across borders, making it difficult to track.[11]

In Hong Kong, almost 14,000 credit card frauds were reported in 2021. This represents a 29% increase from the previous year. For three years running, total losses from online scams amounted to nearly HK$3 billion (approximately US$382 million). In the first four months of 2022, more than 5,000 victims have lost a combined HK$1 billion from online scams. Estimates suggest that by the end of 2022, losses will be approximately HK$3 billion.[12]

In Singapore, victims lost SG$633 million (US$455 million) to scams of various types in 2021. This is a 2.5% increase from the previous year. Phishing scams involving texts that impersonated banks in Singapore have significantly increased from 149 cases in 2020 to 1,021 in 2021.[13] Among the remedial measures taken is to request to relocate bank staff at the Singapore Police Force's Anti-Scam Centre to facilitate freezing of accounts speedily and commence recovery operations. With ISO 20022, banks will be able to know the status of accounts and patterns of transactions with access to enhanced date. This would facilitate the refinement of risk signals.[14]

---

[11]   NICE Actimize/Regulation Asia 'White Paper: Dirty Dealing: Advancing the Fig against Fraud in Asia Pacific', 2022.
[12]   Ibid, p. 4
[13]   Ibid. p. 4.
[14]   Ibid., p. 12.

Mexico's high fraud rates are attributed to, among other things, its high levels of organized crime and drug cartels. Moreover, easy access to US cities along the border is known for the use of counterfeit cards and fraudulent accounts.[15]

Interpol has identified several categories of 'social engineering frauds'[16] involving developing and transition economies. These are scams used by criminals to exploit a person's trust to obtain funds or confidential financial information such as bank account numbers to subsequently commit a fraud. The preferred channel for contact is social media, such as emails rather than through person-to-person contact over the phone. Some of the commonly identified scams are phishing, vishing and SMShing; telecom fraud; access to business emails; romance scams; investment/boiler room fraud; sextortion; and airline ticket fraud. A software developer has monitored over 2 million attacks in three African nations:[17] the number of phishing attacks recorded in South Africa for the first half of 2021 exceeded 1 million at 1,031,006; in Kenya phishing attacks were recorded at 601,557; and in Nigeria 393,569.

Corruption

Unlike credit card and related frauds, corruption has a long history, but what is of increasing concern is the magnitude of the amounts involved and the impact on societies and economies. According to the United Nations Office for Drug Control,[18] corruption, bribery, theft and tax evasion cost developing countries US$1.26 trillion every year.

Petty offences of corruption are usually national in character, whereas large-scale corruption is generally multinational in character at some stage in the lifecycle from conception to execution. In recognition of the transnational implications of corruption, in October 2003 the United Nations adopted the United Nations International Convention against Corruption. It came into force in December 2005. The Convention covers five main areas: preventive measures; criminalization and law enforcement; international cooperation; asset recovery; and technical assistance and information exchange.

---

[15]   See <https://www.forbes.com/sites/halahtouryalai/2012/10/22/countries-with-the-most-card-fraud-u-s-and-mexico/?sh=1f5c05ce4708>.

[16]   See <https://www.interpol.int/en/Crimes/Financial-crime/Social-engineering-scams>.

[17]   See <https://www.premiumtimesng.com/news/more-news/484753-kaspersky-records-over-2-million-phishing-attacks-in-south-africa-kenya-nigeria-in-six-months>.

[18]   See <www.unodc.org>.

The Convention covers many different forms of corruption, such as bribery, trading in influence, abuse of functions, and various acts of corruption in the private sector. An important chapter deals with asset recovery, aimed at returning assets to their rightful owners, including countries from which they had been taken illicitly. More than 180 United Nations Member States are parties to the Convention.

Progress in combatting corruption in developing and transition economies has been relatively slow. The mismanagement of development funds continues to be a matter of great concern to developed countries as well as to funding agencies.

In 2021, the United Nations General Assembly adopted a political declaration entitled 'Our common commitment to effectively addressing challenges and implementing measures to prevent and combat corruption and strengthen international cooperation'.[19] Member States welcomed:

> the creation of the Global Operational Network of Anti-Corruption Law Enforcement Authorities under the auspices of the United Nations Office on Drugs and Crime, the aim of which is to develop a quick, agile and efficient tool for combating cross-border corruption offences, to strengthen communication exchange and peer learning between anti-corruption law enforcement authorities and to complement and coordinate with existing and efficient platforms for international cooperation, such as the INTERPOL/StAR Global Focal Point Network on Asset Recovery. We encourage States to participate in and make best use of this network, as appropriate.[20]

Member States also invited the Conference of the States Parties to the Convention:

> to identify gaps and challenges in the implementation of the Convention by taking into account the results of the Implementation Review Mechanism, as well as any gaps and corruption challenges within the international anti-corruption framework, and to consider any recommendations by States parties to address the gaps and challenges identified in such a way as to improve the Convention and the implementation thereof as may be necessary. In this regard, and as a first step, we further invite the Conference, in the future, after the conclusion of and evaluation of the findings from the second review cycle, to organize a special session of the Conference on all aspects of the asset recovery and return process, with a view to considering all options available under the Convention, including exploring possible areas for improvement to our international asset recovery framework.[21]

---

[19]   A/RES/S-32/1 of 2 June 2021.
[20]   Ibid., para. 78.
[21]   Ibid., para. 82.

In 2021, Chinese President Xi Jinping underlined the need to step up the campaign against corruption. Several legal instruments were enacted to strengthen the regulatory and enforcement system. The 'One Belt One Road' initiative spawned a culture of impunity among some Chinese companies investing overseas. This has led to closer scrutiny of compliance by Chinese companies as well as local counterparts. In September 2022, former Chinese Justice Minister Fu Zhenghua, who had led several high-profile investigations into corruption, had been jailed for life for accepting bribes as a purge of officials intensified ahead of a key Communist Party Congress. Fu, 67, was handed a suspended death sentence that will be commuted to life imprisonment after two years, with no possibility of parole.[22]

Donor countries as well as international agencies such as the International Monetary Fund and the World Bank have underscored the need for recipient countries to have a robust anti-corruption framework that is effectively enforced. This came into sharp focus when Sri Lanka sought international assistance to reschedule debt payments through new loans. The managing director of the International Monetary Fund is on record citing the Sri Lankan case study as a warning signal to other developing and transition economies.[23] Sri Lanka, for instance, issued in October 2022 a White Paper on anti-corruption law reform. The draft law provides, *inter alia*, for officers of the independent Commission on Anti-corruption to be established to arrest without a magisterial order or warrant any person suspected of having carried out an offence under the proposed legislation and to detain such person for a maximum of 24 hours. The draft also permits officers to arrest those who have committed (or against whom there is a reasonable complaint, suspicion or credible information of having committed) any act outside of Sri Lanka which, if carried out in Sri Lanka, would have been punishable under the proposed law.[24] The constitutionality of some of the clauses in the draft bill is likely to be challenged and possibly struck down by the Supreme Court. An overkill situation is unlikely to get support or, in the worst-case scenario, the law will remain unenforced.

---

[22]   See <https://www.reuters.com/world/china/china-sentences-former-justice-minister-death-with-two-year-reprieve-2022-09-22>.

[23]   See <https://asianews.network/sri-lanka-crisis-a-warning-sign-for-many-imf-chief>, 19 July 2022.

[24]   The Sunday Times [Sri Lanka], 9 October 2022, p. 1.

Covid-related fraud

As individuals, communities and countries struggled to cope with the COVID-19 pandemic, criminal organizations lost no time in devising schemes to launder funds or to engage in fraudulent activities. The Financial Action Task Force (FATF), working in tandem with national financial intelligence units, has been in the forefront of activities to track down, monitor and document cases.

Both developed as well as developing countries have been victims. FATF has documented a case study from Brazil[25] that exemplifies the many channels criminals exploit. In Brazil, between April and November 2020, the Federal Police carried out 56 police operations in 17 different states of the federation related to acts of corruption or misapplication of public resources and money laundering. These operations concluded with 133 arrests, 985 search and seizure orders in a range of public contract fraud cases, which together amount to approximately BRL1.9 billion (approximately USD$360 million). The operations varied in size and breadth. The cases involved:

(a)   overpricing of the sale of medical equipment to the detriment of public accounts and society;
(b)   purchases of unlicensed medical equipment;
(c)   irregularities in the bidding waiver contracts for the acquisition of respirators;
(d)   general fraud in public tenders and embezzlement of funds destined to combat COVID-19;
(e)   misuse of public resources to combat the pandemic;
(f)   fraud in contracts for the acquisition of hand gels and masks, medications and diagnostic tests for COVID-19; and
(g)   irregularities in the direct contracting of cleaning, disinfection and asepsis services to combat COVID-19.

The FATF has issued guidance[26] to assist countries to minimize money laundering and terrorist financing risks in the event of a future epidemic.

---

[25]   FATF (2020), Update: COVID-19-related Money Laundering and Terrorist Financing – Risks and Policy Responses, FATF, Paris, France, p. 7.
[26]   FATF (2020), COVID-19-related Money Laundering and Terrorist Financing – Risks and Policy Responses, FATF, Paris, France.

Some key problem areas

Importance of cooperation

Given the fact that it is easy to transcend national frontiers and control systems, international cooperation in the exchange of information, preventing, detecting, prosecuting or extraditing criminals is an important tool in the hands of law enforcement agencies. The need for international cooperation has been underlined by the United Nations, the Council of Europe, Financial Action Task Force, Commonwealth Secretariat, Interpol and several geopolitical groupings. Bilateral agreements also stipulate reciprocal obligations in this area.

Most documented cases of intentional cooperation involve developed and developing countries and transition economies. The following case study exemplifies how several developing countries cooperated to prevent a massive bank fraud.[27]

A US$1 billion scam involving China, Bangladesh, Sri Lanka, the Philippines and US Fed was aborted not so long ago. Sri Lankan authorities had launched a massive probe into a dubious NGO that tried to sneak in millions of US dollars stolen by Chinese hackers from the Bangladesh Central Bank. An alert teller at the Colombo branch of a foreign bank had become suspicious regarding an inward remittance of about US$25 million. The recipient NGO, Shalika Foundation, had been registered here by some outside parties who had left Sri Lanka. The Chinese hackers had broken into the systems of the Bangladesh Central Bank, titled the Bangladesh Bank, stole credentials for payment transfers and then sent, pretending to come from a Bangladeshi official, three dozen requests to the Federal Reserve Bank of New York to move money from the Bangladesh Central Bank account to entities in the Philippines and Sri Lanka. The money was said to have been transferred to casinos in the Philippines and Sri Lanka. The suspicion of the local teller had been alerted when the recipient's name was misspelt as Shalika 'fandation (instead of "foundation")'. The transfers were being made every Friday, which is a holiday in Bangladesh, to escape detection.

As a good example of due diligence and cooperation, in October 2022, Australia arrested two Australians for bribing South Asian, including Sri

---

27   Samath, F. 'Sri Lankan teller helps bust world's biggest bank fraud', The Sunday Times [Sri Lanka], 13 March 2016.

Lankan, officials to secure infrastructure contracts worth millions of dollars. The investigation had lasted almost a decade, spanning several countries.[28]

Problem of extradition

The problem of extradition is a perennial problem. According to Frank Madsen:

> The possibility that a criminal who has fled jurisdiction, would be able to live a quiet, but public life in another jurisdiction outside the reach of the law of the offended country has from the time of the Egyptian pharaoh Ramses II been considered unacceptable and has given rise to a network of extradition treaties. It is almost tautology to state hat extradition is of crucial importance to the success of law enforcement in the fight against transnational crimes, since these by definition concern several countries.[29]

It is often assumed by developing countries that to succeed in an extradition request, the country needs to have 'political clout', particularly if the offender has sought asylum or residence in a developed country. The problem is compounded if the offender is a citizen or permanent visa holder of that country.

The process to initiate and follow up on an extradition request is time-consuming and costly. Internally, there may be politically connected persons who can use influence to stall or delay the procedure. Witnesses may be pressurized into going back on their statements or some may simply 'disappear'.

Towards the future

There is no doubt that developing and transition economies need to step up efforts to deal with financial crime. While it is elementary common sense that law reform needs be given priority, when it comes to reforming laws dealing with financial crime, there are many hurdles and obstacles.

---

[28]   'Australians arrested over alleged Sri Lanka bribes for lucrative contracts', Daily Mirror [Sri Lanka], 12 October 2022, p. 1.

[29]   Madsen, F. 'Policing Transnational Organized Crime- the International Perspective' in Hauck P and Peterke, S. eds. International Law and Transnational Organized Crime, Oxford University Press, Oxford, 2016, p. 503.

It is important to identify from where the pressure for law reform comes or should come from and then have tailor-made solutions to step up pressure:

- Public interest groups – these are groups of individuals and non-governmental organizations seeking to advance their grievances hoping that the lawmakers will take note and do what is needed. Not all public interest groups will advocate for identical changes. To gain credibility, such groups need to build trust and act independently.
- Media exposure – in almost every country the media has played a key role in exposing alleged economic crimes. Investigative reporting has become a specialized vocation.
- Parliamentary debates – parliamentary debates are a helpful source of information on the current state of economic crime and deficiencies in relevant laws and enforcement processes. The need for amendments or for the enactment of new laws will often get highlighted during debates and deliberations. Occasionally countries have established standing committees with the mandate to specifically review the policy and legal framework relating to a specific economic crime, or law and order in a generic sense.
- Academic research and symposia – journals such as the *Journal of Financial Crime* and the *Journal of Money Laundering Control* publish peer-reviewed articles. For researchers, most articles contain useful tips on areas for further investigation from a comparative perspective. The Jesus College Symposia on Economic Crime – now in its 39th year – brings together annually some 2,000 participants from over 90 countries. Participants share their experiences as well as details of ongoing research.
- Bilateral or multilateral partners offering technical assistance – increasingly bilateral and multilateral agencies accord priority to issues of governance and accountability to ensure the proper use of developmental aid.
- Geopolitical groupings – directives, resolutions and charters of various geopolitical groupings have been increasingly paying attention to money laundering, mismanagement of funds, and so on. It was back in 1997 that the Committee on Economic Affairs and Development of the European Parliament prepared a report on the 'Threat to Europe from Economic Crime'.[30] On 15 December 2021, the European Parliament adopted a resolution on the evaluation of preventive measures for avoiding corruption, irregular spending and misuse of EU and national funds in case of emergency funds and crisis-related spending areas.[31] In March 2022, the European Community adopted a Directive on combating money laun-

---

[30]   Doc. 7971.
[31]   (2020/2222(INI)); (2022/C 251/04).

dering by criminal law.[32] To varying extents, geopolitical groupings have stimulated the updating of national legislation in their respective member states.

• Information obtained through the right to information law – in countries that have enacted a right to information law, a political activist may seek vital information that may expose fraudulent or corrupt deals.

Factors that determine the pace of law reform

Political will

Where the political will to stamp out economic crime is lacking, law reform becomes difficult. Even if a bill is presented in parliament, it may well be a watered-down version that is finally passed.

Commitment of political leadership

Where a minister or another member of parliament has mooted the idea of strict laws to combat economic crime, other colleagues may be reluctant to antagonize their 'political friends' – mostly those engaged in corrupt dealings – by lending support, other than that of a cosmetic nature.

Impact on pending investigations

Depending on the political clout of accused in criminal cases, legislators will decide whether or not to support any amendments that may impact on pending cases.

Court orders pursuant to public interest litigation

Courts can question the constitutionality of proposed draft legislation or pending bills and will stall proceedings until a determination is made by court.

Pressure from foreign governments or multinational firms

Changes to legislation may be a precondition to the release of grants and loans by foreign governments or donor agencies. Multinational firms may try to block any legislation that is harmful to their commercial interests.

---

[32]   Directive (EU) 2018/1673 on combating money laundering by criminal law.

Impact on business

Business or trade associations will assess the likely impact of proposed legislative changes and accordingly decide whether or not to lend support.

Effectiveness of mechanisms for enforcement

In most developing economies, law enforcement agencies have limited resources. Support for changes that may affect the status quo of those who benefit from weak existing laws will try to stall the passage of any laws highlighting that it is counterproductive to enact such laws. There is a pressing need for capacity-building, but often this is a low-priority item.

Backlog in drafting

Legal drafting requires special skills, and the office of the legal draftsman may have inadequate staff to handle the volume of work.

Slow parliamentary approval process

The adoption of some bills gets priority, whereas other bills may be referred to various committees to stall the approval process.

Conclusion

All indications seem to suggest that with mounting international pressure, developing and transition economies will fast track the process of updating legislation and enforcement mechanisms to effectively deal with economic crime. At the same time, developed countries are under a moral obligation to ensure that their own nationals and corporate entities follow good governance practices and that there is zero tolerance for exploiting weaknesses in systems in countries with which business transactions are proposed to be done. Where credible evidence exists, developed countries should lend support to efforts to arrest and deport criminals and illegal profits are confiscated and repatriated to lawful owners. There has to be a major paradigm shift to win the war against economic crimes.

4 Corruption and development

Patrick Rappo

1 Corruption and its global impact

Corruption erodes trust, weakens democracy and hampers economic development. The impact of corruption is felt all over the world, often with the poorest areas suffering the most. The World Economic Forum estimates that the global cost of corruption is roughly 5% of global GDP; in 2021, worldwide GDP stood at $96.1 trillion, which means that the cost of corruption equated to $4.8 trillion.[1] Put into more meaningful figures, approximately $455 billion of the $7.35 trillion spent on healthcare annually worldwide is lost each year to fraud and corruption. It is estimated that annually 140,000 deaths in children under 5 can be attributed, in part, to corruption.[2]

Different areas and stages of development projects present different corruption challenges. Public procurement is but one area of weakness: foreign governments and corporations often bribe officials or offer incentives to get lucrative deals. Even in developed countries, there are regular allegations of officials misusing public money or granting public jobs or contracts to their sponsors, friends and families. In Zambia, a report highlighted a six-fold increase from 2016 to 2017 in missing public funds, while also suggesting that the Revenue Authority had failed to collect a significant proportion of mineral royalty tax, suggesting degrees of suspicious activity.[3]

---

[1] Houssam Al Wazzan, 'Global Future Council on Transparency and Anti-Corruption' (*World Economic Forum*, undated) <https://www.weforum.org/communities/gfc-on-transparency-and-anti-corruption> accessed 18 August 2022.

[2] NAP, '*Crossing the Global Quality Chasm: Improving Healthcare Worldwide*' (The National Academies Press, 2018) ISBN: 0-309-47789-1.

[3] Anon., Economist Intelligence, Zambia 'Report highlights growing misuse of public funds' (*Economist Intelligence*, 14 November 2017) <http://country.eiu.com/article.aspx?articleid=666116450&Country=Zambia&topic=Economy&subtopic=Forecast&subsubtopic=Fiscal+policy+outlook> accessed 18 August 2022.

2   Striving to ensure development projects stop falling foul of corruption

There are a wide range of tools available to combat corruption; for many years increased international cooperation has started to develop ideas, frameworks and goals for both national and international implementation. An advantage of collaborating internationally is that countries can benefit from the gains made by others, without having to experiment independently to find ideas that work.

Such international cooperation can be seen in activities such as the OECD's anti-corruption and integrity work,[4] which has led on international efforts to tackle corruption through reforms such as the Anti-Bribery Convention[5] and initiatives covering a spectrum of areas including bribery, procurement, development assistance and more. More recently, the 2030 Agenda for Sustainable Development,[6] adopted by all UN Member States, highlights ongoing international efforts. The strategy recognizes that ending poverty and other deprivations must go hand in hand with efforts to improve health and education, reduce inequality and spur economic growth. At its core are 17 Sustainable Development Goals (SDGs).

In contrast to global frameworks, goals and commitments, we consider it equally important to consider implementation challenges and tested approaches. In this respect, we seek to explore more tangible case studies and change-execution. For example, the Maritime Anti-Corruption Network (MACN)[7] is a global business network working towards the vision of a corruption-free maritime industry, and recently celebrated its tenth anniversary.[8] It operates using guiding principles such as capability-building, collective action and collaboration; organizations such as the MACN offer insightful case studies which highlight cross-cutting themes as well as practical considerations for tackling corruption. For example, the MACN's work in Argentina supports

---

[4]   See <https://www.oecd.org/corruption-integrity/> accessed 18 August 2022.

[5]   See <https://www.oecd.org/daf/anti-bribery/oecdantibriberyconvention.htm> accessed 18 August 2022.

[6]   United Nations General Assembly, 'Agenda for Sustainable Development, Sustainable Development Goals' (United Nations Department of Economic and Social Affairs, 25 September 2015) <https://www.un.org/ga/search/view_doc.asp?symbol=A/RES/70/1&Lang=E> accessed 18 August 2022.

[7]   See <https://macn.dk/> accessed 18 August 2022.

[8]   See <https://macn.dk/taking-account-maritime-anti-corruption-network-outlines-10-years-of-corruption-reporting> accessed 1 September 2022.

the cause for developing robust processes, including digitizing them, alongside promoting transparency and mechanics to resolve grievances and disputes.[9] More broadly, such case studies also allow us to extrapolate important themes to underpin and guide us in tackling corruption in development projects, alongside wider areas such as development bank activities.

In this three-part chapter, we start from the position that there are a number of suggestions of how best to tackle to challenge corruption; however, the following three key pillars have good international recognition as being the best way to tackle corruption effectively:

1. Transparency
2. Digitized Process
3. Social Norms

In our experience, we consider there to be a growing body of evidence behind each of these three pillars, but we ask and explore what the research currently demonstrates and, in particular, how these pillars interact, with a view to identifying and discussing what further research and study is required to better implement anti-corruption measures.

First, we consider *transparency* and the drive for open-access data, publicly available records, registers and similar reforms as crucial in ongoing and future efforts to combat corruption. We examine beneficial ownership as but one facet of a worldwide transparency agenda and explore the further benefits to be gained from studying the effectiveness of current implementation efforts of the same.

---

[9]   One example of the MACN's work is collective action in Argentina, resulting in the adoption of a new regulatory framework for dry bulk shipping, reducing corruption risks. In this case, issues with inspector discretion being unclear, unspecific and not objective, as well as recording inspections via paper records (and various other factors), resulted in conditions which facilitated bribery. Following fieldwork, in collaboration with a local partner, MACN developed key points for a new, feasible and integrity-oriented system. After public consultation, a new system reduced discretion, used cross-checks to increase integrity and provided an escalation process for disputes as well as an e-governance system which further digitized and enhanced the transparency and process rigour to tackle corruption. In doing so, the MACN introduced greater transparency through a more robust process – utilizing technology – and navigated social behaviours by providing wider training and communication materials to help embed new practices.

Second, *process and digitization* can be powerful instruments to help achieve anti-corruption goals. Research has shown that when governments have invested in digitization and, in some cases, automation of their systems, transparency increases and the window for corruption narrows. We explore what further research is needed to make the most of the potential value of process digitization, alongside a better understanding of processes and entry points of corruption, within the context of current post-procurement corruption.

Finally, having reflected on where digitization can take us, we turn to the need to better understand *social norms* to complement transparency and digitized process. This understanding is required to holistically tackle corruption by ensuring that we fully identify, manage and reduce corruption. Within this context, we explore the need for a better understanding of social norms, cultures and the contexts in which corruption manifests.

In doing so, we hope to generate debate, discussion and prompt focused research anchored on our three pillars, which can help to make meaningful progress in the fight against corruption in development projects and the breadth of activities this entails.

3 The transparency spotlight: beneficial ownership

3.1 Background

Transparency has long been at the core of thematic analyses of corruption and one of the first tools to challenge and reduce corruption. The drive for transparency itself has been championed by international bodies such as the Financial Action Task Force (FATF), who published 'transparency of legal persons and arrangements' recommendations in 2004 (updated regularly since)[10] and guidance on transparency and beneficial ownership in October 2014.

A policy of transparency is driven by the recognition of a worldwide problem of anonymously owned companies underpinning corrupt and criminal financial transactions. Such entities were used in 70% of grand corruption cases

---

[10]   Financial Action Task Force, 'FATF 40 Recommendations' (*Financial Action Task Force*, October 2003, as updated) <https://www.fatf-gafi.org/publications/fatfrecommendations/documents/the40recommendationspublishedoctober2004.html> accessed 18 August 2022.

reviewed by the Stolen Assets Recovery Initiatives and are one of the oldest tricks in the book for moving, laundering and spending 'dirty' money.[11]

3.2 Current implementation

Worldwide efforts to increase beneficial ownership transparency provide useful case studies of a developing area of reform in the fight against corruption and the translation of policy into implemented legal reform.

In support of the FATF's latest iteration of its 40 Recommendations and its drive for beneficial ownership transparency (Recommendation 24),[12] Transparency International argues that governments shining a light on anonymous company ownership make it harder for corrupt individuals to hide their connections to illicit flows of capital.[13] Governments are achieving this by creating public registers of the true beneficial owners of companies or other assets through public beneficial ownership registers, but Transparency International also suggests that authorities must tackle corruption by rectifying any harm caused via the recovery of stolen assets. This would assist in prosecutions and act as a deterrent to would-be criminals.[14]

Looking back to the UK Government BIS Department 2014 impact assessment of the implementation of the UK's public beneficial ownership register, which is often cited as a standard for developing countries to aspire to and/or build

---

[11]   Emile van der Does de Willebois; Emily M. Halter; Robert A. Harrison; Ji Won Park; J.C. Sharman, 'The Puppet Masters: How the Corrupt Use Legal Structures to Hide Stolen Assets and What to Do About It' (*Stolen Asset Recovery Initiative; The World Bank; UNODC*, 2011) <https://star.worldbank.org/sites/star/files/puppetmastersv1.pdf> accessed 18 August 2022.

[12]   Financial Action Task Force, 'Public Statement on revisions to R.24' (*Financial Action Task Force*, 4 March 2022) <https://www.fatf-gafi.org/publications/fatfrecommendations/documents/r24-statement-march-2022.html> accessed 18 August 2022.

[13]   Transparency International, 'Progress: Financial Action Task Force Adopts New Standard on Transparency in Company Ownership' (*Transparency International*, 7 March 2022) <https://www.transparency.org/en/press/financial-action-task-force-adopts-new-standard-transparency-company-beneficial-ownership> accessed 18 August 2022.

[14]   Transparency International, 'Recommendations on Beneficial Ownership for OGP Action Plans' <https://images.transparencycdn.org/images/Rec-on-Beneficial-Ownership-Transparency-for-OGP-action-plans-FINAL.pdf> accessed 18 August 2022.

upon,[15] it was stated that 'there is little quantified data about the benefits from this policy proposal'. The impact assessment nevertheless hoped for reductions in crime, law enforcement inefficiencies and due diligence costs for firms.

Fast forward to 2020 and a World Bank Group global report[16] further considers beneficial ownership transparency within its 'selected policy tools government uses' theme, dedicating a chapter to the subject. Here, it was remarked that the transparency spotlight was also used against the anonymous corporate world, which conceals corrupt practices and proceeds, such as by virtue of the release of the Panama Papers and Paradise Papers in 2016 and 2017. The report discusses how the use of public registers is still relatively new but is beginning to have a two-fold impact: helping to enforce illicit enrichment laws and helping to detect and prevent conflicts of interest in public procurement.

One such example of beneficial ownership registers is the UK's establishment of a 'Register of Overseas Entities', which came into force on 1 August 2022 and introduced requirements to provide beneficial ownership information of overseas entities holding UK property interests, building on the UK's existing 'persons with significant control' and money laundering beneficial ownership requirements.

3.3   Improving future implementation

Almost 10 years on, we begin to amass our frameworks and policy approaches into more practical change through the introduction and refining of registers, AML requirements and other means of focusing the transparency spotlight; we are at an important juncture to both learn from what has been implemented and better evolve frameworks, policies and measures into sharper tools to fight the impact of corruption on development projects and similar activities. There is a need to develop a better and more practical understanding of how approaches, tools and methods may help maximize the intensity and impact

---

[15]   Department for Innovation and Skills, 'Transparency & Trust – Enhanced Transparency of Company Beneficial Ownership' (*Her Majesty's Government*, 2014) <https://assets.publishing.service.gov.uk/government/uploads/system/uploads/attachment_data/file/434546/bis-15-320-enhanced-transparency-of-company-beneficial-ownership-enactment-impact-assessment.pdf> accessed 18 August 2022.

[16]   World Bank Group, 'Enhancing Government Effectiveness and Transparency, the Fight Against Corruption' (*World Bank Group*, September 2020) <https://documents1.worldbank.org/curated/en/235541600116631094/pdf/Enhancing-Government-Effectiveness-and-Transparency-The-Fight-Against-Corruption.pdf> accessed 18 August 2022.

of the public ownership spotlight, building upon frameworks in place and focusing on the most effective means of implementation.

Commenting upon the current impact of beneficial ownership transparency, the World Bank identifies both a need for a framework but also, perhaps more importantly, a greater understanding of which tools or approaches are most effective.[17] Similarly, a U4 and Transparency International publication from 2020 reflects on beneficial ownership registers being a policy area 'still in its nascence' and remarks that, 'much evidence will be needed before a robust ex-post evaluation of their effects can be undertaken'.[18] What this evidence looks like, the scale of it and the potential for informing future policy and implementation is of value and warrants further study.

For instance, ongoing analysis of the effectiveness of different tools and approaches is needed,[19] which could include more practical considerations, such as what the scope of such registers should be, and minimum standards across the world to help ensure that consistent levels of public information further disable corrupt practices through anonymity. The question of implementation effectiveness, therefore, should be considered further to help guide and improve progress in an area where progress is currently uneven and inconsistent.

Areas for further examination include an assessment of what information and data matter most in such registers; for example, Global Witness and Open Ownership have identified areas for improvement, having examined and commented on the UK's public beneficial ownership register.[20] It is reported that Ghana has amended its Companies Act to not set a defining beneficial ownership threshold in certain instances, and the Nigerian Ministry of Justice

---

[17] Ibid.

[18] Theo Van der Merwe, 'Beneficial ownership registers: progress to date' (*U4 Anti-Corruption Resource Centre, Transparency International*, 8 April 2020) <https://knowledgehub.transparency.org/assets/uploads/helpdesk/Beneficial-ownership-registers_2020_PR.pdf> accessed 18 August 2022.

[19] World Bank Group, 'Enhancing Government Effectiveness and Transparency, the Fight Against Corruption' (*World Bank Group*, September 2020) <https://documents1.worldbank.org/curated/en/235541600116631094/pdf/Enhancing-Government-Effectiveness-and-Transparency-The-Fight-Against-Corruption.pdf> accessed 18 August 2022.

[20] Theo Van der Merwe, 'Beneficial ownership registers: progress to date' (*U4 Anti-Corruption Resource Centre, Transparency International*, 8 April 2020) <https://knowledgehub.transparency.org/assets/uploads/helpdesk/Beneficial-ownership-registers_2020_PR.pdf> accessed 18 August 2022.

has argued for a reduction from the UK's 25% threshold. This highlights a tension between beneficial ownership thresholds generally, but also a tension with overly onerous reporting requirements, which may impact levels of compliance and the quality of data collected on such registers.

Understanding more tangible practices, such as the Extractive Industries Transparency Initiative (EITI)[21] and its work in the extractives sector, also helps frame the value of transparency and its social use cases. Looking to the EITI's work in Ghana and the Opening Extractives programme as an example, the Registrar General's Department and Ghana EITI trained 30 civil society advocates, journalists and citizens on accessing and using beneficial ownership information to inform investigative reporting and data-driven advocacy.[22] It is clear that there is great scope for initiatives enhancing the use and focus of beneficial ownership information in a holistic way, informing government, private sector and civil society use cases.

Another crucial insight from one study reveals that an increase in the number of rules only seems likely to promote more defensiveness, depersonalization and boilerplate compliance, also feeding reporting fatigue, in which key stakeholders within firms become indifferent, tired, or hostile in the face of additional regulations. This is an important counter-consideration on what to further study in terms of effective implementation; legal reform to further enact transparency of information cannot operate in a vacuum and further research can help motivate further engagement and, ultimately, effectiveness, in achieving the intended objective.[23]

3.4   Areas of further study: the private sector

In a similar vein and in the context of beneficial ownership, another study highlights a gap in current knowledge of beneficial ownership transparency. Further research and data is needed to focus beneficial ownership transparency efforts on the role of the private sector – specifically, the role of corporate

---

[21]   See <https://eiti.org/> accessed 18 August 2022.

[22]   Extractive Industries Transparency Initiative, 'Progress Report' (*Extractive Industries Transparency Initiative*, 2022) <https://eiti.org/sites/default/files/2022 -06/EITI%20Progress%20Report%202022.pdf> accessed 18 August 2022. And see <https://eiti.org/opening-extractives> accessed 18 August 2022.

[23]   Mark Fenwick, Erik P.M. Vermeulen, 'Focus 14: Disclosure of Beneficial Ownership after the Panama Papers' (*ICF Corporate Governance Knowledge Publication*, 2016) <https://openknowledge.worldbank.org/bitstream/handle/ 10986/25408/109535-WP-Focus-14-PUBLIC.pdf?sequence=1&isAllowed=y> accessed 18 August 2022.

services providers and their interaction with beneficial ownership registers.[24] Calling for more research in how nominee service providers react to and develop their services in light of this ever brighter beneficial ownership spotlight offers clues into how to better implement and reform beneficial ownership transparency in developing countries. Such countries could otherwise be seen as 'easier' jurisdictions, navigable with less holistic or stringent beneficial ownership requirements which may undermine the impact of such reforms regionally, if not globally.

Understanding an apparent correlation with what is described as a 'highly significant'[25] statistical difference goes beyond understanding the implications of reforms and how governments can increase the pace and robustness of such transparency measures in country. This area speaks to a more commercial and practical landscape beneath the policy and legal framework that is being developed and implemented.

As the *Signatures for Sale* report states: 'Over its now 30-year history, the AML policy community has spent much more time and effort composing and diffusing formal rules than it has assessing whether these rules actually make any difference.'[26]

To understand whether the rules do 'make any difference', global themes, trends and data need to be grappled with and more robustly investigated. The disproportionate appearance of nominee services in countries requiring registration of beneficial ownership[27] serves as a valuable insight into how corporates and their beneficial owners are reacting to the prospect of having the transparency spotlight shone on their previously private arrangements, namely by finding new ways to circumvent the requirement to be transparent.

This would be but one piece of a more holistic and concerted effort to gather evidence and understand how beneficial ownership information is in fact used by organizations and where gaps or challenges remain. To do so should serve multiple benefits and assist both lobbying efforts to implement more beneficial

---

[24]   Daniel Nielson, Jason Sharman, ' Signatures for Sale: How Nominee Services for Shell Companies Are Abused to Conceal Beneficial Owners' (*StAR, World Bank Group UNODC*, 2022) <https://star.worldbank.org/publications/signatures -sale-how-nominee-services-shell-companies-are-abused-conceal-beneficial> accessed 18 August 2022.

[25]   Ibid.

[26]   Ibid.

[27]   Ibid.

ownership transparency measures in the first instance, such as national public registers or even potentially a global asset register.[28] Such a study should aim to help refine the practicalities, design and implementation of such registers, increasing their effectiveness, for example, by introducing additional controls, such as verification requirements and closing off loopholes to improve the quality of information provided.

That said, efforts to increase transparency are unlikely to be a complete solution to corruption, not least because of corruption's complex and multifactorial nature. Institutional structures and systems provide new entry points and pathways for corruption, especially for those with the money and motivation to find them. To tackle this, a firm and ever-evolving understanding and embedding of process is also needed. To achieve this, greater certainty and scrutiny of established process is required, just as the MACN did with dock inspection work in Argentina. Moreover, digitization should be utilized to at least improve, if not redesign and automate, these systems and structures in a manner that is inherently transparent and further reduces corruption risk. Until this is better researched and implemented, while we recognize the value and importance of transparency, efforts to reduce corruption by increasing transparency will only lead to partial successes.

4   Procurement and corruption

Public procurement is a societally significant process which remains blighted by corruption. Much thought, effort and expense has been put into combatting corruption in this field and into the creation of more transparent tender processes for public contracts and related development activities of significant size and value. Examples of potentially affected public projects include transport infrastructure, water supplies, healthcare systems, telecommunications infrastructure, and power and energy infrastructure, including where projects involve cross-border activities and suppliers.

However, failure to identify and address all of the entry points of corruption within the lifecycle of a public project, including post-award project activities, has enabled corruption to evolve and persist. Overspending in public projects, whether by way of payment of inflated prices to contractors (in return for

---

[28]   See <https://www.gisreportsonline.com/who-we-are> accessed 1 September 2022.

personal favours) or by having to re-spend to rectify problems in the work of underqualified contractors, eats into national and transnational budgets and resources. This invariably limits funding and resources available for other public projects; as a result, even sectors free from corruption will be unable to develop as they otherwise could have if all government contracts were awarded fairly following a genuinely competitive tender process.

In this section, the embedding of process, coupled with digitization and alongside transparency, within procurement is explored to assess how a holistic approach can better address corruption, as an area which is in need of further study.

4.1   Corruption in procurement

Over the past two decades procurement processes have come under close scrutiny from academics, politicians and lobbyists. Legislation has been introduced across the world to set strict procurement procedures and establish institutions seeking to ensure accountability and transparency.[29] There has also been a push towards e-procurement, whereby tender and award processes are managed through online portals, leveraging digitization to increase efficiency and minimize opportunities for manipulation.[30] Such systems have facilitated transitions to simpler, more structured and transparent procurement processes; however, as studies in Kenya have demonstrated, automated systems remain susceptible to fraud and corruption and are by no means a silver bullet.[31]

Increased procurement-related data has inspired innovative solutions to corruption in procurement at relatively low administrative cost. The World Bank has partnered with cities and states in Brazil to develop an artificial intelligence system capable of identifying potentially fraudulent awards of public contracts. The system looks for 225 red flags extrapolated from a data set of 250 million

---

[29]   OECD, 'Preventing Corruption in Public Procurement' (*OECD*, 2016), <https://www.oecd.org/gov/ethics/Corruption-Public-Procurement-Brochure.pdf> accessed 18 August 2022.

[30]   United Nations Office on Drugs and Crime, 'Procurement and Corruption in Small Island Developing States: Challenges and Emerging Practice' (*United Nations*, December 2016) <unodc.org/documents/corruption/Publications/2016/V1608451.pdf> accessed 18 August 2022.

[31]   David Chesire Barngetuny, 'Effects of e-Procurement on Supply Chain Management Performance in Elgeyo-Marakwet County' (*International Academic Journals*, 7 November 2015) <https://www.iajournals.org/articles/iajpscm_v1_i5_99_120.pdf> accessed 18 August 2022.

data points. Utilizing digitization in this way optimizes detection of corruption in public office without demanding the dedication of substantial state funds or personnel.[32]

However, despite the scrutiny which has been directed at procurement and the successful application of transparency and digitization tools to the procurement process, corruption has not been eradicated. The government of the UK, a country that is number 18 in the Corruption Perceptions Index and which has a transparent and robust public procurement policy, has seen allegations that it handled procurement for personal protective equipment during the Covid-19 pandemic with, 'systemic bias towards those with connections to the party of government in Westminster'.[33] The Transparency International report into the UK government's public health response to Covid-19, the largest rapid response development project the UK has faced for decades, found that 'critical safeguards for protecting the public purse have been thrown aside without adequate justification'.[34] While it does not suggest that ministers were guilty of misconduct, it does point to the ease with which longstanding anti-corruption safeguards can be set aside and how quickly corruption seeks to re-establish itself when the ability to apply effective monitoring (as a key process) is reduced, whether by circumstance or design.

4.2   Corruption post-procurement

If corruption still emerges in the procurement process where concerted anti-corruption efforts have been made, what then of post-procurement activities where it is known, as was highlighted in a study into the Odebrecht Brazilian construction firm case, that 'corruption in the post tender stage has attracted less research than corruption during auctions'.[35]

---

[32]   2020. 'Artificial Intelligence in the Public Sector | Maximizing Opportunities, Managing Risks' EFI Insight-Governance. Washington, DC: World Bank <https://openknowledge.worldbank.org/bitstream/handle/10986/35317/Artificial-Intelligence-in-the-Public-Sector-Maximizing-Opportunities-Managing-Risks.pdf?sequence=1&isAllowed=y> accessed 18 August 2022.

[33]   Transparency International, 'Track and Trace: Identifying Corruption Risks in UK Public Procurement for the Covid-19 Pandemic' (*Transparency International,* April 2021) <https://www.transparency.org.uk/track-and-trace-uk-PPE-procurement-corruption-risk-VIP-lane> accessed 18 August 2022.

[34]   Ibid.

[35]   Nicolas Campos; Eduardo Engel; Ronald D. Fischer; Alexander Galetovic, 'Renegotiations and Corruption in Infrastructure: The Oderbrecht Case' (*Università degli Studi di Padova,* April 2019) <https://economia.unipd.it/sites/economia.unipd.it/files/20190230.pdf> accessed 18 August 2022.

Post-award corruption poses unique challenges. The execution phase of a project is often a much less public affair than the tendering process. Rather than multiple parties and, in some cases, anti-corruption authorities being involved, these phases can often just involve a small number of individuals from a particular government department and contractors. A live project thus provides countless opportunities for fraud to occur discreetly. Large-scale public projects will often involve hundreds of invoices and countless work-streams. Approving false costs or accepting minor irregularities (which reduce costs) is easy to do and difficult to trace. These conditions constrain transparency and monitoring, creating conditions conducive to corruption.

While corruption at the award stage of procurement is almost always financially motivated, once a contract is awarded, a number of different pressures come into play that can push politicians and public servants to buckle to the demands of fraudulent contractors. If a project is of particular public importance, there will be significant pressure for it to be completed in a timely manner. Politicians will want to avoid the reputational consequences of delay and civil servants will see successful completion of the project as important to their prospects of career progression. These pressures can incentivize the concealment of mistakes, the acceptance of sub-quality work and it therefore becomes an easier decision to agree to contractor demands for higher fees.[36]

Equally, nepotism can appear with detrimental effects on wealth distribution and lead to the creation of a self-supporting network capable of entrenching corrupt behaviours. Added to that picture, the lower sums and relatively low risk of detection post-award makes corruption of this kind accessible to individuals who may not have the risk appetite for 'higher risk, higher reward' bribery or involvement in corrupt practices during the tender process, further undermining the behavioural changes a transparent process and tender stage would hope to inculcate.

4.3   Avenues of further research

The focus on procurement has hitherto been a sensible approach; the scope for large sums to be removed at later stages of a project is much reduced if the procurement stage has been conducted robustly. It is also clear that research

---

[36]   Dr Mihály Fazekas; Dr Elizabeth Dávid-Barrett, 'Corruption Risks in UK Public Procurement and New Anti-Corruption Tools' (*Government Transparency Institute*, November 2015, Budapest, Hungary) <https://www.govtransparency .eu/wp-content/uploads/2016/10/Fazekas-David-Barrett_Public-procurement -review_public_151113.pdf> accessed 18 August 2022.

into procurement must continue, and the existing body of procurement data must be analysed to identify where corruption remains and, crucially, weak points where it may re-emerge. Corruption manifests in seemingly transparent, digitized and robust systems, and more research is needed to understand why this is so and what further prevention measures can be implemented. As the Covid-19 pandemic demonstrated, events may at any time override the best processes and reduce the effectiveness of any or all of the anti-corruption limbs we have identified. Backstops are lacking to limit adverse impacts, and this is an urgent area that needs more robust study to better guide post-award practice.

The importance of post-award corruption should not be understated. The UN Procurement Practitioners Handbook dedicates a chapter to contract management, a key component of post-procurement activities. The handbook provides a useful roundup of core principles and practical guidance, including file and documentation steps, monitoring and control, and change management,[37] and the 2020 World Bank Group recognizes 'Governments are forever in search of new approaches and tools that can help identify loopholes and entry points for corrupt activities',[38] reiterating there are ongoing efforts to improve understanding and enhance implementation efforts.

In this positive climate, further study should be dedicated to identifying the true nature and extent of post-award corruption; in particular, how to actively monitor corruption throughout the lifecycle of a project to ensure efforts to curb corruption at the award stage do not merely serve to displace corruption down the line. Armed with better information, research into how monitoring can be made more holistic and enforcement more focused can provide, as identified by Oxford Insights, an 'in-depth and systematic assessment of the volume and quality of data'.[39] From there, gaps can be identified and solutions designed to make use of what is available. The use of big or open data, and

---

[37]   'UN Procurement: Practitioner's Handbook' (*United Nations*, October 2017) <https://unprocurement.de/fileadmin/Unprocurement/PDFs/UN_Procurement _Practitioner_s_Handbook-vOct2017.pdf> accessed 18 August 2022.

[38]   World Bank Group, 'Enhancing Government Effectiveness and Transparency, the Fight Against Corruption' (*World Bank Group*, September 2020) <https:// documents1.worldbank.org/curated/en/235541600116631094/pdf/Enhancing -Government-Effectiveness-and-Transparency-The-Fight-Against-Corruption .pdf> accessed 18 August 2022.

[39]   Andre Petheram; Walter Pasquarelli; Richard Stirling, 'The Next Generation of Anti-Corruption Tools: Big Data, Open Data & Artificial Intelligence' (*Oxford Insights*, May 2019) <https://static1.squarespace.com/static/58b2e92c1e5b6c8 28058484e/t/5ced49ccc8302518cb27f64b/1559054797862/Research+report+

artificial intelligence, could further help equip us with better information and more effective monitoring, which, in turn, enable more focused enforcement efforts.

The case studies we have considered reveal that our pillars of anti-corruption identified at the outset of this chapter work most effectively when they are supporting one another. A holistic approach to monitoring procurement projects will increase transparency, and public access to data can enable further identification of areas where new processes, digitization and automation can be introduced.

Equipped with the knowledge that, when opportunities for corruption are closed at a particular stage in a project, corrupt actors will seek out other entry points, governments, academics and anti-corruption institutions can develop a comprehensive awareness of corruption at every stage of a project's lifecycle and initiate discussions on how to combat the more subtle instances of illegitimacy that occur post-award. This should include areas that were free of corruption prior to the intervention. Research must also address why transparency, automation and data interventions are not, on their own, entirely effective in changing the motivation to act corruptly.

5   Social norms and corruption

5.1   Background

Corruption flourishes under systems where there is a lack of control, enforcement and transparency. Any intervention must tackle this fertile ground; however, even robust and transparent systems applying best practice are not always sufficient to combat corruption. Uganda presents a useful case study for Cheyanne Scharbatke-Church and Diana Chigas in their 2019 work, *Understanding Social Norms: A reference guide for policy and practice.* Uganda ranks 144 in the Corruption Perceptions Index 2021, with a score of just 27:

> Yet Uganda has an impressive array of legal mechanisms to prevent and punish corruption. There is an Anti-Corruption Court and transparency, oversight, and disciplinary mechanisms such as the Judicial Services Commission and the Inspectorate General, police disciplinary courts, and a human rights and corruption complaints desk, not to mention training and education for integrity.

2019_+The+Next+Generation+of+Anti-Corruption+Tools_++Big+Data%2C+ Open+Data+%26++Artificial+Intelligence.pdf> accessed 18 August 2022.

The missing piece in the analysis, they argue, is the impact of the social norms which still support corrupt behaviours, and which equip corruption with the impetus and ingenuity to breach the dams put in place to stop it.[40]

Social norms and their role in perpetuating corrupt systems have thus become an important topic for anti-corruption academics, researchers and practitioners. There is increasing recognition that behavioural science is a key tool in understanding how corrupt practices are embedded in social structures at macro- and micro-economic levels such that instituting best practice policies and procedures – including education and training, audits and utilizing digitization to remove human interference – does not necessarily, or entirely, resolve entrenched and systemic corruption.

5.2   The role of monitoring

Effective monitoring and transparency can reduce corruption at the point of the intervention. This was demonstrated by a case study on the effectiveness of transparency and monitoring on corruption in road-building projects in Indonesia in 2007, which compared projects facing a 100% probability of being subject to an audit, with projects facing only a 4% probability of being audited.[41] In the group facing guaranteed audits, invoice and payment corruption was reduced. An important part of the success of the study was that it addressed social norms directly; the audits were not only conducted in the time and manner they had been promised, but the results were read in public at open village meetings, resulting in social sanctions for corrupt actors. In this controlled environment, the researcher was able to deliver the promised audits to the community and to deliver the results in the manner the community had been led to expect, creating trust and accountability.

Social norms fostering corruption rely on the mutual expectations of the participants – what do my peers expect of me? What do I expect of my peers? How will I be rewarded? How will I be punished? By pushing the review of the audits

---

[40]   Cheyanne Scharbatke-Church; Diana Chigas, 'Social norms, corruption & fragility: Understanding social norms – a reference guide for policy and practice' (*The Fletcher School of Law and Diplomacy, Tufts University; Henry J. Leir Institute*, September 2019) <https://reliefweb.int/report/world/social-norms-corruption -fragility-understanding-social-norms-reference-guide-policy-and> accessed 18 August 2022.

[41]   Benjamin A. Olken, 'Monitoring Corruption: Evidence from a Field Experiment in Indonesia' (*Harvard University and National Bureau of Economic Research; Journal of Political Economy*, 2007) <https://economics.mit.edu/files/2913> accessed 18 August 2022.

into the community, the traditional expectations of the community are directly challenged and reset, creating a new social norm. Where previously bringing home additional resources for the family would have been a source of indirect pressure to continue corrupt practices – and the collusion of colleagues a form of direct pressure – the community is now engaged in actively monitoring and punishing dishonest behaviours for the good of the community, generating alternative social pressures that challenge corruption. Monitoring, transparency and effective enforcement have therefore been demonstrated as having a strong anti-corruption effect when coupled with action that directly influences social norms. Here, the context in which corruption was taking place was changed *and* the context of social pressure in the community reconfigured.

However, positioning social norms against the other drivers at play in the Indonesian example is instructive. The academic conditions in Indonesia allowed the auditors to deliver the 100% probability of audit required by the study – transparency was therefore able to help achieve the expected results of reducing corruption. Outside of these conditions, however, auditors are not operating under academic conditions and are social beings, capable of being susceptible to corruption themselves. This is especially so if the auditors are subject to the same social norms that govern corrupt behaviour as other system participants. The concern is therefore that introducing auditors to a process could simply add an extra stage at which money can be extracted from the legitimate system in the form of fraud or bribes.

The corollary to the success of the study in reducing corruption in the payment of invoices was that corruption in other areas of the project increased – for example, the awarding of contracts to family members, project leaders or village officials. Thus, as is already accepted, a corrupt system will attract corrupt actors; but here it is demonstrated that corrupt actors already within a system may prevent and circumvent anti-corruption interventions. As we have seen in relation to procurement, by focusing interventions on one area of a project or system without understanding the social norms which create the complex web of motivations and incentives behind the corrupt behaviour, well-designed and well-implemented interventions at a certain entry point to a project will cause a ripple effect, resulting in corruption unfolding elsewhere in the chain.

Corruption is a dynamic and adaptive process with rules and actions governed by attitudes and conventions and enforced by social pressure – these, together, describe the social norms that must be unravelled for lasting and meaningful change. The World Bank's 2020 Global Report notes:

> [the] incentives for corruption and the vulnerabilities that can be exploited need to be better understood first at a sectoral/functional level, before drilling down to a specific national/local level. Some [civil society organizations] and international organizations are already beginning to mine this area for insights, but more work remains to be done.[42]

5.3   Role models

Choosing effective role models can be an important driver in changing social norms and is one way to foster an independent and honest audit body. 'Islands of integrity', described by the British Academy as key individuals or coalitions of willing actors, can be promoted and harnessed within a corrupt system as sites around which honest practices coalesce.[43] Such persons or groups of persons fulfil their appointed functions without corruption and can, if supported, change social norms by offering different expectations and emboldening others to shake off practices which they find uncomfortable.

Such in-situ role models can achieve a great deal, but research, 'on islands of integrity and documented empirical evidence on their impact in the broad context is very scarce. Moreover, their impact is context dependent and requires case-by-case analysis.'[44] The private sector also has a role to play in shaping social norms – the value of institutions successfully avoids corruption when operating in an environment with normalized corruption. Bangladeshi Grameen Bank has been studied for its proactive corruption-mitigating culture, processes and structure, highlighting the importance of organizational-level activity, as opposed to national, and the role of institutional models in success-

---

[42]   World Bank Group, 'Enhancing Government Effectiveness and Transparency, the Fight Against Corruption' (*World Bank Group*, September 2020) <https://documents1.worldbank.org/curated/en/235541600116631094/pdf/Enhancing-Government-Effectiveness-and-Transparency-The-Fight-Against-Corruption.pdf> accessed 18 August 2022.

[43]   See   <https://www.thebritishacademy.ac.uk/projects/sustainable-development-islands-integrity-politics-corruption-reduction/> accessed 18 August 2022.

[44]   United Nations Office on Drugs and Crime, 'Holistic Integrity Frameworks to Address Corruption' (*United Nations Pacific Regional Anti-Corruption (UN-PRAC) Project, a joint initiative by the United Nations Office on Drugs and Crime (UNODC) and United Nations Development Programme (UNDP), supported by the Australian Government and the New Zealand Aid Programme*, January 2021) <https://www.unodc.org/documents/southeastasiaandpacific//pacific/2021/UN-PRAC_Paper_-_Holistic_Integrity_Frameworks_to_Address_Corruption.pdf> accessed 18 August 2022.

fully combating corruption.[45] Such institutional activity can also lead to organizational isomorphism and the spread of positive behaviours across competitor organizations, resulting in wider anti-corrupt standards across a market, such as in the case study of the Nepalese banking sector and the impact of foreign investment, joint ventures and the subsequent competition from incumbent banks.[46]

Imposing role models from out of the country or from elite groups, on the other hand, can feel condescending and didactic to the target audience, and even, at worst, colonial. The result can be the entrenching of corrupt behaviour further, even when drawing expertise from countries with lower levels of corruption with positive expertise to share. Any intervention to challenge social norms must necessarily involve an understanding of and sensitivity towards the attitudes of the target community and involve local actors as partners.

As described in the World Bank 2020 report:

> An administrative reform is unlikely to succeed if the main source of energy and leadership for it comes from outside. A locally grounded policy intervention is also less likely to have unintended side effects. International development agencies should therefore not play a leading role and they should not dictate the content, pace and direction of the reforms.

Ideas of general application that anti-corruption practitioners can parachute in to localized projects, therefore, are few and far between when tackling corruption from a social norms perspective. Successful direct engagement with a project cannot be short-cut by avoiding in-depth sector and jurisdictional knowledge. However, research does also show that there are interventions that work to influence social norms on a peer-to-peer basis that do not necessarily rely on deep cultural knowledge, though they are, in another sense, targeted and sensitive.

Tax Inspectors Without Borders (TIWB) was set up in 2015 by the OECD and UNDP 'to enable sharing of tax audit knowledge and skills with tax

---

45   Mohammad I. Azim; Ron Kluvers 'Resisting Corruption in Grameen Bank', (*Journal of Business Ethics,* May 2019) https://journals.scholarsportal.info/details ?uri=/01674544/v156i0003/591_rcigb.xml> accessed 01 September 2022.

46   Nnaoke Ufere et al., 'Why is bribery pervasive among firms in sub-Saharan African countries? Multi-industry empirical evidence of organizational isomorphism' (*Journal of Business Research* 2020). See <https://www.london.edu/think/ can-investing-in-frontier-markets-tackle-corruption> accessed 7 September 2022.

administrations in developing countries through a targeted, real time 'learning by doing' approach'.[47] Working only where they are requested to, expert tax officials from another country are sent to work directly with the tax officials of the host country, providing not only specific advice on actual cases, but also, inevitably, sharing best practice and cultural norms in the process. Since its inception, it has helped to collect over US$1.4 billion in additional tax revenues and US$3.9 billion in tax assessed.[48]

At the time of writing in 2022, there are 49 ongoing peer-to-peer projects organized by TIWB including, for example, Her Majesty's Revenue and Customs in the UK supporting the Egyptian Ministry of Finance. The successes of TIWB could serve as a blueprint for peer-to-peer engagement in anti-corruption as itself an example of best practice engagement with corruption and development.

5.4   Developing our understanding

What seems clear is that, before planning an anti-corruption intervention in a specific sector or location, a practitioner must understand the historic and social context of the system of corruption in question to mitigate the potential for unintended consequences. What is required is a 'more systematic understanding of behavioural patterns, and experiments with innovative approaches, [which] can make anti-corruption efforts more effective'.[49] However, the Indonesian road-building study discussed above also raises questions about whether it is possible to understand in advance what alternative route corruption will take through a system if blocked at a specific point. Increased nepotism elsewhere in the procurement chain was an unintended consequence in this specific project in this location, but what can be extrapolated by the resolute anti-corruption practitioner scanning the horizon for unforeseen consequences in other interventions?

[47]   See <http://www.tiwb.org/about/> accessed 18 August 2022.

[48]   See   <https://www.oecd.org/tax/tax-inspectors-without-borders-continues-to-significantly-boost-domestic-revenue-mobilisation-in-spite-of-covid-19-crisis.htm> accessed 18 August 2022.

[49]   World Bank Group, 'Enhancing Government Effectiveness and Transparency, the Fight Against Corruption' (*World Bank Group*, September 2020) <https://documents1.worldbank.org/curated/en/235541600116631094/pdf/Enhancing-Government-Effectiveness-and-Transparency-The-Fight-Against-Corruption.pdf> accessed 18 August 2022.

More research is needed into other live examples where a specific entry point has been chosen for a specific measure – are there any generalities that can be extrapolated or applied? What frameworks can be developed that are of universal application? Can a dynamic system of monitoring be developed, applicable across sectors and jurisdictions, to spot and remediate corruption hotspots in real time? Effective monitoring must be ongoing and inform both day-to-day decision-making and the re-evaluation of strategic decisions. A static approach simply asking, 'are we achieving the goals we set?' does not go far enough to match the dynamic and adaptive nature of the corruption it seeks to tackle.

The Social Norms Learning Collaborative's 2021 paper, *Monitoring Shifts in Social Norms: A Guidance Note for Program Implementers*, sets out the need for further research in this area, arguing that, while recent years have seen a surge in interest in social norms and efforts have been made to highlight 'best practices for both shifting norms in programs and the measurement and evaluation of social norms [...] there has been a lack of consensus and guidance on how to systematically monitor social norms shifts during program implementation'.[50] The report goes on to discuss approaches and provides a guide for monitoring social norms in the lifecycle of a project; however, it leaves open the question as to how to incorporate the results into adaptive change management. Further research can be conducted into how to incorporate ongoing social norm monitoring into adaptive long-term programme monitoring, focusing on outcomes along the chain to avoid the pitfalls of siloed successes.

In 2019 Scharbatke-Church and Chigas argued that the interplay of the many possible drivers of corruption must be examined in any analysis of social norms to determine the right approach to create the best anti-corruption programme.[51] It is now necessary to apply the same logic to the monitoring and ongoing implementation stages of anti-corruption programmes. For example, as raised by the Indonesian study, to what extent can audits reduce corruption and continue to reap benefits overtime, without corruption emerging within

---

[50] The Social Norms Learning Collaborative. Monitoring Shifts in Social Norms: A Guidance Note for Program Implementers. April 2021. Washington, D.C. <https://www.alignplatform.org/sites/default/files/2021-04/lc_monitoring_shifts _in_social_norms_a_guidance_note_eng.pdf> accessed 18 August 2022.

[51] Cheyanne Scharbatke-Church; Diana Chigas, 'Social norms, corruption & fragility: Understanding social norms – a reference guide for policy and practice' (*The Fletcher School of Law and Diplomacy, Tufts University; Henry J. Leir Institute*, September 2019) <https://reliefweb.int/report/world/social-norms-corruption -fragility-understanding-social-norms-reference-guide-policy-and> accessed 18 August 2022.

the new regulatory framework? As identified by Marquette and Peiffer (2018), 'unintended consequences – welcome or unwelcome – receive little attention in anti-corruption academic and policy debates. This is a significant gap. For example, without knowing much about when and why benign side effects may have occurred, policy-makers cannot learn how they might be able to support them in future.'[52] This is a salutary reflection which speaks to all three of our pillars, not just social norms.

There are also potentially fruitful areas for research when addressing another question raised above, namely how to share best practice without alienating people and creating the unintended consequence of further entrenching social norms. A 2018 report, *The Future of Peer-to-Peer Learning and Partnerships in the New Development Agenda* by Effective Institutions Platform (EIP) and National School of Government International, highlights several other examples of public sector peer-to-peer learning, including UK civil servants supporting skills development, organizational structures and working practices to assist in the reform of the Kyrgyz civil service.[53]

To what extent and in what other sectors can this model and the example of TIWB be replicated? EIP describes peer learning as 'a potentially powerful way of sharing knowledge about doing public sector reform. This learning involves individuals exchanging knowledge and experience with each other, and diffusing this learning back to their organisations to ensure an impact—at scale—on reform initiatives.'[54] Private sector industry bodies are well placed to share best practice amongst their members; can these existing structures be harnessed to provide peer-to-peer support? Can private sector companies in development projects and commercial business operating in the developing world share best

---

52   Heather Marquette; Caryn Peiffer, "Islands of integrity'? Reductions in bribery in Uganda and South Africa and lessons for anti-corruption policy and practice' (*Developmental Leadership Program, University of Birmingham,* October 20181) <https://research.birmingham.ac.uk/en/publications/islands-of-integrity-reductions-in-bribery-in-uganda-and-south-af> accessed 18 August 2022.

53   Effective Institutions Platform; National School of Government International, 'The Future of Peer-to-Peer Learning and Partnerships in the New Development Agenda' (*Effective Institutions Platform; National School of Government International,* 2018) <https://www.effectiveinstitutions.org/files/The_Future _of_Peer_to_Peer_Partnerships_in_the_New_Development_Agenda.PDF> accessed 18 August 2022.

54   Effective Institutions Platform, 'A Guide to Peer-to-Peer Learning: How to make peer-to-peer support and learning effective in the public sector?' (*Effective Institutions Platform,* 2016) <https://www.effectiveinstitutions.org/files/The_EIP _P_to_P_Learning_Guide.pdf> accessed 18 August 2022.

practice across specific teams and engagement points? On the other hand, is there a greater risk of social norms being influenced in the 'wrong' direction in the private sector, with corrupt practices feeding back into the very organizations which had held themselves up as examples of best practice? What safeguards would need to be in place to mitigate both this potential risk and the competition and markets implications of such collaboration?

6 Conclusion

Corruption is undoubtedly an issue that continues to plague development across the globe. Given the breadth and depth of its impact on development activities, both financial and non-financial, a cross-party and multidisciplinary approach is required to continue making inroads in reducing corruption. This requires not only a 'top–down' international and governmental approach, but also a cross-societal and collaborative approach bringing together the private sector, NGOs, industry bodies and other groups. Equally, a 'bottom–up' understanding of the impact of corruption and the underlying motives, circumstances and social conditions in which corruption continues is necessary.

We started this chapter by looking at what we consider to be foundational pillars to combat corruption, namely: transparency, digitized process and social norms. However, we need to further unpack these pillars, conduct more research and better understand where they can be most effective. This is imperative to improving our odds of success and, moreover, to discern what bespoke measures and measures of general application we can implement to make reforms truly effective. Tackling corruption needs a practical focus on implementation, consequences and impact.

Understanding how such practical measures can be identified, designed and implemented is, however, where further research is required across the spectrum, and collaboration is necessary across all key protagonists to assess the impact of initiatives both before, during and after implementation. To achieve this, we have identified a range of topics, underpinned by our three pillars for success.

First, research is needed to understand how best to focus our reforms and the implementation of transparency measures. Studying the impact of ongoing reforms such as beneficial ownership registers and the additional bells and whistles that should, or should not, be attached to such regimes, alongside how businesses and the private sector navigate the same, offers an insight into effectiveness and impact.

Second, the future of the fight against corruption needs to better understand and identify the entry points for corruption within our processes, particularly in the post-award stages of projects, and how to enhance those processes to ensure greater transparency and accountability. Without such identification, we cannot really begin to design the solutions. On the one hand, we know robust, clear and integrity-centric processes can help guide reforms across sectors and development activities, particularly where means of accountability are improved through mechanisms such as whistleblowing and appeals processes; on the other, where and how to best implement such measures requires further study.

Finally, while transparency and process digitization can make meaningful inroads, efforts will nevertheless fall short if social norms remain unaddressed and unchanged, including where we hold on to an idea that corruption is caused solely by 'bad apples' we can remove from the system through automation. In order to alleviate the effects of corruption on development, we must undertake research to find effective, holistic and adaptive ways to dismantle and refashion social norms where they are breeding corruption, to harness and encourage social norms which encourage probity and honesty, alongside transparency and process measures.

We hope this chapter, its review of themes, case studies and research, provides a useful insight to guide future research efforts in the fight against corruption in development projects, alongside development bank activities, and we would encourage every opportunity to do so.

5 Anti-money laundering, suspect wealth and development

Dominic Thomas-James

Introduction

Much has been written about the causes of economic crime and its impact on development. Whether it is public sector corruption, embezzlement, or the funding of terror groups, the effects of financially motivated criminality are as broad as they are perhaps self-evident in the erosion and undermining of every possible hallmark of democracy, social functioning and institutional development. So much so, financial crime is at the very forefront of the global community's agenda. With each passing year, we see more rules, increased standards, more watchdog bodies and compliance officers, renaming and re-mandating of domestic organizations, as well as more and more international, non-governmental, charitable, research, and not-for-profit organizations joining the fight. While collective measures to shared problems is, of course, a key hallmark of globalization, one has to consider the realities of the vast sums of suspect wealth relative to the meagre amounts ever seized, recovered and reintegrated. One therefore has to consider whether more rules, or 'too many cooks in the kitchen', is indeed causing a problem by trying to solve one.

Many international instruments explicitly set out the effects of economic crime on development. Good examples include the United Nations Sustainable Development Goals ('SDG'), in particular SDG 16. While we perhaps *think* we know the impact from a conceptual standpoint, the true cost is much deeper. Moreover, the more frequently we see reported stories such as the Panama Papers, and the successive media reports on financial institutions' breaches of anti-money laundering ('AML') controls, can we be sure that progress is being made? Within the discourse on economic crime and development, oftentimes attention is – perhaps understandably – rooted in the notion of economic crime *in* the developing world. In other words, the widespread effects of graft, grand corruption, theft and abuse of public office in the world's poorest countries.[1] The word 'kleptocracy' has become a commonplace term in the development and international relations setting. Of course, the effects of this are self-evident: if a despotic regime pilfers public funds in favour of personal gain, then clearly that country's development is flawed. As a former president of the World Bank, James Wolfensöhn, put it, 'the causes of financial crisis and poverty are one and the same ... [if countries] do not have good governance [and] if they do not confront the issue of corruption ... their development is fundamentally flawed and will not last'.[2] Not only do these things have direct effects on resource allocation and public revenue, but more broadly it undermines key development pathways – such as institutional development in the legal and regulatory setting, empowerment of law enforcement, trustworthy appeals and complaints procedures, competitive marketplaces, and advancement in education leading to economic development, to name a few. These issues of course rightly hold paramountcy in the development discourse, and much has been written on corruption as a 'cancer' and at the heart of so many of the world's problems. Indeed, in the foreword of the United Nations Convention Against Corruption, it is described as an 'insidious plague that has a wide range of corrosive effects on society', while pointing to the inhibiting of development and sustaining poverty.[3]

An area that remains under-researched in the development setting is the role played by so-called offshore financial centres ('OFC') in terms of economic crime. The phrase 'offshore' is not very well understood, less so the complexities of the offshore finance and business industry. Exacerbated by events like the offshore data leaks,[4] the offshore world is firmly in the cross-hairs of the global community, many of whom think that so-called tax havens serve no useful economic purpose.[5] Building on earlier research on this interesting group of jurisdictions,[6] this chapter contends that there is a seriously lacking

---

[1]   See, for background, Sharman, J. C. (2017) *Despot's Guide to Wealth Management*, Ithaca, NY: Cornell U. Press.

[2]   Address to the Board of Governors, World Bank Group, Joint Annual Discussion, 28–30 Sept 1999, Press Release No. 2 [5].

[3]   Foreword to the UNCAC.

[4]   I.e. the Panama Papers, the Paradise Papers and the Pandora Papers: International Consortium of Investigative Journalists.

[5]   Oxfam (2016) 'Tax Havens Serve No Useful Economic Purpose: 300 Economists Tell World Leaders'. Available: https://www.oxfam.org/en/press-releases/tax-havens-serve-no-useful-economic-purpose-300-economists-tell-world-leaders (accessed 1 August 2022).

[6]   See Thomas-James, D. (2021) *Offshore Financial Centres and the Law: Suspect Wealth in British Overseas Territories*, Oxford, Abingdon: Routledge.

discussion within the development setting about the development concerns of island nations that have entered into the offshore and business services market. Across myriad issues relating to economic crime – be that anti-money laundering, corruption, abuse of offshore services, etc – there is a strong perception that offshore jurisdictions are harmful actors in the global community through such offerings, or that they serve no useful purpose, and therefore they are contributing to development challenges elsewhere. What this chapter hopes to capture and present are some of the development challenges of the offshore jurisdictions themselves. The purpose of this is to provide avenues of inquiry in terms of a research agenda, and better contextualize or explain the compliance records (or otherwise) of offshore jurisdictions. It is therefore hoped that this chapter contributes better understanding about these strategically important jurisdictions.

Concerns about money laundering and suspect wealth

It is first necessary to set out some of the international concerns about the impact of economic crimes like money laundering on development. Economic crime can include many types of interrelated misconduct – be it corruption and bribery, laundering of the proceeds of crime, terrorism financing, tax misconduct, theft and embezzlement, abuse of public office, serious organized crime like drug trafficking, or fraud and market abuse.[7] As alluded to, the true cost and extent of financially motivated misconduct can never be understood, given that greed in the human condition takes on many forms. For example, thinking about bribery often rests solely on monetary value – i.e., the paying of a bribe – while other nuances within the subject such as trading favours and influence, or profiting from a fiduciary duty or conflict of interest, become side-lined. Notwithstanding the difficulty of measuring money laundering's true impact or extent, various international bodies have attempted to estimate the problem – including the UN Office on Drugs and Crime, which estimates that between US$800 billion to US$2 trillion is laundered every year. Of course, the range this represents is considerable – which perhaps, actually, demonstrates the challenges with estimates on this area. Kar and Spanjers, in

---

[7]   For background on financial crimes, see Rider, B. A. K. (2015) *Research Handbook on International Financial Crime*, Cheltenham: Edward Elgar.

a 2015 UN study, estimated that some US$1.1 trillion from corruption and tax evasion flowed illicitly from developing jurisdictions.[8]

Money laundering is a facilitative type of crime which ensures that crime can remain an enterprise, or that misconduct can be concealed. There are, of course, many things that laundering might be trying to cover, whether it is laundering bribes through a series of shell companies, or utilizing phoenix companies to pay money into, withdraw, and then close before needing to submit returns, or using a legitimate business – such as a café – to launder drug money to make the money look like it came from legitimate custom. The international standard-bearer on money laundering norms, the Financial Action Task Force ('FATF'), defines money laundering as the processing of criminal proceeds to conceal illegal origin. Concerns about money laundering pertain to its effect on the financial system, its ability to sustain other, serious criminality, and its ability to undermine legitimate business. Indeed, section 1D of the UK Financial Services and Markets Act 2000 contains provisions regarding integrity and the need to ensure that the UK's financial marketplace is not used for purposes connected to financial crime.

Money laundering was, essentially, an offence developed to go after crimes like drug trafficking. There has been increasing attention on money laundering as an academic discipline, but also in terms of professional activity within the remit of compliance officers and other corporate governance professionals. AML is now a firm part of corporate governance, with internal controls and strategies being necessary for many types of business, and various categories of business being required to register for money laundering supervision, such as real estate agents or art market professionals.[9] Indeed, the FATF recommendations emphasize the risks apparent for designated non-financial businesses and professions ('DNFBPs'). Global attention on AML can be traced back to the 1970s and 1980s onwards with the so-called war on drugs and later the war on terrorism, which necessitated an ethos of 'starving the terrorists' or 'starving the criminals' of their resources and funding.[10] This ethos can find its root in

---

[8] Kar, D., and Spanjers, J. (2015) Illicit Financial Flows from Developing Countries: 2004–2013, Global Financial Integrity. Available: https://www.gfintegrity.org/wp-content/uploads/2015/12/IFF-Update_2015-Final-1.pdf (accessed 1 August 2022).

[9] See: Money Laundering and Terrorist Financing (Amendment) Regulations 2019, and Money Laundering, Terrorist Financing and Transfer of Funds (information on the payer) Regulations 2017.

[10] US Treasury Department (9.2002) 'Contributions by the Department of the Treasury to the Financial War on Terrorism: Fact Sheet'. Available: https://www

criminological thinking in terms of deterrence and related theories of criminal justice. Not only does rooting out the proceeds of crime make crime as an action choice less desirable, but it also carries the added benefit of assisting law enforcement and investigators from an intelligence standpoint. Oftentimes, money seized in county-lines drug dealing operations may *prima facie* pale in comparison with those familiar global estimate figures published by bodies like the UN about the international costs of money laundering. Yet, even a seizure of several thousands of pounds in a given case may be enough to disrupt an organized crime gang temporarily or even permanently, or, yet, push them to cut corners in their operations. The ability to encourage operational vulnerability in this sense is self-evident as an enforcement tool, thereby highlighting the deterrent function of law – if, indeed, AML carries that aim.

Concerns about money laundering and terrorism financing are firmly part of the international financial crime movement. At the European Union ('EU') level, for instance, a series of directives on money laundering have been enacted,[11] with which states have to comply and implement minimum AML standards (for example, as part of the 5th Directive implementing a publicly accessible beneficial ownership register, which was upgraded from the 4th AML Directive which prescribed that states could operate a central or public register). Within this movement, harmonization is an important feature that ensures the approach to shared challenges carries some sense of alignment. In this regard, the FATF standards[12] have become accepted global rules. The 40+9 AML and counter-terrorism financing ('CFT') recommendations manifest as soft law given the status of FATF, yet non-compliance with them, or indeed the FATF review and upgrade process more broadly, is essentially 'non-optional' and compliance therewith is a key hallmark of a country's global perception as to how they respond to the challenges posed by money laundering and terrorism financing. The standards themselves presuppose a very significant degree of compliance, and the organization operates a list of deficient countries who have been held to be non-compliant. The standards are constantly subject to revisions, as was seen with the consultation on beneficial ownership registers in recent years and a revision of Recommendation 24.[13] Countries have to not

---

.treasury.gov/press-center/press-releases/documents/2002910184556291211.pdf (accessed 1 August 2022).

[11] See: EU Directive (EU) 2018/843; and formerly 2015/849.

[12] The FATF Recommendations 2012.

[13] See FATF Revisions to Recommendation 24 and the Interpretive Note – Public Consultation. Available: https://www.fatf-gafi.org/media/fatf/documents/recommendations/pdfs/Pdf-file_R24-Beneficial-Ownership-Public-Consultation.pdf and also FATF Public Statement on Revisions to Recommendation 24, 4 March

only achieve technical compliance with these global standards (e.g., criminalizing money laundering), but are also judged on effectiveness of implementation, which is a broader review process that necessitates jurisdictions to engage in national risk assessments, among other initiatives, in preparation for the mutual evaluation and follow-up processes by peers in the FATF network. This is where cracks certainly start to form in terms of jurisdictions achieving compliance on paper versus in practice. While it should be an obvious conclusion, a one-size-fits-all approach is not always appropriate in the context of assessing how certain countries are doing in terms of their adherence to the global AML order. While standardization may well underpin any chance of success of a global system of rules for money laundering, the costs of implementing and achieving compliance with the recommendations are often significant. Sadly, if the UN estimate is just the tip of the iceberg, the reality is that these standards yield little in terms of results as compared with the sheer degree of suspicious illicit flows.

It is worth remarking on the concept of suspect wealth – something I have formerly defined as wealth that carries an inference of being somehow suspicious and should be explained. Suspect wealth can emanate from illicit activity like money laundering, corruption, terrorism financing, tax crimes, fraud or market abuse. Yet, increasingly, the discourse is taking aim at conduct, such as aggressive tax avoidance, which may have similar end results as crimes such as tax evasion. Suspect wealth may be wealth entering a jurisdiction under the guise of investment, yet without much information forthcoming as to the origins or ultimate beneficial owner of that wealth. Suspect wealth may also be wealth fleeing some sort of civil, societal or matrimonial injunction. In the area of tax avoidance, suspect wealth may be wealth that states have an interest in in terms of closing tax avoidance loopholes and thereby generating more by way of taxable revenue. It is therefore broader than wealth which can be solely aligned with the proceeds of a particular predicate crime – such as drug dealing for example. This is, however, where issues start to arise on the basis that drawing lines between illegality and its proceeds is a fundamental principle of fairness. In other words, just because something may look suspicious, there has to be evidence of the same and to a high hurdle – as was seen lacking in the case of *NCA v Baker*, of which more later. Why are we interested in broader notions of suspect wealth rather than simply the proceeds of crime? It is because it is having a serious effect on policy and legislation as desirable outcomes. For example, the media stories following the Panama and Paradise

2022. Available: https://www.fatf-gafi.org/publications/fatfrecommendations/documents/r24-statement-march-2022.html (accessed 10 August 2022).

Papers data leaks were clearly as much to do with serious money laundering as they were about the tax affairs of athletes. There is only so much legislation can cure, without over-parameterizing the aims and objectives so as to make them obsolete.

Certain standards, or even compliance more generally, can be challenging for certain jurisdictions based on an array of development challenges, which shall be explored in this chapter. This chapter progresses to consider a certain type of jurisdiction that is often perceived as being facilitators of financial crime – namely, offshore financial centres or so-called 'tax havens'. This category of jurisdiction presents a considerable problem in the discourse. Due to long-held criticisms about their status and perceived role as enabling the problems often considered in a developmental context, they are often first in line in terms of bearing condemnation. Yet, the development of such jurisdictions represents a considerably under-researched problem itself – given that various challenges shared by such jurisdictions may go some way in explaining not only their development into business marketplaces and therefore the reasons why they have diversified their economies into offshore centres, but also their records of compliance to date with international AML and other standards. If certain development issues identified in this chapter act as inhibitors to the implementation of such standards, this presents considerable scope for increasing the discussion about OFCs rather than resting on longstanding perceptions about them which often lead to problematic policymaking.

Offshore and development

Despite a steep development curve for many offshore jurisdictions, from barter-based economies in some instances to world-leading service providers in a matter of decades, the subject of their development remains under-researched. Even despite some offshore jurisdictions being middle-income jurisdictions, many residual challenges remain which are common to all. This section considers by way of example British Overseas Territories, which, of the 14, 7 have financial and business sectors which are therefore of relevance to this discussion.[14] Many are now considered wealthy or middle-income jurisdictions and, particularly pertinent regarding the latter, are therefore ineligible for development aid.

---

[14]   Anguilla, Bermuda, the BVI, the Cayman Islands, Gibraltar, the TCI, Montserrat.

Many island nations developed professional service sectors and offshore financial centres as a means of economic diversification by the mid-1980s and 1990s, which represented a growing trend in the Caribbean region during this period. By the mid-1980s, many island nations in the Caribbean had entered into this market, including the British Virgin Islands (BVI), Turks and Caicos Islands (TCI), Antigua and Barbuda, to name a few. Momentum was certainly gathering towards a sense of greater financial independence[15] in the case of formerly (or, still) dependent territories, gearing towards sustainable development – away from over-reliance on certain industries like agriculture or fishing to the provision of business and offshore financial services. Contrary to popular belief, this was not simply a nefarious plan concocted to exploit the growing onshore deregulation of financial services during this period, but rather a means for some jurisdictions – with complex and nuanced colonial histories – to diversify their economies, achieve sustainable development, and start to secure their place in the international community. Historically, this came in the context of the dissolving British Empire post-war, which necessitated a rethinking of jurisdictions' level of autonomy, future economic sustainability and prosperity. Such was modelled on a product and service offering. Taken against a backdrop of declining development programmes and bilateral aid initiatives during the 1980s and 1990s, small islands were able to establish these kinds of offerings which, in some instances, has turned them into world-leading service providers in a matter of years: such as the Cayman Islands, which is now in the highest wealth per capita across the region – a similar story to Bermuda, a jurisdiction whose reinsurance market is consistently ranked as leading. As Freyer and Morriss (2013) observe of the development of the Cayman Islands as a financial centre, they developed a regulatory system that allowed them to achieve more diversification and economic development than their peers.[16] It has to be noted that many island nations embarked upon this diversification journey with technical support and encouragement from larger jurisdictions such as the UK, particularly as regards legal drafting and reform, constitutional development, and the building of legal and other civic institutions. It is interesting, however, to contrast the development of jurisdictions within this group of territories. For instance, Bermuda has a per capita GDP of US$116,890 which, essentially, makes it one of the wealthiest countries in the world. Its financial and business services

15   Kudrle, R. T. (2016) 'Tax Havens and the Transparency Wave of International Tax Legalization', *University of Pennsylvania Journal of International Law*, 37(4): 1153–1182, 1155.
16   Freyer, T. A., and Morriss, P. A. (2013) 'Creating Cayman as an Offshore Financial Centre: Structure and Strategy Since 1960', *Arizona State Law Journal*, 45: 1297–1398, 1300.

sector contributes some 39% of GDP.[17] Despite its reinsurance industry being consistently ranked among the world's leading markets, Bermuda continues to suffer from deep-rooted economic and social challenges, such as living standards and wage gaps, homelessness and crime, as well as some of the aforesaid challenges with hurricanes and a relatively narrow economy. Anguilla, in a similar vein, continues to also suffer with challenges that often go overlooked by the international community. It has a relatively high GDP at US$21,068 per capita and is therefore too wealthy to be eligible for UK aid.[18] Recent challenges include its banking sector being placed under regulatory control of the Eastern Caribbean Central Bank, who found Anguilla's indigenous banks to be insolvent and placed them under receivership[19] for fear of a collapse occurring. Moreover, Anguilla, like many of its fellow island nations, suffers from dependency on neighbouring islands – logistically, Anguilla has no deep ports for the same level of international cruise traffic as other Caribbean destinations and its airport is of limited size as regards the same. According to its own government, as recently as 2017, Anguilla was considered to have the least developed public health facilities under a British flag.[20] Its legal and institutional development also raises challenges, with desperately needed constitutional reform having consequence on the development of modern laws, jurisprudence in the courts, and protracted implementation of modern statutes such as anti-bribery laws.

The issue of economic crime and misconduct *in* offshore jurisdictions – or mere allegations of them – can also have ravaging effects on the country's development. For instance, misconduct in public life has stunted the development of some such jurisdictions – an example being the Turks and Caicos Islands. In TCI, two British-instigated Commissions of Inquiry in a period of three decades saw the islands unilaterally come under two periods of direct

---

17   See: Bermuda Government (2017) 'Department of Statistics, Digest of Statistics 2017, Table 6.1'. Available: https://www.gov.bm/sites/default/files/2017-Digest -of-Statistics.pdf (accessed 5 December 2021), 2.

18   DfID (1 November 2018) 'UK Secures Change to International Aid Rules: Restrictions to Britain's Aid Support to Countries Affected by Crises and Natural Disasters that Severely Impact their Economy are Lifted', Press Release.

19   Caribbean Development Bank (2016) 'Loan & Project Summary: Anguilla Bank Resolution – Bridge Bank Capitalisation Loan'. Available: https://www.caribank .org/publications-and-resources/resource-library/board-papers/loans-grants -and-projectsummaries/anguilla-bank-resolution-bridge-bank-capitalisation -loan (accessed 10 December 2021).

20   Anguilla Government London Office (2017) 'Anguilla and Brexit: Britain's Forgotten E.U. Border'. Available: https://westindiacommittee.org/anguillabrexit -britains-forgotten-eu-border/ (accessed 10 February 2022).

rule based on Commission findings relating to ministerial misconduct.[21] In the BVI, in 2021/22, a similar Commission was led, with recommendations to impose direct rule, which was not invoked by the UK parliament. For a jurisdiction to face a Commission of Inquiry carries significant reputational concern, given the international media interest in it. After all, such allegations fuel the long-held offshore stereotype, rightly or wrongly. However, in the case of TCI, for a jurisdiction to effectively lose its sovereignty over such allegations – twice – is a sobering reminder that allegations and findings relating to economic crime and misconduct can have serious effects on development. In the latest instance of direct rule for TCI following the Sir Robin Auld Commission of Inquiry, its constitution was suspended, the right to trial by jury essentially disbanded, and there were serious concerns about taxation without representation.

One explanation as to the limited research on island nations that have developed as financial centres is that in many there are no higher education or research institutes. Combined this with the challenges of 'brain drain' – a phrase coined by the British Royal Society in the 1950s describing the outflow of professionals in the fields of science and technology to places like the US and Canada[22] – as well as strict immigration policies and traditional protectionist stance on citizenship or worker and residency permits, it is easy to see why some industries struggle to recruit personnel. Indeed, for younger people in the islands, the lack of higher education institutes necessitates overseas travel for work and training, particularly so for professions such as law and finance. The risk as far as domestic recruitment goes remains in terms of those students, newly qualified, staying overseas rather than returning home to practice.

Many offshore jurisdictions suffer from the same sorts of development issues – regardless of their individual levels of development. For example, even highly developed jurisdictions like Bermuda still suffer from relatively narrow economies with over-reliance on tourism, financial and professional services. Many of them also lack research establishments of the kind that research into their economic development might occur. There is also a general lack of scholarly interest at the international levels, despite how 'problematic' they are claimed to be by legislatures and transparency groups the world over. Their

---

21   For background on the two Commissions of Inquiry (the 1986 Commission led by Louis Blom-Cooper QC and the 2008/9 Commission led by Sir Robin Auld QC) see, Thomas-James, D. (2021) *above n6*, in particular Chapter 6.
22   Dodani, S., and LaPorte, R. E. (2005) 'Brain Drain from Developing Countries: How Can Brain Drain be Converted into Wisdom Gain?' *Journal of the Royal Society of Medicine*, 98(11): 487–491, 488.

geographic positioning – many being small, relatively homogenous, archipe-lagic islands in, for instance, the Caribbean or north Atlantic – raises serious concerns about connectivity, remoteness, and dependence on neighbouring countries for basics and luxuries. For a given island, it is the case that crucial things such as healthcare, postal service, or international arrivals are wholly or largely dependent upon neighbouring islands. Environmentally, many share challenges with their location and being prone to natural and environmental disasters, including hurricanes every few years. Many are located within tropic cyclone zones. During the 2017 hurricanes that affected several islands, including TCI, Anguilla and BVI, many fundamental hallmarks of functioning society – such as the legal system or integral government/civil service buildings – were upended and destroyed. As the then Attorney General for Anguilla, John McKendrick KC, recalled in the annual Inner Temple yearbook, he and many others were forced to live in temporary accommodation without access to mains utilities for some four months.[23] Despite rapid rebuilding efforts, these challenges resonate for years to come, not least the reputational impact on tourism.

Many of the challenges faced by such jurisdictions are often ignored by their international critics. Successive offshore data leaks paint a very damaging picture of offshore jurisdictions; but it is a picture – or perception – they have long been familiar with. For the international community – who may only have a perception about such jurisdictions from media reports or influential bodies that have agendas squarely aimed against the offshore world – greater thinking is needed as it relates to policy on the basis that these islands, for their many similarities and shared challenges, are different and at different stages, with fundamentally different capacity levels. For those who have been implicated internationally as being uncooperative, while these challenges do not justify the same, they may well provide some explanation. The next section considers some recent and ongoing areas of AML and economic crime com-pliance, as they relate offshore.

Compliance efforts

There are some areas worth discussing as examples of compliance in the offshore world. In the aftermath of the Panama and Paradise Papers, critics of

---

23   McKendrick, J. 'A Tropical Attorney General', Inner Temple Year Book 2018–2019, [134–135].

offshore and legislatures alike seemed perplexed at the idea that UK Overseas Territories, for instance, did not have public registers of beneficial ownership such as the UK's Persons with Significant Control register.

Eroding the ability to take advantage of 'form over substance' is another key area of the global AML framework, and one which many OFCs have taken on board in recent years. Focus on transparency initiatives in the wake of events like the offshore data leaks is perhaps inevitable, but at times focus drifts away from other functions which may further those same aims. For example, as the well-documented, and internally acknowledged, challenges that exist with the UK's own register of persons with significant control (notwithstanding its public nature), registers will take considerable time and resources to achieve not only compliance in a technical sense, but also the extent to which countries can achieve effectiveness in using the model for its stated purpose. One area worth considering is economic substance laws. These are designed to increase momentum against profit-shifting and aggressive tax avoidance practices. Emerging from the EU's Code of Conduct Group on business taxation's recent investigation into the tax policies of EU and third countries, the laws (which carry differences depending on the jurisdiction) essentially require entities registered there to have adequate operating expenditure relating to the relevant activities, enough suitably qualified personnel, and that the entity must essentially be directed and managed in the jurisdiction, as well as having its core income-generating activity therein. Importantly, the activities which tend to fall under these frameworks include banking, insurance, management of funds, leasing, financing, headquarters, shipping and distribution, intellectual property and holding services. Examples of OFCs that have implemented such laws in recent years include the Turks and Caicos Islands,[24] the British Virgin Islands,[25] Anguilla,[26] Bermuda,[27] the Cayman Islands,[28] and the Channel Islands. Elsewhere, we see progression in jurisdictions such as Panama, Belize, UAE, Barbados and Mauritius,[29] to name a few jurisdictions. The effect of economic substance requirements seeks to ensure that entities demonstrate

---

[24] See, for TCI: Companies and Limited Partnerships (Economic Substance) Ordinance 2018.
[25] See, for BVI: Economic Substance (Companies and Limited Partnerships) Act 2018.
[26] See, for Anguilla: the Companies (Economic Substance) Regulations 2019 and Companies (Amendment) Act 2019 (Economic Substance).
[27] See, for Bermuda: the Economic Substance Act 2018.
[28] See, for Cayman Islands: the Tax Cooperation (Economic Substance) Act (2021 revision).
[29] PWC Economic Substance for 2021. Available: https://www.pwc.com/jg/en/services/tax/updates/economic-substance-2021.html (accessed 10 August 2022).

adequate economic substance in a jurisdiction for their prescribed relevant activities, so that they should not be taxed elsewhere for the same.

Similarly, in the wake of the Panama and Paradise Papers, significant attention was placed on the notion of transparency as an effective tool for fighting money laundering. It has taken on somewhat of a silver-bullet complex, in terms of the likely effects. In the debate on the public register amendment relating to UK Overseas Territories in the Sanctions and Anti-Money Laundering Act, one of the amendment's architects, Rt. Hon. Andrew Mitchell MP, averred that closed registers do not allow the dots to be joined up.[30] Despite initial resistance from many of the Overseas Territories – doubtless fuelled by the non-optional nature of this unilateral legislative ultimatum which requires them to implement such registers (regardless of the extent of their incorporations and services sectors) by the end of 2023 – the territories eventually made commitments in line with this becoming a global standard. The latter point, however, seems a considerable way off – and even once this is achieved for companies, it seems difficult to see where the initiative ends in terms of the increasing number of registers and the significant degrees of both compliance and capacity they presuppose, as we are seeing with the latest register in the UK for overseas entities owning property.[31]

Indeed, in November 2022, the Court of Justice of the European Union, in joined cases C-37/20 | Luxembourg Business Registers and C-601/20 | Sovim[32] handed down judgment in a matter considering the validity of the public register provisions of the EU AML Directive. Importantly, it questioned the extent to which this provision of the Directive, which prescribes public accessibility to ultimate beneficial ownership registers of company information, conflicted with fundamental rights under the Charter of Fundamental Rights of the European Union, namely the right to private life and the right to protection of personal data. In the wake of this decision, some registers in the EU were taken offline. The decision demonstrates that a global standard remains wholly unresolved in this area, and raises questions relating to privacy, proportionality and data protection. It will therefore be interesting to monitor this development

---

[30]   HC Deb (1 May 2018) Vol 640, Col 203, Rt. Hon. Andrew Mitchell MP.
[31]   See: Economic Crime (Transparency and Enforcement) Act 2022, part 1; and, for background, House of Commons Library Research Briefing (13 June 2022) 'The Register of Overseas Entities: Five Things you Need to Know'. Available: https://commonslibrary.parliament.uk/the-register-of-overseas-entities-five-things-you-need-to-know/ (accessed 1 August 2022).
[32]   Press Release 188/22. Available: https://curia.europa.eu/jcms/upload/docs/application/pdf/2022-11/cp220188en.pdf (accessed 31 May 2023).

and the extent to which this decision may impact not only EU jurisdictions, but also others.

Problem and paradox and other issues for a research agenda

Reputational criticism towards OFCs is nothing new and can be traced back to the OECD-led anti-tax haven campaigns from the 1990s and 2000s. Nowadays, a campaign with those same sentiments is led by international transparency groups, tax justice bodies, charities, investigative reporters and other watchdog commentators. We have seen increased attention placed on OFCs by legislatures and anti-tax haven campaigners alike in the wake of the aforesaid offshore data leaks. Criticisms against offshore centres pertain to their perceived role in international finance and a long-held, common view that they are harmful actors in the global financial system. Such typically relate to their knowing or inadvertent receipt of suspicious wealth, facilitation of fiscal advantage, lack of cooperation, lax regulation and limited engagement with the international community on global norms.

While many of the criticisms levelled at so-called offshore jurisdictions might be warranted, continuing to frame such jurisdictions under one umbrella is causing confusion, rather than contributing clarity to a complex issue. As was evident in the media stories surrounding the Panama and Paradise Papers, as well as the reliance by some UK lawmakers on their probative value, it is unclear precisely *what* the offshore problem is or consists of. For example, it is unclear whether we are interested in the fiscal planning activities of athletes, or corrupt officials from developing countries embezzling public funds, or both? Are we interested in an actor owning property interests through an offshore trust for both privacy and fiscal reasons, or an organized crime group abusing the same for nefarious gain and the sustaining of organized crime? Of course, the picture is not entirely that simple, yet for any law or direction in policy-making to succeed, effectively parameterizing one's aims and objectives is paramount – rather than just relying on default impressions of 'offshore' to guide thinking. Offshore finance is not very well understood, nor are the fiscal affairs of ultra-high-net-worth individuals or corporations. Sentiments pertaining to fairness tend to displace any real depth of understanding as to such activity and the legitimate practices or uses thereof.

This issue was seen in the recent English High Court case of *NCA v Baker*,[33] the first major instance of an unexplained wealth order ('UWO') in the UK since the passage of the Criminal Finances Act in 2018. In *Baker* there was considerable attention placed on the suspicion surrounding offshore entities and complex structures. This focus was where investigative efforts fell short of the high hurdle required by the courts in such cases. After all, UWOs are civil matters that do not presuppose a conviction or the same level of suspicion in the criminal context and are, essentially, reverse burden-shifting. Importantly, the High Court in this case emphasized that there are legitimate uses of offshore structures. As Lang J emphasized at 97: 'The use of complex offshore corporate structures or trusts is not, without more, a ground for believing that they have been set up, or are being used, for wrongful purposes, such as money laundering.' Additionally, while acknowledging that offshore structures can be used and abused by criminals, Lang J emphasized some of the standard uses of offshore structures:

> There are lawful reasons – privacy, security, tax mitigation – why very wealthy people invest their capital in complex offshore corporate structures or trusts. Of course, such structures may also be used to disguise money laundering, but there must be some additional evidential basis for such a belief, going beyond the complex structures used.

With new thinking about disposing of cases relating to money laundering and suspect wealth, such as greater use of civil recourse such as UWOs, conceptualizing and profiling white-collar offenders is important from many directions of scholarship – be that criminology, sociology, penology or other criminal justice thinking. Moreover, understanding how best to dispose of, and deter, cases through the legal system or other mechanisms has led to a variety of initiatives, perhaps the largest pertaining to corporate governance, compliance and oversight in financial and related institutions. Many commentators pose that when the true cost of compliance is laid out, is it particularly worth it?[34] To better tackle this issue, our thinking about cultures of economically driven crime has to consider the extent to which the disruption, prosecution (or recourse through other legal fora) and disposal of cases actually serves foundational principles of theories such as deterrence – be that on an individual or general basis. In various key AML and anti-economic crime areas, we are seeing a departure from the traditional criminal law and its procedure, towards

---

[33]   NCA v Baker and ors [2020] EWHC 822 (Admin).
[34]   See, for example, *Financial Review* (6 August 2022) 'Anti-Money Laundering Is a Joke'. Available: https://www.afr.com/chanticleer/anti-money-laundering-is-a-joke-20220805-p5b7ho (accessed 10 August 2022).

new initiatives such as deferred prosecution agreements ('DPAs'), which we have seen in cases recently brought by the Serious Fraud Office in the UK against major companies like Airbus or Rolls Royce.[35] Further, we see other initiatives such as civil UWOs targeting the asset-holder (i.e., a politically exposed person, person involved in serious crime, or their family and close associates) to provide a legitimate explanation as to the source of the assets which are considered by law enforcement to be disproportionate to their known level of income or wealth.[36] We are also seeing increasing reliance by legislatures on the work of investigative reporters and the media in the wake of data leaks such as the Panama and Paradise Papers.[37] Reputational castigation of the kind seen in consequent media stories perhaps smacks of the by-gone punitive functions of 'shaming' and 'banishing'. While there are multiple routes to get to the same destination, caution ought to be given to the sheer onslaught of new principles, standards, rules and organizations that administer or monitor them. Rules, such as FATF principles considered in this chapter, may well create a one-stop rulebook; yet the fact that these are constantly updated, or that new organizations and bodies appear to be frequently created or renamed, may confuse rather than clarify the way towards that same destination.

Of course, the initiatives may well yet show considerable benefit in the interdiction of money laundering and economic crime. DPAs, for instance, target culture within an institution to enhance oversight and related controls, and free up significant human and capital resources for other investigations. UWOs enable the targeting of suspicious assets without the need to accompany this with criminal proceedings or a criminal conviction, per the traditional approach under the Proceeds of Crime Act. Yet, as with the latter, they remain astonishingly underutilized by those statutory bodies empowered to use them, relative to earlier predictions during the bill stage. This

---

[35] See, for example, Serious Fraud Office (31 January 2020) 'SFO enters into €991m DPA with Airbus as part of a €3.6bn global resolution'. Available: https://www.sfo.gov.uk/2020/01/31/sfo-enters-into-e991m-deferred-prosecution-agreement-with-airbus-as-part-of-a-e3-6bn-global-resolution/ (accessed 1 August 2022); and SFO (17 January 2017) 'SFO completes £497.25m DPA with Rolls-Royce PLC'. Available: https://www.sfo.gov.uk/2017/01/17/sfo-completes-497-25m-deferred-prosecution-agreement-rolls-royce-plc/ (accessed 1 August 2022).

[36] See: Thomas-James, D. (2017) 'Unexplained Wealth Orders in the Criminal Finances Bill: a suitable measure to tackle unaccountable wealth in the UK?', *J. of Financial Crime*, 24(2): 178–180.

[37] For example, Dame Margaret Hodge MP stated '[We] have the Guardian and Panorama to thank for their brilliant investigative work and for placing the data relevant to us under public scrutiny', HC Deb (13 November 2017) Vol 631, Col 55.

ever-changing landscape poses an important question: namely, the extent to which there is alignment in thinking between newer and older models. At the moment, there is a real risk that innovation modelled largely on convenience or resources proceeds without the foundations of why a particular behaviour may be considered criminal in the first place, and why society has an obligation to try and deter such behaviour and ensure against recidivism. The NCA UWO investigation of Hussein[38] is a good example, where property was simply forfeited by the recipient. A legitimate question a white-collar offender may ask is if there is the ability to essentially settle something, then is there a motivation to rebuild, restock and simply repeat the conduct in the first place? We also have to think more about the extent to which deterrence is being served by non-conviction-based disposals of cases. For UWOs, while one part of the problem may be addressed, and value realized, understanding the motivations as to the offending in the first place may go unconsidered and, rather, assumed to be 'just financial'. Indeed, eminent criminologist Edwin Sutherland's formulation of the white-collar criminal goes further and invokes things such as power and status, rather than just 'getting rich quick' (something such offenders may already be, or be well practised in becoming in terms of making fortunes, losing them, and repeating).

Finally, the issue of transparency as an effective tool in tackling money laundering needs much more research attention. Transparency efforts are often seen as a silver bullet in terms of their effect. Transparency in the AML setting, such as through registers of beneficial ownership (be that for companies, properties, overseas entities, or trusts) all sound like they will move the AML framework in the right direction; but law on the books alone cannot achieve this – as the UK's own register has demonstrated with its well-documented flaws.[39] In 2022, reforms were announced at UK Companies House addressing some of the challenges of the register, such as limited use of technology and lack of independent verification. As the aforementioned commitments by British

---

[38] See: NCA (18 July 2019) 'NCA secures first serious organised crime Unexplained wealth Order for property worth £10 million'. Available: https://www.nationalcrimeagency.gov.uk/news/nca-secures-first-serious -organised-crime-unexplained-wealth-order-for-property-worth-10-million #:~:text=News-,NCA%20secures%20first%20serious%20organised%20crime %20Unexplained%20Wealth,property%20worth%20%C2%A310%20million& text=A%20businessman%20with%20suspected%20links,%C2%A310%20million %20property%20empire (accessed 1 August 2022).

[39] UK Gov, DBEIS, Corporate Transparency and Register Reform White Paper (Feb 2022). Available: https://assets.publishing.service.gov.uk/government/uploads/ system/uploads/attachment_data/file/1060726/corporate-transparency-white -paper.pdf (accessed 1 August 2022).

Overseas Territories and Crown Dependencies indicate, some may well be able to achieve both technical compliance and effective implementation of this standard within a reasonable timeframe, but for others yet to even have functioning central registries, it is difficult to see how such commitments may serve those transparency aims. Indeed, even if compliance is achieved, the UK model – even with the infinite resources and loudest bark of all the major global AML players – suggests that public registers themselves may not serve any useful purpose once they are established. Even if a sophisticated system of verification is observed, which took the UK some six years to essentially acknowledge the pitfalls of its own register in this regard, there are a whole raft of issues that remain and loopholes potentially exposed – such as those relating to fractional beneficial ownership, thereby obviating a requirement to show one particular beneficial owner (a feature sometimes seen in complex estate planning). The UK Register of Overseas Entities is another example in this regard of detached thinking – with its maximum financial penalty for non-compliance with the reporting requirements being up to £2,500 per day.[40] Given the type of luxury property the Act presumably seeks to relate, even the maximum penalty may only be a percentage value of the properties concerned and perhaps seen as a simple cost in addition to high professional fees for advising on the same. Transparency also presupposes honesty during the reporting requirements. If the aim is to disrupt criminality, a register whose utility rests on the honesty of representations made, and therefore the accuracy of the data therein, in the hands of its users without independent verification, is hopeful at best in terms of meeting its aims. Simply put, even if they are told to, nefarious actors will not play the transparency game with regards to their entities or assets.

Concluding thoughts

This chapter has sought to contribute to the development discourse regarding AML and suspect wealth and, in particular, the role of the offshore world. It has identified various challenges faced by small island nations in the development context, which are issues that should be considered alongside their compliance records, particularly when considering law and policy that affects them all as a group of jurisdictions (rather than individual ones, which is often not the case despite their considerable differences and stages of development). The chapter has also flagged some other AML-related areas such as UWOs and registers of beneficial ownership. It leaves the reader with three suggestions for

---

[40] Section 8(2), Economic Crime (Transparency and Enforcement) Act 2022.

further research. First, a one-size-fits-all approach for small island jurisdictions that share the 'offshore' label is inappropriate and will not yield the types of results that global AML and transparency initiatives hope to achieve. Viewing and researching them as individual jurisdictions will generate a more nuanced understanding of their models, their sectors (many not even having prominent incorporation or trust service sectors), and challenges regarding their development. More work needs to be done to understand the development journeys and their ongoing challenges as a means of contextualizing their commitment to international standards but also their efforts in terms of implementation. Third, in the global AML and anti-economic crime movement, more research needs to be done to understand the complexities of the offshore world, to avoid conflating prejudiced suspicions with typical offshore-related activity. It is not sufficient for the discourse, and indeed in the context of investigations, to simply revert to offshore stereotypes as a means of buttressing a position. Finally, the AML movement has at its heart an increasing momentum towards use of transparency across many areas – most notably registers of ultimate ownership and control of legal persons. Transparency in and of itself may well sound positive, but it rests on overly simplistic ground in terms of how transparency may operate and what its objectives are. More research is needed into transparency as a tool, but also its status relative to fundamental legal safeguards (as the aforesaid Court of Justice of the European Union case indicates) and, simply put, to ensure a distinction between that which is substantively 'of interest', and that which is merely 'interesting'.

6   International interventions and sovereignty

Rohan Clarke

Introduction

Illicit markets are globally integrated. Advances in financial technology (FinTech) now facilitate instantaneous and anonymous cross-border movements of virtual assets and illicit financial flows. The typologies of economic crimes are also evolving, amidst the emergence of an increasingly sophisticated international network of legal, financial and tech-savvy professional enablers. These developments in the illicit global economy have come to subvert states' traditional exclusive control over activities within their territorial borders. But so have subversive money launderers, be they high-net-worth individuals (HNWIs) and power-wielding elites, multinational corporations, tax dodgers, jet-setting kleptocrats, or criminal and terrorist networks. These clandestine actors, operating across state borders, have undermined the rule of law, stability, sustainable development and ultimately the sovereignty of many developing countries. Whether spearheaded by the Financial Action Task Force (FATF), other institutional actors, transnational regulatory networks, or unilaterally or multilaterally by states, there is an evolving suite of international interventions to counter economic crimes and reduce impunity for both state and non-state actors intent on either enabling or participating in illicit economic activities. There is not always agreement on whether these counter-measures are the most effective, proportionate or dissuasive. The propriety of some of these interventions has particularly been questioned, from the standpoint of the sovereignty of those developing countries that bear the brunt of their regulatory obligations. Since the 1990s, for instance, international interventions have been primarily targeted at developing countries either perceived as high risk for money laundering or assessed to have strategic deficiencies in their anti-money laundering and counter-terrorist financing (AML/CFT) regimes. Accurately or not, developing countries are presumed more likely to shirk their regulatory responsibilities, whether legitimately ascribed or not. Regardless, the sovereignty of developing countries is perceived to be under 'siege' both from insidious internal threats posed by perpetrators and enablers

of economically motivated misconduct as well as from transnational AML/
CFT regulatory interventions.

Against this background, the twenty-first century globalized security landscape has given rise to unprecedented demands for political, legal and institutional ordering and other modes of international interventions to supress illicit
economic activities. These demands, presumably, are markedly different from
those in seventeenth-century Europe in which the idea of sovereignty emerged
in tandem with the modern nation-state. In a cosmopolitan post-War international legal order, the bedrock norms of consent, reciprocity, mutual respect,
sovereign equality, justice and multilateralism[1] have evidently come to be
regarded with varying degrees of normative significance. This is especially the
case in the context of transnational efforts to fight economic crimes. Although
academically contested, the idea of sovereignty has shown a particular vital-
ity in contemporary discourses on global regulatory governance. Through
well-grounded analysis, centred around a series of probing questions about
the empirical content, practical utility, and normative value of sovereignty,
the objective is to suggest a research agenda that may generate fresh ways of
thinking about international interventions and the marginality of sovereignty.
The hope is that such a research agenda may amplify the need to recentre
sovereignty as a development idea in transnational regulatory governance,
without compromising the integrity of the global financial system or efforts to
hold perpetrators of economic crimes to account.

The idea of sovereignty – what is it?

A research agenda on economic crime and development would have to pick up
the mantle of recasting sovereignty as intrinsically a sustainable development
idea. Sovereignty, at its core, refers to a state's claim to the exclusive right to
make rules within its territorial borders, without external control or intervention.[2] Juridically legitimate and concrete manifestations of state sovereignty
therefore include the decision of some developing states to pursue regulatory

---

[1]   Ted Piccone, 'Why International Law Serves U.S. National Interests' (Brookings
       Institute 2017).
[2]   Janice E Thomson, 'State Sovereignty in International Relations: Bridging
       the Gap between Theory and Empirical...' (1995) 39 International Studies
       Quarterly 213; Alan Hudson, 'Beyond the Borders: Globalisation, Sovereignty
       and Extraterritoriality' in David Newman (ed), *Boundaries, territory and postmo-
       dernity* (Frank Cass Publishers 1999).

arbitrage and competitive deregulation to attract international mobile capital from onshore jurisdictions. Many established offshore financial and corporate services sectors, backed by banking secrecy and confidentiality laws, and that afforded varying degrees of transparency in their beneficial ownership regimes. But so is the issuance of golden passports by several European countries to high-net-worth individuals (HNWI), including from former USSR and Russia, some of whom have abused their access to the City of London's financial and real estate sector for money laundering. Albeit a bedrock constitutive principle of international law and global governance, the idea of sovereignty has been theoretically and politically contested particularly in the post-War international legal order. Its meaning is often contingent on why, by whom, when, and how it is deployed.[3] This has implications for the perceived permissibility and legitimacy of transnational regulatory interventions to tackle economic crimes. The idea of state sovereignty can be traced to the Treaty of Westphalia (1648), which recognized modern nation-states as juridically mutually exclusive territorial entities, each having absolute and exclusive power and authority within their respective territories.[4] As a form of seventeenth-century political and legal ordering of inter-state relations, it ascribed juridical equality to all sovereign states, as well as several core legal rights and obligations, regardless of size or material capabilities, on admission to the international community of states.[5] These rights include respect for a state's territorial integrity, non-interference in its domestic affairs and the right to self-determination (economic or political). Sorensen usefully distinguishes between two dimensions of sovereignty – the constitutive (legal) and the regulatory (empirical).[6]

The constitutive content of sovereignty has remained largely fixed since the seventeenth century. It is tied to the criteria for international recognition of statehood, namely, a nation-state had to have a clearly delimited territory, a permanent population, stable government and constitutional independence

3   Michael Fakhri, 'Third World Sovereignty, Indigenous Sovereignty, and Food Sovereignty: Living with Sovereignty despite the Map' (2018) 9 Transnational Legal Theory 218.

4   Antony Anghie, 'The Evolution of International Law: Colonial and Postcolonial Realities' (2006) 27 Third World Quarterly 739; J Samuel Barkin and Bruce Cronin, 'The State and the Nation: Changing Norms and the Rules of Sovereignty in International Relations' (1994) 48 International Organization 107; Thomson (n 2).

5   Georg Sørensen, 'Sovereignty: Change and Continuity in a Fundamental Institution' (1999) 47 Political Studies 590; Robert H Jackson, *Quasi-States: Sovereignty, International Relations and the Third World* (Transferred to digital reprint, Cambridge Univ Pr 1990).

6   Sørensen (n 5).

of other states.[7] The sovereign nation-state was therefore not subject to any external authority higher than its own. It is this orthodox focus on the legal content of sovereignty that has led some to conclude that sovereignty is not being materially eroded,[8] even by international interventions targeted at economic crimes. Thus, every state has a right to non-intervention in its domestic affairs by other states and a corresponding duty to refrain from interfering in others' domestic affairs.[9] It follows that where a state's exercise of politico-legal authority, or its omission to do so, creates cross-border risks to the integrity of the international payment and financial systems or, the national interests, of other states, the onus is on that state to take remedial actions. Such interventions may be taken individually or consensually in collaboration with other states and transnational institutional actors. It is uncontroversial to suppose that states have a collective moral, if not legal, responsibility to fight economically motivated misconduct. The core international legal instruments targeting illicit finance – namely the 1988 Vienna Convention, the United Nations Convention against Transnational Organized Crime (2003) and the United Nations Convention against Corruption (2005) – almost have universal ratification. These conventions expressly provide for the criminalization of laundering of the proceeds of crime, and the establishment of comprehensive domestic regulatory and supervisory regime for financial institutions (FIs) and designated non-financial businesses and professions (DNFBPs), including the requirements for customer due diligence (CDD), record-keeping, reporting suspicious transactions, and for international cooperation on information exchange, technical assistance and mutual legal assistance. However, the instruments have expressly provided that obligations much be discharged in a manner consistent with the principles of sovereign equality and territorial integrity of states and non-intervention in the domestic affairs of other states (e.g., Article 4 of UNCAC). Thus, theoretical arguments of a state's unfettered right to exercise its sovereignty, even if it enables economic crimes or contravenes its international obligations, would not productively advance the discourse on international interventions aimed at eliminating safe havens for illicit finance.

The regulative content of sovereignty has been dynamic in the post-War, and especially in the post-9/11, international legal order. This dimension is variously defined either in terms of the state's empirical capacity to control, or exercise exclusive political authority over actors and activities within or across

---

[7]   ibid.
[8]   Barkin and Cronin (n 4).
[9]   Jackson (n 5); Sørensen (n 5) 598.

its borders.[10] Of course, the empirical sovereignty of seventeenth-century nation-states cannot be matched by that of post-colonial developing states.[11] Developing countries are therefore constrained by asymmetrical power relations in enforcing sovereignty claims in transnational AML/CFT governance. They are less integrated in the global financial system and, hence, are dependent on correspondent banking relations (CBRs) with international banks in advanced financial centres. This has often been leveraged to secure their compliance for intrusive AML/CFT regulatory and legislative expectations of powerful foreign regulators and law enforcement agencies. Divergences in technical compliance with FATF International Standards and effectiveness ratings between developing countries and richer countries are likely to be attributable to disparate resource capabilities.

A research agenda on economic crime and development would therefore need to address the regulatory risks posed by the resource capabilities of poorer countries in terms of their disempowerment. In other words, being under-resourced will cyclically result in low effectiveness ratings, black/grey-listing and increased monitored to address strategic deficiencies in their respective national AML/CFT regimes that impinge their sovereignty in very significant ways. In view of the challenges presented by the regulatory content of developing countries' sovereignty, such a research agenda may very well need to seriously explore whether developing countries require special and differential treatment and timelines to implement FATF AML/CFT standards, and to interrogate the policy coherence of the 'levelling the playing field' ethos of global AML/CFT governance. Particularly as AML/CFT compliance costs soar – especially for poorer countries that would naturally be assessed higher risk for money laundering due to structural factors such as geographic location, high levels of informality, and lower levels of financial development and penetration of regulatory technology (RegTech) – this should be an urgent undertaking. Unless addressed, the asymmetrical material and power capabilities along the Global North/South axis will continue to normalize a variety of international interventions within post-War development discourses, which prejudice developing states' sovereignty.[12] Thus, in reality, despite sovereign equality, it is material resources and power capabilities that determine a state's ability to assert or defend its sovereignty.[13] Consequently, interstate relations,

---

[10]   Sørensen (n 5); Thomson (n 2).
[11]   Sørensen (n 5).
[12]   ibid.
[13]   Thomson (n 2).

state practices, and forces external to the state, shape and recursively reconstitute the regulative content of sovereignty.[14]

The challenge, therefore, is to determine how to resolve problematic forms of international interventions to suppress economic crimes that prejudice the empirical sovereignty of developing countries. For present purposes, international interventions are broadly understood. They would encompass coercive OECD anti-money laundering blacklisting practices under its discontinued Non-Cooperative Countries and Territories Initiative (NCCTs), FATF grey-listing, and the EU's designation of high-risk third countries with strategic deficiencies in their AML/CFT regimes that pose significant threats to its financial system. Other disciplining practices, such as rankings and ratings by international watchdogs or compliance prescriptions by regulatory networks such as Egmont Group of Financial Intelligence Units based on financial sector surveillance, would qualify. So would conditional technical assistance to developing countries to comply with international standards to counter economic crimes. Thus, where interventions such as conditioned technical assistance require internal structural adjustments or restrict the policy choices or policy autonomy of governments, they might undermine the sovereignty of recipient developing states.[15] There is a view that political and economic conditionalities are often assumed in the context of negotiated, and therefore consensual, agreements and are consequently compatible with non-intervention. But could there be circumstances in which a state's free consent is arguably vitiated by necessity, of accessing the international financial and payment systems for instance? Or, should full and effective consent be reasonably inferred from reluctant acquiescence derived from their constrained choice? Even if conditioned aid, to which they consent, arguably leaves developing countries' politico-legal independence intact,[16] it would be difficult to argue that such interventions have not normalized interference in their internal regulatory affairs and, by extension, have curtailed empirical aspects of their sovereignty. More problematic forms of international interventions include the extension of extraterritorial regulatory and enforcement jurisdiction through long-arm

---

14   ibid.
15   David N Plank, 'Aid, Debt, and the End of Sovereignty: Mozambique and Its Donors' (1993) 31 The Journal of Modern African Studies 407; David Williams, 'Aid and Sovereignty: Quasi-States and the International Financial Institutions' (2000) 26 Review of International Studies 557; David Williams, *The World Bank and Social Transformation in International Politics: Liberalism, Governance and Sovereignty* (Routledge 2008).
16   William Brown, 'Sovereignty Matters: Africa, Donors, and the Aid Relationship' (2013) 112 African Affairs 262.

AML/CFT statutes to coercively influence developing countries' legislative, policymaking and regulatory activities. These state practices have become prevalent in transnational AML/CFT regulatory governance.

Does it matter?

States of the Global South have always insisted that their sovereignty should matter. The 1955 Bandung Conference of African and Asian countries, representing more than half of the world's population, was a watershed moment in calling for an anti-hegemonic post-War international legal order in which developing countries' sovereignty would matter. At Bandung, developing countries demanded the right to be consulted by Western powers on international policy decisions that affect the Global South. In essence, they demanded respect. These normative claims to sovereignty and sovereignty equality persisted in the third world's bid for a new international economic order (NIEO) to counter imperialistic interventions in their domestic affairs, and change the rules of international law to become more supportive of their development.[17] These efforts culminated in the United Nations' adoption of the Charter of Economic Rights and Duties of States (1974), which saw sovereignty assuming an economic dimension and becoming tied to the right to development.[18] Article 7 of the Charter of Rights and Duties of States, for instance, provides that every state has the right to choose its means and goal of development.

It is in the context of developing countries' ongoing quest for self-determination of their sustainable development policies and pathways, and ultimately to secure respect for their sovereignty, that their marginality in transnational efforts to drive up financial integrity and fight economic crimes ought to be analysed. On the one hand, the United Nations 2030 Sustainable Development Agenda and Sustainable Development Goal 16 in particular set as targets, by 2030, significantly reducing illicit financial flows, corruption and bribery, strengthening the recovery and return of stolen assets, and combating all forms of organized crime. On the other hand, high-risk regulatory activities such as liberal tax regimes, economic citizenship programmes, offshore financial services sector buttressed by banking secrecy and confidential laws, and inno-

---

[17]   Antony Anghie, 'Sovereignty and the Postcolonial State', *Imperialism, Sovereignty and the Making of International Law*, vol 37 (Cambridge University Press 2005).
[18]   Alan M Simon and Spencer Weber Waller, 'A Theory of Economic Sovereignty: An Alternative to Extraterritorial Jurisdictional Disputes Essay' [1986] Stanford Journal of International Law 337.

vative trust vehicles, which are being exploited for money laundering, were pursued by many developing countries absent much credible development alternatives. These policies were driven by the need to mobile international capital to finance their development, by innovatively leveraging their economic sovereignty. Similar policies were pursued by advanced financial centres, such as Wyoming, Nevada and Delaware in the United States, and across Europe, such as in Andorra, Cyprus, Gibraltar, Liechtenstein, Luxembourg, Malta, Monaco, Montenegro, San Marino, and Switzerland. While the risk of abuse of such financial and corporate services are generally high regardless of the jurisdiction in which they are hosted, the sovereignty of states of the Global South would appear to matter less than their developed counterparts in transnational AML/CFT governance. How to bridge this gap and promote fairness, mutual respect, and integrity in transnational regulatory interventions to tackle economically motivated crime must, therefore, form a critical dimension of a research agenda on economic crime and development. The sovereignty of developing countries has not mattered, in several important respects.

International AML/CFT rules

The international rule of law, as a principle of global governance, is essential for sustainable development. However, the misuse of deeply penetrative international AML/CFT political standards as law is normatively problematic as it impinges on the sovereignty of disproportionately targeted developing countries. Intuitively, these states' full and effective participation in the global AML/CFT regime is critical to the regime's effectiveness since they are presumed to be high-risk jurisdictions for illicit finance. International 'hard' law on countering illicit finance preserves state sovereignty, as it is premised on state consent in terms of the assumption of legislative, supervisory and enforcement obligations. Consent not only preserves the legitimacy of international rules, but incentivizes compliance and affords states the opportunity to vet those rules to ensure they are compatible with their development interests.[19] Consent further preserves a state's policy space to determine how to balance the allocation of scarce resources between fighting economic crimes in line with national risk assessments and financing other social sectors. However, the misuse of 'non-consensual' forms of international 'soft' law to impose AML/CFT obligations on states has become normalized. The role of international 'hard' law is

---

[19]   Andrew Guzman, 'The Consent Problem in International Law' <https://escholarship.org/uc/item/04x8x174> accessed 23 October 2021.

being supplanted by more pragmatic use of international 'soft law' standards.[20] The increasingly digitized global illicit economy, changing typologies of economic crimes and money laundering channels, increasingly sophisticated criminal actors and tech-savvy professional enablers, and crypto-laundering have necessitated faster, more flexible and responsive international interventions. However, respect for developing countries' sovereignty requires their full and effective participation in international rule-making processes. The FATF International Standards were developed without the Global South's full and effective participation and coercively diffused globally.

The enforcement of FATF International Standards as prescriptive rules, albeit conceptualized as guidance, means that these international soft law standards often exceed AML/CFT obligations states assumed under relevant treaty law. While more flexible and responsive, to the extent that the FATF International Standards were promulgated by the exclusive club of rich OECD countries, they prejudice the principles of sovereign equality, territorial integrity and non-interference in the domestic affairs of other states. Additionally, the FATF International Standards are constantly being updated. Failure to keep pace with regulatory expectations and compliance with evolving international 'soft law' AML/CFT standards, due to resource constraints, have resulted in poorer developing countries being de-risked and excluded from international capital markets.[21] The continuing loss of correspondent banking relationships (CBRs) with financial intermediaries in advanced financial centres has severely disrupted money and value transfer services and remittance flows in regions such as the Caribbean.[22] De-risking exacerbates financial exclusion and undermine developing countries' advances toward achieving the SDGs. Thus, the elaboration of transnational rules and regulatory standards, in such a non-participatory manner, reproduces the subordinate status of states of the

---

[20] David Kennedy, 'Law, Expertise and Global Political Economy' (2018) 23 Tilburg Law Review 109.

[21] Julia Black and David Rouch, 'The Development of the Global Markets as Rule-Makers: Engagement and Legitimacy' (2008) 2 Law and Financial Markets Review 218.

[22] Caribbean Policy Research Institute (CAPRI), 'The Correspondent Banking Problem: Impact of de-Banking Practices on Caribbean Economies' (The Caribbean Policy Research Institute 2016) <https://capricaribbean.org/documents/correspondent-banking-problem> accessed 12 March 2020; Caribbean Development Bank, 'Decline in Correspondent Banking Relationships: Economic and Social Impacts on the Caribbean and Possible Solutions' (Caribbean Development Bank 2016) <http://www.caribank.org/wp-content/uploads/2016/05/CorrespondentBanking_May6-1.pdf>.

Global South.[23] What are seen as legitimate, or at least excusable, interventions in the internal affairs of other states have thus become pliable.[24] No doubt, this trivialization of developing countries' sovereignty is attributable to the shift in locus of transnational AML/CFT standards from international treaty law to non-consensual soft law and the latter's coercive enforcement. This is a slippery slope for the international rule of law on illicit finance.

International institutions and practices

Article 10 of the Charter of Rights and Duties of States reaffirms that all states are juridically equal and have the right to participate fully and effectively in international decision-making. This would include decision-making on transnational efforts to fight economically motivated misconduct and protect the integrity of the global financial and payment systems. Likewise, SDG 16 provides for the development of effective, accountable and transparent institutions at all levels. SDG 16 further provides for ensuring responsive, inclusive, participatory and representative decision-making at all levels. Yet, despite the FATF International Standards shaping the legal, supervisory, and enforcement regimes of over 200 sovereign states and jurisdictions around the world, the FATF has no international legal standing. This is an anomaly in global governance. A research agenda on economic crime and development would therefore need to seriously examine options for institutional design to democratize the FATF. This would affirm the Global South's normative claim that global governance ought to be premised on a more just and equitable basis, and respect sovereign equality, non-intervention and non-hegemony.[25] Transnational AML/CFT regulatory governance has taken a cosmopolitan turn. A multiplicity of powerful non-state actors and regulators have disempowered states and eroded their sovereignty,[26] in very significant ways in the fight against economic crimes. Non-governmental organizations (NGOs), international institutions and transnational regulatory networks (TRNs) of varying legal standing, and populated by unaccountable experts and technocrats, have sought to compel sovereign states to comply, or account for non-compliance, with non-consensual international AML/CFT and anti-corruption 'soft law' standards. These international 'watchdogs', along with powerful onshore reg-

---

23   Anghie (n 17).
24   Barkin and Cronin (n 4).
25   Simon and Waller (n 18).
26   Kennedy (n 20).

ulators of the EU and OECD Member States, have often resorted to coercive unilateral blacklisting, rankings, ratings and other disciplining strategies to hold sovereign developing countries to higher levels of financial integrity. The impacts of such disciplining practices have been most felt by developing countries with offshore financial centres (OFCs).[27] Beginning in the late 1990s and early 2000s, there was a simultaneous assault on Caribbean OFCs, in particular, under the FATF Non-Cooperative Countries and Territories Initiative that effectively was a 'blacklist' of jurisdictions for money laundering purposes, and under the OECD Harmful Tax Competition campaign. Under these initiatives, Commonwealth Caribbean 'tax havens'[28] were discriminatorily and arbitrarily targeted for blacklisting,[29] as though their sovereignty did not matter.

Continued grey-listing of many developing countries as 'non-cooperative' or 'high-risk' jurisdictions for the purposes of money laundering have unintentionally threatened their sustainable development.[30] Such practices continue to treat their sovereignty as if it does not matter. This has been echoed, for instance, by a senior Caribbean legal expert on offshore matters who has insisted that the global AML/CFT regime has been used as a 'red herring' for preventing capital flight from onshore advanced financial centres.[31] This is not far-fetched. In 1994, the policy that underpinned the campaign against OFCs was framed in one of the first seminal International Monetary Fund reports on OFCs, almost exclusively in terms of addressing 'the migration of financial activity from major financial centres to these offshore markets,' and on the basis that 'OFCs have challenged the supremacy of large industrial countries' financial centres

---

[27] Rose-Marie Belle Antoine, 'The Caribbean Offshore Financial Services Revolution – A Bold, Futuristic Initiative Requiring Brave Leadership' (Trinidad & Tobago, 5 May 2015).

[28] Brigitte Unger and Joras Ferwerda, 'Regulating Money Laundering and Tax Havens: The Role of Blacklisting' (Tjalling C Koopmans Research Institute 2008).

[29] Jason C Sharman and Gregory Rawlings, 'Deconstructing National Tax Blacklists: Removing Obstacles to Cross-Border Trade in Financial Services – A Report Prepared for the Society of Trust and Estate Practitioners' (Society of Trust and Estate Practitioners 2005).

[30] Matthew Collin and others, 'Unintended Consequences of Anti-Money Laundering Policies for Poor Countries – A CGD Working Group Report' (Centre for Global Development 2015); Vijaya Ramachandran, 'Mitigating the Effects of De-Risking in Emerging Markets to Preserve Remittance Flows' (2016) 22 *EMCompass, International Finance Corporation, Washington DC* <https://openknowledge.worldbank.org/handle/10986/30348>.

[31] Rose-Marie Belle Antoine, 'Keynote Address – Enablers of Financial Crime: Tax, Finance and Societies' (Copenhagen Business School Tax Group 2021).

with their array of tax and regulatory incentives to non-resident investors'.[32] This tension between global AML/CFT and global tax policy, from the late 1990s, persists. The reputational consequences and quasi-sanctions to which tropical offshore jurisdictions have been subjected[33] has never been directed at similar financial centres onshore, such as Andorra, Ireland, Lichtenstein, Luxembourg, Monaco, and Switzerland. In fact, Luxembourg and Switzerland had refused to endorse the OECD's 'Harmful Tax Competition Initiative' Report in 1998, and Austria, Belgium, and Luxembourg did not agree to automatic exchange of information mandated by the EU Directive on the Taxation of Savings (2005).[34] For these liberal onshore financial centres, already integrated into the global payment and financial systems, it would appear that their sovereignty matters more.

Another problematic form of intervention in the area of transnational AML/ CFT governance that has brought into question the extent to which the sovereignty of developing countries matter, is the expansive extraterritorial extension of legal, regulatory and enforcement jurisdiction to counter transnational economic crime threats. The spatiality of regulatory rules tends to mirror the spatiality of geopolitical power and regulatory hegemony.[35] The United States, for instance, has framed its interests fighting economic crimes globally, in line with its control of the SWIFT system, the global volume of US-denominated financial transactions and its international hegemony. The US federal government has projected its federal legal and regulatory reach accordingly. This form of international intervention is often perceived as illegitimate interference with the sovereign jurisdiction of other states.[36] Section 6308 of the US Anti-Money Laundering Act 2020, which builds on the USA PATRIOT Act, has expanded the authority of the US Treasury and the Department of Justice (DOJ) to issue subpoenas to foreign banks for records related to their US correspondent accounts. They may also request records of any account at the foreign bank, including records held in a foreign country. Additionally, subpoenas may be issued to foreign banks in connection with any US criminal investigation or civil forfeiture action, including but not limited to federal money laundering investigations. The propriety of these unliteral interventions, and their broader

---

[32] Marcel Cassard, 'The Role of Offshore Centers in International Financial Intermediation' (International Monetary Fund 1994) 1.

[33] Steven Dean and Attiya Waris, 'Ten Truths about Tax Havens: Inclusion and the "Liberia" Problem' (2021) 70 Emory Law Journal.

[34] David Spencer, 'The UN: A Forum for Global Tax Issues? (Part 1)' [2006] International Taxation 42.

[35] Hudson (n 2).

[36] ibid.

implications for transnational AML/CFT regulatory governance, must therefore be addressed on any research agenda on economic crime and development, not least because their intrusiveness disempowers weaker states' legal and regulatory decision-making. Such unilateral interventions operate outside of institutionally embedded multilateral processes for developing countries to render account for shortcomings in compliance with the FATF International Standards, such as regional peer-review or mutual evaluation processes. Consequently, they undermine the sovereignty of targeted countries.

Why should sovereignty matter?

A research agenda on economic crime and development would need to reinforce respect for state sovereignty and the right to non-intervention by states in others' internal regulatory affairs, as a legitimate international legal expectation. Despite the risk-based approach (RBA) to implementing FATF International Standards, the costs associated with maintaining domestic AML/CFT regimes remains excessive. There is need for scaling up AML/CFT technical assistance and RegTech transfer to developing countries, to mitigate lower technical compliance and effectiveness ranking of their domestic AML/CFT regime. This requires effective international cooperation and mature partnerships in the context of transnational AML/CFT governance. For this reason, state sovereignty should matter. Coercive disciplining practices and exclusionary legal, political and institutional processes will only lead to reluctant acquiescence to FATF International Standards that lacks enduring support. A commitment to respecting state sovereignty and the need to safeguard the integrity of the global financial system from money laundering and other illicit economic activities are not mutually exclusive. The question then becomes how to constructively balance both. How can this balance be struck in ways that might productively promote genuine AML/CFT policy ownership and improve the overall effectiveness of global AML/CFT efforts? The answer might well lie in promoting genuine development partnerships to support the fight against economic crimes. Judging from unintended sustainable development consequences of transnational AML/CFT regulation, international interventions and other countermeasures that are not premised on genuine and mature partnerships between developing countries and advanced economies have generally been unproductive. Genuine development partnerships are premised on equality and mutual respect.[37] They must show an openness to genuine co-learning along the Global North/South axis, rather than promote top–down agenda-setting, policymaking and conferral of regulatory, supervisory and enforcement responsibilities.

Conceptualizing a research agenda on economic crime and development to promote meaningful development partnerships, which respect developing countries' sovereignty, in the context of transnational AML/CFT efforts, is no easy task. The regulatory interests at stake, along the onshore/offshore and Global North/South axes, are divisive. Those partnerships would be overshadowed by the asymmetrical power relations, coercive blacklisting and 'naming and shaming' practices that have characterized transnational AML/CFT governance, especially post-9/11. Indeed, there is a view that 'genuine partnerships' between rich and poor countries based on equality and mutual respect are impractical as long as donor countries are 'in possession of the purse' and recipient countries 'the begging bowl'.[38] Furthermore, genuine partnerships in which sovereignty matters might not necessarily serve the interests of powerful actors in global governance. Such partnerships would require that donors cede power or accountability over the use of development assistance and erode their influence.[39] It is useful to recall, in this regard, that the discourse on development partnerships was meant to signal a move away from over-prescriptive and interventionist development strategies for poorer countries. Reframing aid relations as 'partnerships' between donor and recipient developing countries was meant to convey a sense of the reversal of asymmetrical power relations within the institutions, processes and structures of global governance to give recipient countries 'ownership' over development policies, ensure the alignment of assistance with recipient countries' national priorities, and ultimately preserve their agency.[40] From the current state of affairs with blacklisting and naming and shaming, there is some pessimism as to whether powerful states will genuinely respect the regulatory policy space and autonomy of developing countries they deem high-risk for money laundering and to be practising harmful taxation.

Institutionalized Global North/South partnerships in the field of transnational AML/CFT regulatory governance is underdeveloped and understudied. For

---

[37]   Steve Kayizzi-Mugerwa, 'Africa and the Donor Community: From Conditionality to Partnership' (1998) 10 Journal of International Development 219.

[38]   Rita Abrahamsen, 'The Power of Partnerships in Global Governance' (2004) 25 Third World Quarterly 1453, 1454.

[39]   Abrahamsen (n 38).

[40]   ibid.

present purposes, this might be usefully examined in the context of one of the longest institutionalized Global North/South development cooperation frameworks – European Union (EU)–Organisation of African, Caribbean and Pacific Group States (OACPS) Strategic Partnership buttressed by successive Lomé Conventions and now the Cotonou Partnership Agreement. The OACPS has been highly critical of the EU's unilateral and punitive approach of 'blacklisting' third countries it designates as non-cooperative for taxation and AML/CFT purposes. OACPS President-in-Chief, Uhuru Muigai Kenyatta, President of the Republic of Kenya, has written to Charles Michell, President of the European Council, Ursula Von der Leyen, President of the European Commission, and David Sassoli, President of the European Parliament, condemning the EU's unilateral blacklisting practices which, in his view, tarnish the images of affected countries and disrupt their cross-border financial flows. At the regional level of the Caribbean Community (CARICOM), heads of state and government continue to strongly criticize the EU's harmful backlisting practices as 'unilateral, arbitrary and non-transparent'.[41] CARICOM has lamented the EU's 'unwillingness to take into account the substantial progress made by CARICOM Member States at compliance with global standards'.[42] CARICOM has also condemned the fact that 'along with the unprecedented task of staging a post-COVID-19 economic recovery, these CARICOM States now have the added the burden of being subjected to the EU's discriminatory tactics'.[43] More recently, Barbados Prime Minister Mia Mottley has described the island's listing as 'unjustified and disproportionate'.[44] The OACPS itself has often claimed that the EU's listing practices do not adequately take account of country contexts. The OACPS has also taken issue with divergences between the FATF grey list and EU AML/CFT list. For instance, OACPS countries are convinced that political considerations, rather than pure technical AML/CFT and tax transparency weaknesses determine the EU's listings, as countries of strategic importance to the EU, such as Albania, Turkey, and the United Arab Emirates (UAE), are on the FATF grey list of monitored jurisdictions but not on that of the EU.

Despite a longstanding strategic partnership, it is only fairly recently that the OACPS has sought to have discussions on AML/CFT and tax transparency

---

[41] Caribbean Council (The), 'Barbados, CARICOM Strongly Object to EU Finance Ministers' Blacklisting Decision' [2020] *Caribbean Insight* <https://www.caribbean-council.org/barbados-caricom-strongly-object-to-eu-finance-ministers-blacklisting-decision/> accessed 22 April 2021.

[42] ibid.

[43] ibid.

[44] ibid.

issues mainstreamed within political dialogue within the context of the existing multilateral development cooperation framework of the Cotonou Partnership Agreement.[45] Amidst the reputational and sustainable development consequences of blacklisting, and the EU's unwillingness to engage diplomatically, the OACPS has established an Ad Hoc Ministerial Contact Group on the EU List of Non-Cooperative Tax Jurisdictions and List of Third Countries on Anti-Money Laundering and Countering the Financing of Terrorism (AML/CFT). The Contact Group was established to engage in dialogue with the EU on its approach to designating non-cooperative tax jurisdictions and third countries with strategic AML/CFT deficiencies that are perceived to threaten the integrity of the EU financial system. What is rather interesting is that the OACPS has called for such political engagement on financial and AML/CFT governance to be mainstreamed within EU–OACPS joint institutions and the OACPS–EU development partnership. The OACPS has further called for policy coherence with the UN framework for international tax reform, which is more inclusive and transparent, and for a UN body to be established to ensure greater inclusion of developing countries in international rule-making processes on international tax and AML/CFT governance. In essence, they have demanded respect, and that their sovereignty should matter.

The frailty of EU–OACPS institutionalized engagement on AML/CFT and tax transparency matters highlights developing countries' frustration with the scant regard paid to their sovereignty in the context of interventions to fight economic crimes. The EU having weaponized the disbursement of disaster relief to small Caribbean islands ravished by hurricane Irma in 2017, for instance, by unilaterally setting strict timetables to which devastated countries were to meet AML/CFT and tax transparency expectations, hardly counts as a commitment to 'genuine partnership' in fighting economic crimes. The EU does, however, financially support the Caribbean Financial Action Task Force and effort to build regional AML/CFT capacity. But global AML/CFT agenda-setting by exclusive groups of powerful actors who then 'partner' with recipient developing countries to support their compliance with international AML/CFT standards promulgated without their full and effective participation is problematic. Understandably, therefore, there is a view that Global North/South 'partnerships' simply 'whitewash' coercive practices and conditioned development assistance. The assumption is that such partnerships mask continued international interventions in developing countries' regulatory

---

[45]   Organisation of African, Caribbean and Pacific Group of States Secretariat. OACPS escalates action on unilateral publication of EU Blacklist. Brussels, 3 July 2020.

affairs behind a veil of legitimacy, rather than transferring power to recipient countries.[46] From this perspective, Global North/South partnerships are a form of liberal rule and disciplining veiled under promises of self-management by, and respect for the agency of, recipient states, through strategies of cooperation and inclusion rather than through overt coercion.[47] Any research agenda on economic crime and development must therefore explore how such development partnerships could be productively leveraged to ensure mutual accountability and respect for sovereignty, fairness, proportionality, and policy ownership in transnational AML/CFT and arrangements across the Global North/South axis. This is ultimately the case for international moral leadership in AML/CFT regulatory governance. A research agenda on economic crime and development would also need to consider how such partnerships can be incentivized if poorer, weaker, and smaller developing states' compliance, even if attributable to reluctant acquiescence, is being secured anyway through unilateral blacklisting, grey-listing, 'naming and shaming', and other forms of coercive international interventions.

Conclusion

In summary, one of the main challenges for a research agenda on economic crime and development is to imagine alternative futures for the global governance of economic crimes – futures that are development-centric, principled by fairness and proportionality of international interventions, and respecting of sovereignty and sovereign equality of developing countries. Ideas of sovereignty and sovereign equality, which permeate most areas of global governance, have been markedly uninfluential in transnational AML/CFT regulatory governance, especially post-9/11. Yet, what degree of sovereignty can be reasonably expected in an interconnected world with globalized economic crime risks cannot easily be answered. How can the international community productively leverage the power of partnerships to better accommodate the legitimate expectation of developing countries for their sovereignty to matter?

---

[46]   Gordon Crawford, 'Partnership or Power? Deconstructing the "Partnership for Governance Reform" in Indonesia' (2003) 24 Third World Quarterly 139.
[47]   Abrahamsen (n 38); Jennifer M Brinkerhoff, *Partnership for International Development: Rhetoric or Results?* (Lynne Rienner Publishers 2002); Crawford (n 46); Andi Mallarangeng and Peter Van Tuijl, 'Partnership for Governance Reform in Indonesia: Breaking New Ground or Dressing up in the Emperor's New Clothes?: A Response to a Critical Review' (2004) 25 Third World Quarterly 919.

Is this even realistic within the prevailing asymmetrical power structures embedded within the international legal ordering and institutional design for global economic crime governance? Can sufficient appetite be generated to take on these contentious issues if the compliance of developing countries with international 'soft law' AML/CFT standards and foreign regulatory expectations is being secured anyway, albeit through coercive and other problematic disciplining practices? It is these unresolved normative, legal and policy issues which account for the reluctant acquiescence of many developing countries to the FATF's international 'soft law' standards and, in addition, to their expensive implementation. To assume that that developing countries have an inertia towards honouring their collective responsibilities to combat economically motivated misconduct would be facile. In the final analysis, at least empirically, the idea of sovereignty does not appear to matter in the context of international interventions to curb economic crimes, but it should. Perhaps, only by deliberately establishing a research agenda that mainstreams development ideas in the transnational regulatory governance of illicit finance can one hope to rescue the sovereignty of developing countries from the slippery slope of international interventions.

7 Governance, integrity and sustainability – joining the dots?

Chizu Nakajima

Introduction

Much discussion in the international arena is dominated by all matters relating to sustainability in recent years. Taking it narrowly, some focus on environmental issues, others on sustainable development, particularly as we have now had 17 goals articulated in the form of the United Nations Sustainable Development Goals since 2015, or even more specifically in terms of 'environment, social and governance' (ESG) matters in the investment management community. And the significant role that companies play has been recognized, as was predicted at the turn of the century by the then president of the World Bank, who stated, 'The proper governance of companies will become as crucial to the world economy as the proper governing of countries.'[1] Nevertheless, notwithstanding the increasing interest and debate in the various global fora and business circles, relatively less attention has been given by scholars in the relevant fields that attempts to join up issues relating to the governance of companies, matters of integrity and development, partly due to the siloed way in which research is conducted, and partly due to the complexity that such an attempt would bring. This chapter is not designed to comprehensively capture what has been achieved thus far in research but to focus on some developments and to attempt to highlight a number of issues to add to the growing research agenda, through a legal/institutional lens.

The financial turmoil that began in 2007 and the ensuing financial crisis prompted calls for remedial measures which, in turn, led to a spate of regulatory reforms, or at least attempts at reform, on both sides of the Atlantic. The world of corporate governance did not escape political and media scrutiny, and

---

[1] As was stated by James Wolfensohn, former president of the World Bank, *The Economist*, 2 January 1999, at 38.

resulting consultation documents and interim and final reports with various recommendations for change have been countless.

Nevertheless, one fundamental issue that has not been addressed in much depth – until relatively recently and only when we began to pay more attention to other stakeholders in connection with sustainability – is in regard to the dominance of shareholder primacy in the thinking of both business leaders and academics for the last few decades. It has been pointed out, 'Throughout the 1980s and 1990s in the U.S. and U.K., the logic of shareholder value maximization became the guiding principle, informing the top management strategic decision making in listed firms as well as (and because of) the way institutional shareholders evaluated their performance.'[2] Indeed, shareholder primacy, shareholder value maximization and profit maximization have, often, been used synonymously and interchangeably in discussion. Those advocating shareholder focus often refer to the article by Professor Milton Friedman, a Nobel laureate economist, published in 1970, in which he famously states, 'there is one and only one social responsibility of business – to use its resources and engage in activities designed to increase its profits ....' However, this on its own is, in fact, a misquote. What is omitted, deliberately or unintentionally, is what follows in the same sentence, which states: 'so long as it stays within the rules of the game, which is to say, engages in open and free competition without deception or fraud.'[3] In other words, Professor Friedman was not advocating the type of behaviour manifested in many a corporate collapse, such as Enron and WorldCom earlier this century, and bank failures and ensuing revelations of unacceptable practices not only in the financial services sector but right across the board and globally.

Notwithstanding the misquote, as has been observed by scholars, 'the concept of shareholder primacy and the concomitant insistence that the only real purpose of the corporation is to deliver shareholder value has become an almost universal principle of corporate governance and often goes unchallenged',[4] thus becoming a 'rational myth'.[5] A number of law scholars have

---

[2]   J. Lok, 'Institutional Logics and Identity Projects' (2010) 53 *Academy of Management Journal* 1305, at 1305.

[3]   M. Friedman, 'The Social Responsibility of Business is to Increase its Profits', *The New York Times Magazine*, September 13, 1970.

[4]   T. Clarke, *Corporate Governance: Cycles of Innovation, Crisis and Reform* (2022) Sage Publications, Thousand Oaks, at 108.

[5]   On rational myth, see, for example, L. B. Edelman, C. Uggen and H. S. Erlanger, 'The Endogeneity of Legal Regulation: Grievance Procedures as Rational Myth' (1999) 105 *American Journal of Sociology* 406.

questioned this premise, pointing out that the company law of these countries, where shareholder primacy is perceived to be dominant, does not require directors to maximize shareholder value.[6] Indeed, more recently, a substantial report prepared by an international law firm at the request of the United Nations Environment Programme Finance Group, has concluded, after extensive comparative legal research of key jurisdictions, that there are no legal obstacles for the investment management sector to take into consideration environment, social and governance matters in their decision-making, and further states that the report's findings 'will help dispel the all-too-common misunderstanding that fiduciary responsibility is restricted by law, and solely and in a narrow sense, to seeking maximization of financial returns'.[7]

Nevertheless, as has been observed,[8] those who have entered the corporate governance debate in the last few decades, given the predominant message found in mainstream academic commentary and discussions in the business media, would easily have been led to believe that shareholders are the only *raison d'être* of the company, and that the board's sole duty is to serve the interests of the company's shareholders, and the best way to fulfil this is to maximize the value of the company's shares. Some leading US corporate lawyers have even gone as far as to claim that it is 'the end of history for corporate law' by

---

[6]   See, for example, M. Blair and L. Stout, 'Director Accountability and the Mediating Role of the Corporate Board' (2001) 79 *Washington University Law Quarterly* 403, in regard to the US. In regard to the UK, see, for example, D. Collison, S. Cross, J. Ferguson, D. Power and L. Stevenson, *Shareholder Primacy in UK Corporate Law: The Exploration of the Rationale and Evidence* (2011) Council of the Association of Chartered Certified Accountants, London, and A. Keay, 'Moving Towards Stakeholderism? Constituency Statutes, Enlightened Shareholder Value and All That: Much Ado About Little?', http://dx.doi.org/10.2139/ssrn.1530990. In regard to Australia, for example, see M.A. Anderson, M. Jones, S. Marshall, R. Mitchell and I. Ramsay, 'Shareholder Primacy and Directors' Duties: An Australian Perspective' (2008) 8 *Journal of Corporate Law Studies* 161.

[7]   United Nations Environment Programme Finance Initiative and Freshfields Bruckhaus Deringer, *A Legal Framework for the Integration of Environment, Social and Governance into Institutional Investment* (October 2005), at 3, highlighting the misunderstanding of an English case, *Cowan v Scargill* [1985] Ch 270. In this report, the relevant laws of France, Germany, Italy, Japan, Spain, UK and USA are examined. See also a more recent report, Freshfields Bruckhaus Deringer, 'A Legal Framework for Impact – Sustainability Impact in Investor Decision Making' (2021), commissioned by UNEP FI, The Generation Foundation and PRI.

[8]   M. Blair and L. Stout, *ibid,* at 405.

stating that a global consensus is converging on this approach:[9] that is, to make 'corporate managers strongly accountable to shareholder interests and, at least in direct terms, only to those interests',[10] in order to maximize social welfare on the part of business enterprises.

Drivers of corporate governance debate and resulting short-termism

What has been the driver of the corporate governance debate in the last few decades? Much of the policy, advocated by various intergovernmental organizations, emphasizes the importance of corporate governance on the basis that 'quality corporate governance contributes to thriving financial markets', which, in turn, 'contribute to national economic success'.[11]

Indeed, based on the above-mentioned logic, incentive mechanisms, such as executive share option schemes, have been widely implemented so as to align the interests of the management with those of the company's shareholders. Notwithstanding the logic behind these incentive mechanisms, they have led to a number of 'unintended consequences', such as short-termism on the part of management[12] and more egregious practices, including executive share

---

[9]   Although the application of the institutional theory to corporate governance research has moved some scholars away from pursuing a universal corporate governance model by enabling them to identify various institutions that result in different corporate governance practices and their outcomes, shareholder primacy remains central to their discussion. For discussion of institutional approach to corporate governance research, see, for example, I. Filatotchev and C. Nakajima, 'Internal and External Corporate Governance: An Interface between an Organization and its Environment' (2010) 21 *British Journal of Management* 591 and I. Filatotchev, G. Jackson and C. Nakajima, 'Corporate Governance and National Institutions: A Review and Emerging Research Agenda' (2012) *Asia Pacific Journal of Management*, https://doi.org/10.1007/s10490-012-9293-9.

[10]   H. Hansmann and R. Kraakman, 'The End of History for Corporate Law' in J. N. Gordon and M. J. Roe (eds.). *Convergence and Persistence in Corporate Governance* (2004) Cambridge University Press, Cambridge, at 42–43.

[11]   F. B. Cross and R.A. Prentice, *Law and Corporate Finance* (2007) Edward Elgar, Cheltenham, at 7.

[12]   See, for example, R.A. Posner, 'Are American CEOs Overpaid, and, If So, What If Anything Should Be Done About It?' (2009) 58 *Duke Law Journal* 1013, at 1026–27, pointing out that share options have the effect of making executives focus on the short term.

option backdating,[13] thereby bringing into question the integrity of corporate leaders and undermining confidence in systems and mechanisms that have been introduced to ensure that they maintained and protected the integrity of their companies.

The post-mortem of the financial crisis and of the ensuing global economic downturn has pointed to short-termism that permeates across business sectors,[14] caused by business decisions being made increasingly on the basis of short-term shareholder value maximization.[15] Indeed, in the continuing debate as to whether bank lending or equity markets is a better source of corporate finance, which predates the last financial crisis, concern has been expressed that reliance on equity markets might fuel companies' short-term focus. It has, nevertheless, been dismissed on the basis that 'empirical research generally bears out the importance of developed and free equity markets'.[16] Therefore, the majority of measures that were introduced post-financial crisis appear to continue to revolve around shareholder primacy.

Notwithstanding the lack of appetite for any fundamental rethink of the existing capital markets system, a number of measures have been introduced in order to counter short-termism. One such example is the UK's Stewardship Code. While encouraging institutional shareholders, who look after individuals' wealth such as pension funds, to take a longer-term view on their investments is a welcome move, institutional investors themselves have been judged on a shorter-term basis in regard to their performance and, therefore, as the

---

[13] See, for example, N. Bishara and C. Schipani, 'Strengthening the Ties that Bind: Preventing Corruption in the Executive Suite' (2009) 88 *Journal of Business Ethics* 765.

[14] See, for example, remarks by Sheila C. Bair, Chairman of the US Federal Deposit Insurance Corporation of the to the National Press Club, Washington, DC, June 24, 2011, https://archive.fdic.gov/view/fdic/1673 (accessed 26 October 2022).

[15] See D. Krehmeyer, M. Orsagh, and K. N. Schacht, *Breaking the Short-Term Cycle: Discussion and Recommendations on How Corporate Leaders, Asset Managers, Investors, and Analysts Can Refocus on Long-Term Value* (2006), CFA Institute, quoting a survey, published in J. R. Graham, C. R. Harvey, and S. Rajgopal, 'The Economic Implications of Corporate Financial Reporting' (2005) 40 *Journal of Accounting and Economics* 3, of more than 400 financial executives, in which 80% of the respondents indicated that they would decrease discretionary spending on such areas as research and development, advertising, maintenance, and hiring in order to meet short-term earnings targets and more than 50% stated they would delay new projects, even if it meant sacrifices in value creation.

[16] F. B. Cross and R.A. Prentice, *Law and Corporate Finance* (2007) Edward Elgar, Cheltenham, at 5.

Kay Review in 2012 highlighted, their ability to engage with the companies in which they invest has been questioned.[17]

The counterbalancing voices against the singular focus on shareholder primacy have, in the past, been dismissed as lacking in substance to be viable alternatives to the shareholder primacy model.[18] They may be further muted as a result of the continuing economic woes in Japan and a series of Eurozone crises impacting negatively on the economies of those countries that represent the Rhenish model of corporate governance, such as Germany, France, Italy, and Spain, where more attention is given to the interests of a wider group of stakeholders and focusing more on sales, market share, headcount and long-term ownership.[19]

It has been noted that there is politically and economically motivated opposition to moving away from shareholder-centric corporate governance in the countries where shareholder primacy prevails, due to the focus on the company as an economic entity, the function of law as enhancer of trade freedom, the political policy to promote competition, and the market for corporate control facilitated by hostile takeovers.[20] Indeed, as the aforementioned Kay Review observes, the resulting short-term views taken by the company management is not due to what the law states but stems from the misunderstanding of 'British law', pointing out that some directors erroneously think that 'their duties can be reduced to an obligation to achieve the highest possible share price in the short-term'.[21]

As has been discussed above, the support for shareholder primacy has been further reinforced by law and economics literature, following the logic that

---

[17]   See generally, The *Kay Review of the UK Equity Markets and Long-Term Decision Making: Interim Report*, February 2012, BIS, UK, and The *Kay Review of the UK Equity Markets and Long-Term Decision Making: Final Report*, July 2012, BIS, UK.

[18]   See, for example, H. Hansmann And R. Kraakman, *Ibid.,* at 36–42.

[19]   M. Blowfield and A. Murray, *Corporate Responsibility: A Critical Introduction* (2008) Oxford University Press, Oxford, at 19.

[20]   C. Nakajima, 'Corporate Governance and Responsibility' in B. Rider (ed.) *Research Handbook on International Financial Crime* (2015) at 158. See also A. Keay, *ibid.,* at 52, A. Sundram, and A. Inkpen, 'The Corporate Objective Revisited' 15 Organization Science 350 at 352 and S. Deakin, 'The Coming Transformation of Shareholder Value' (2005) 13 Corporate Governance: An International Review 11.

[21]   The *Kay Review of the UK Equity Markets and Long-Term Decision Making: Final Report*, July 2012, BIS, UK, at 57.

good corporate governance enhancing shareholder value will lead to thriving financial markets, which in turn will ensure economic growth,[22] a view which has been very much endorsed, at least in the past, by intergovernmental organizations, such as the World Bank.[23]

The continuing soul-searching debate

Post-financial crisis, there have been an increasing number of 'AGM revolts' where shareholders have voted against executive remuneration, attracting much media attention. And the UK government in the Queen's Speech in May 2012 included a proposal for legislation to make shareholders' votes in regard to remuneration binding.[24] Shareholders remain a focus of attention in the current debate on corporate governance reform, and given that not only the media and political attention but the persistence of academic research focused on shareholder wealth maximization, this trend is set to continue. In the current economic climate, there appears to be no sign that the debate will shift its attention to more fundamental questions, such as in whose interests should a company be run[25] and what is a company for?[26] And notwithstanding the criticism of 'audit capture' or the 'financialization' of corporate governance, the dearth of literature addressing these fundamental issues post-financial crisis, and the lack of proper soul searching in regard to, for example, UK company law and governance, continue. Rare exceptions can be found in a report, published by the Council of the Association of Chartered Certified Accountants (ACCA) in 2011,[27] in which it recommends 'a re-examination of central aspects of company law in the UK', on the basis that the findings from

---

22   See, for example, F. B. Cross and R.A. Prentice, *Law and Corporate Finance* (2007) Edward Elgar, Cheltenham, at 7.

23   See, for example, A. Demirguc-Kunt and V. Maksimovic, 'Law, Finance and Firm Growth' (1998) 53 *Journal of Finance* 2107.

24   Department for Business and Innovation, Queen's Speech 2012 (9 May 2012) available at https://www.gov.uk/government/speeches/the-queen-s-speech-2012 (accessed 30 October 2022).

25   See, for example, C. Nakajima and W. Harry, 'Is the Desire to Embed Corporate Social Responsibility within Organizations at a Crossroads?' (2012) 42(3) *International Studies of Management & Organization* 3.

26   C. Handy, 'What is a Company For?' *Michael Shanks Memorial Lecture* (5 December 1990), published in (March 1991) 139 (5416) *RSA Journal* 231.

27   D. Collison, S. Cross, J. Ferguson, D. Power and L. Stevenson, *Shareholder Primacy in UK Corporate Law: The Exploration of the Rationale and Evidence* (2011) Council of the Association of Chartered Certified Accountants, London.

the extensive literature review and empirical work suggest that the question 'in whose interests should companies be run?' was not seriously examined as part of the Company Law Review (CLR).[28] It argues that maximizing shareholder value (MSV):

> as an established corporate objective, and the accompanying shareholder-value rhetoric have arguably contributed to the recent financial crisis through the pursuit of a single objective at the expense of long-term prosperity and wider social consid- erations. In particular, there is evidence to suggest that Anglo-American countries have a 'case to answer' in regard to their consistently poor measures of social well-being relative to those of other developed economies that typically pursue a 'stakeholder', rather than a 'shareholder' model of capitalism. This evidence was not considered as part of the CLR.[29]

The report raised a further four issues as meriting re-examination in the future review of UK company law. First, the need for greater corporate accountability and for reconsidering the introduction of the Operating and Financial Review. Second, a recommendation made by the CLR, but not adopted by the govern- ment, for a standing body keeping company law under review. The third and fourth issues were 'linked to potentially perverse consequences of maximising shareholder value', namely the regulations governing the market for corporate control in the UK, and the level of directors' remuneration.[30]

Another initiative in soul searching has been led by the Institute of Chartered Accountants for England and Wales, in the form of *Dialogue in Corporate Governance: New Challenges*, comprising five fundamental questions in regard to corporate governance in the UK,[31] the first question being, 'What should companies be responsible for?' which was launched in April 2013. The primary concern of the first question, as the ICAEW states, 'is the responsibilities of companies rather than the mutual responsibilities between companies, boards and shareholders that are defined for example in the UK Companies Act 2006 and the UK Corporate Governance and Stewardship Codes'.[32] And in the context of this initiative, the scope of companies to be considered was set wider

---

[28]   *Ibid.*, at 6.
[29]   *Ibid.*
[30]   *Ibid.*
[31]   ICAEW, *Dialogue in Corporate Governance: New Challenges*, available at https://www.icaew.com/technical/corporate-governance/principles/dialogue-in -corporate-governance (accessed 9 November 2022).
[32]   ICAEW, *What Should Companies Be Responsible for?*, available at https://www .icaew.com/-/media/corporate/files/technical/corporate-governance/dialogue-in -corporate-governance/what-should-companies-be-responsible-for.ashx?la=en (accessed 9 November 2022).

than what is the norm in corporate governance discussion, which tended to focus on publicly listed companies. This wider scope is somewhat prophetic, as a few years later, as a result of the catastrophic collapse in 2018 of Carillion, a large private company, which sent shock waves across the UK business sector, prompted the government to review the status quo.[33]

The first question posed in the ICAEW initiative is reminiscent of the lecture on 'What is a company for?' given by Professor Charles Handy in 1990, who stated that the systems required reform in such a way as to allow each 'corporate community' to decide its own purpose.[34] His lecture also included the following prophetic statement, which resonates with many post-financial crisis comments:

> My long-term worry is that property prevails over community. As the world shrinks and companies aim for global reach, property will inexorably annex communities ... the Anglo-American system which, I have argued, works less well for everyone than the German or Japanese models, may prevail, driving the whole world into a fever of short-term speculation, forcing companies to become asset traders rather than wealth producers...[35]

The ICAEW initiative may also immediately provoke the recital of Professor Milton Friedman's oft-quoted statement, which has been mentioned earlier.

The ICAEW paper identifies four fundamental responsibilities owed by companies, namely: achieving a business purpose; behaving in a socially acceptable way; meeting legal and regulatory requirements; and stating how responsibilities are met. The ICAEW, while accepting that compared with 'a responsibility to serve shareholders alone', addressing multiple responsibilities 'makes life too complicated', the primary reason for which the Company Law Review decided against the pluralist approach and in favour of shareholder primacy (albeit with the additional introduction of 'enlightened shareholder value'), it

---

33   See the initial consultation, Department for Business, Energy and Industrial Strategy, 'Insolvency and Corporate Governance: Government Response' (20 March 2018) and the final report, 'Insolvency and Corporate Governance: Government Response' (26 August 2018). For discussion, see C. Nakajima, 'Corporate Failures and Governance – The Ongoing Debate' (2018) 39 (5) *The Company Lawyer*, 137.

34   C. Handy, 'What is a Company For?' *Michael Shanks Memorial Lecture* (5 December 1990), published in (March 1991) 139 (5416) *RSA Journal* 231.

35   *Ibid.*, at 238.

asserts, 'Life, whether for individuals or organizations, is complicated because it involves accepting the need to balance different responsibilities.'[36]

Indeed, the present author concurs with the ICAEW's view and would ask why simplicity should be a matter of priority. We live in a complex world of globalization and interdependence. While there is outrage against spiralling executive pay, those who think they deserve astronomical sums surely should, at least, be expected to justify their enormous pay packages on the basis that they are an extremely rare breed of extraordinarily gifted individuals, who can deal with complex issues and prioritize and balance different interests that are both internal and external to the organizations which they are charged to lead.

Furthermore, it is respectfully submitted that the continuing tendency in scholarship to keep 'corporate governance' and 'corporate (social) responsibility' as distinctly separate subjects to be studied independently requires careful review[37] as, indeed, the world of practice has long abandoned such distinction, particularly as the nascent concept of ESG, discussed below, matures. The siloed approach of scholars may well suit advocates of agency theory who wish to focus solely on the relationship between management and shareholders, dismissing relationships with and interests of other stakeholders as outside the remit of corporate governance and an unnecessary distraction to managerial focus and therefore to their own research agenda. On the other hand, advocates of corporate social responsibility (CSR) or corporate responsibility (CR), particularly those who see this area as purely voluntary, find it of crucial importance to keep the corporate governance debate outside their remit of discussion and consideration. While a certain degree of categorization may be useful when it comes to academic course delivery and therefore the sales of appropriately titled textbooks, it may serve as unnecessary hindrance to ascertaining what companies (and their management) need to be taking into consideration in running their businesses.

Looking at issues that company management now face from the perspective of those who are concerned with legal risks and their implications confronting contemporary business, the debate in regard to whether shareholder primacy

---

[36] ICAEW, *What Should Companies Be Responsible for?*, available at https://www
.icaew.com/-/media/corporate/files/technical/corporate-governance/dialogue-in
-corporate-governance/what-should-companies-be-responsible-for.ashx?la=en
(accessed 9 November 2022), at 5.

[37] For further discussion, see C. Nakajima and W. Harry, 'Is the Desire to Embed
Corporate Social Responsibility within Organizations at a Crossroads?' (2012) 42
(3) *International Studies of Management & Organization* 3.

or stakeholder theory should prevail in corporate governance, or whether C(S)R should remain in the realm of voluntary action, seems a matter of relative insignificance nowadays. Indeed, even if we confined our argument to the initial definition that 'corporate governance is about the system by which companies are directed and controlled',[38] which forms the basis of the current UK Corporate Governance Code, it would be tolerably clear that such system could not be concerned solely with shareholder interests, let alone shareholder value maximization. Furthermore, one only needs to look at the areas listed as those covered by CSR standards, such as natural environment, labour, money laundering, bribery and corruption, and human rights,[39] to realize that these areas are highly regulated and therefore no longer 'voluntary', particularly if the management does not wish the company to engage in illegal activities and/ or to be subjected to legal and regulatory sanctions.

Paradigm shift to wider stakeholder interests and beyond

Those who wish to continue to pursue CSR purely as voluntary often refer to the pronouncement made by the European Commission in 2001 that CSR is 'a concept whereby companies integrate social and environmental concerns in their business operations and in their interaction with their stakeholders on a voluntary basis'.[40] This is now superseded by the Commission's new definition, which states it as 'the responsibility of enterprises for their impacts on society'.[41] The Commission goes on to emphasize:

> Respect for applicable legislation, and for collective agreements between social partners, is a prerequisite for meeting that responsibility. To fully meet their corporate social responsibility, enterprises should have in place a process to integrate social, environmental, ethical, human rights and consumer concerns into their business operations and core strategy in close collaboration with their stakeholders....[42]

---

[38]   Committee on the Financial Aspects of Corporate Governance (Cadbury Committee), *Report of the Committee on the Financial Aspects of Corporate Governance* (1992) London, at 15.

[39]   See generally, for example, M. Blowfield and A. Murray, *Corporate Responsibility* (2011, 2nd edn.) Oxford University Press, Oxford.

[40]   European Commission, Green Paper COM (2001) 366, at 6.

[41]   European Commission, *A renewed EU strategy 2011–14 for Corporate Social Responsibility* COM (2011) 681 final, at 6.

[42]   *Ibid.*

This resonates with the observation made by a leading scholar in corporate governance, stating, 'Bridging the great divide between corporate governance and corporate social and environmental responsibility is the next great challenge for business.'[43] And 'that only a fundamental redesign of corporate forms, objectives and value measures can fully meet the realities of responsibility'.[44]

This brings us back to the aforementioned Professor Handy's lecture in 1990, in which he challenged the existing corporate forms, objectives and performance metrics, and advocated an overhaul that allows companies to be run in a sustainable manner so as not to 'endanger our children's future'.[45]

And, as for the ICAEW initiative, it also casts the net wider and distinguishes it from 'conventional corporate governance thinking which tends to view companies in terms of their responsibilities to shareholders and investors'.[46] It supports its approach of setting a broad range of corporate responsibilities on the basis that this would better address various challenges to corporate behaviour and culture in recent years, such as in regard to executive remuneration, short-termism, distrust of the listed company model, aggressive tax avoidance, lack of diversity and legislative delays.[47] The ICAEW also anticipates challenges to their proposal on the basis that: it will make life too complicated (as mentioned above); companies will not be able to fill expectation gaps created by irreconcilable responsibilities owed to different parties, forcing them to make difficult decisions; it deviates from the enlightened shareholder value enshrined under the Companies Act 2006; and intermediaries focused on short-term financial gains will value companies pursuing responsibilities at the expense of financial gains.[48]

Those concerns notwithstanding, the ICAEW asserts that taking on a broad range of responsibilities will enable a company to remain 'agile in adapting to the environments where it does business and should be better at anticipating and even eliminating potential expectation gaps' and to benefit from 'a solid foundation for building and maintaining trust'.[49] The present author fully sup-

---

[43]   T. Clarke, *International Corporate Governance: A Comparative Approach* (2nd edn., 2017) Routledge, London, at 411.
[44]   *Ibid.*
[45]   C. Handy, *supra*, at 238.
[46]   ICAEW, *supra.*, at 5.
[47]   *Ibid.*, at 4–5.
[48]   *Ibid.*, at 5–6.
[49]   *Ibid.*, at 6.

ports this approach, which challenges a number of rational myths, discussed earlier, such as shareholder primacy.[50]

Corporate governance, integrity and sustainability in a global setting

International political moves to draw attention to business impact on the triple bottom line[51] have produced a plethora of international and regional agreements, which, in turn, have encouraged governments to implement CSR through the introduction of national legislation. The resulting laws and regulations, imposing increasing and wide-ranging business obligations concerning environmental, social, and governance issues, have formalized what were once mainly voluntary corporate actions into legal requirements.

This significant shift, although exploited by non-government organizations to put pressure on misbehaving corporations, is not widely appreciated by corporate management and academic researchers, as they continue to emphasize the voluntary nature of CSR.[52] Nevertheless, judicial recognition and acceptance of the importance of CSR as a matter of public policy have been progressing just as fast as legislative developments in this area. As a result, corporations' voluntary initiatives in CSR can have significant legal implications. For example, codes of conduct and compliance programmes can set the standards of care that are legally expected of businesses.

Equally, when these CSR initiatives are publicized, the courts may hold them to be binding on the corporation and, if what has been publicized is found to be untrue, the corporation in question may incur liability for misrepresentation and false advertising. It is argued that legislation influences the substance, implementation, and communication of CSR and that the current

---

[50] See also C. Nakajima, 'Shareholder Primacy Revisited' (2012) 33 *The Company Lawyer* 193.
[51] See J. Elkington, *Cannibals with Forks: The Triple Bottom Line of the 21st Century Business* (1998) New Society, Stony Creek, CT.
[52] T. Dyllick and K. Hockerts, 'Beyond the Business Case for Corporate Sustainability' (2002) 11 (2) *Business Strategy and the Environment* 130, and R. Steurer, M.E. Langer, A. Konrad and A. Martinuzzi, 'Corporations, Stakeholders and Sustainable Development: A Theoretical Exploration of Business-Society Relations' (2005) 61 (3) *Journal of Business Ethics* 263.

normative CSR may constitute pre-formal law.[53] Others recognize the role of law as 'metaregulation',[54] which attempts to make corporations 'want to do what they should do'.[55] These relatively recent developments call for further theory-building within the field of CSR by integrating previous strategy- and governance-focused research with elements of institutional theory that are related to policy, law, and regulation. The legal foundations of CSR may create institutional constraints on managerial discretion in this field and shift emphasis from strategic choices to compliance elements. However, by legally internalizing CSR, management may convert these institutional constraints to facilitators of corporate goals that are aligned with the interests of a wider community of stakeholders and consideration for environmental and longer-term corporate interests. The pursuit of goals may previously have been constrained by a narrower perspective on shareholder primacy.

Currently, differences between private commerce and government interests are non-existent in certain countries. Therefore, 'pretending that corporate governance will somehow be good enough to protect the interest of developed world investors is, in some cases, laughable'.[56] What is important for twenty-first-century business is to respond to the global move towards the control of misbehaving organizations by implementing 'legally embedded' CSR policy and practice.

In the past few decades, research on corporate governance has been dominated by agency theory,[57] the central premise of which has been that managers as agents of shareholders as their principals can engage in self-serving behaviour that may be detrimental to shareholders' wealth maximization because of the difference in access to firm-specific information. It is, therefore, primarily concerned with efficiency outcomes of various corporate governance mechanisms from the perspective of shareholders, who invest resources and seek

---

[53] K. Buhmann, 'Corporate Social Responsibility: What Role for Law? Some Aspects of Law and CSR' (2004) 6 (2) *Corporate Governance* 188.

[54] C. Parker, J. Braithwaite, C. Scott, and N. Lacey, *Regulating Law* (2004) Oxford: Oxford University Press.

[55] P. Selznick, *The Communitarian Persuasion* (2002) Washington, DC: Woodrow Wilson Center Press, at 102.

[56] K.D. King, *Losing Control* (2011) London, Yale University Press, at 89.

[57] See E.F. Fama, 'Agency Problems and the Theory of the Firm.' (1980) 88 (2) *Journal of Political Economy* 288, E.F. Fama and M.C. Jensen, 'Separation of Ownership and Control' (1983) 26 (2) *Journal of Law and Economics* 26 (2) 301, and M.C. Jensen and W.H. Meckling, 'Theory of the Firm: Managerial Behavior, Agency Costs, and Ownership Structure' (1976) 3 (4) *Journal of Financial Economics* 305.

maximum return on their investment. Institutional theory has contextualized the universalistic agency perspective by studying corporate governance as a system of interdependent elements supported or undermined by various other institutions,[58] and some argue for a more holistic, institutionally embedded governance framework to analyse organizational outcomes of various governance practices.[59]

Although the development of institutional perspective in corporate governance research has complemented the more universalistic agency perspective by recognizing the differences in national institutions from country to country that may affect corporate governance outcomes, we should not be too quick to condemn countries that lack national institutions that are complementary to efficient corporate governance outcomes. Countries with national institutions that are complementary to efficient corporate governance outcomes may not be so forthcoming in joining forces with the rest of the world. For example, in global environmental protection, for domestic economic or political reasons, countries may well turn a blind eye to other countries and corporations that are 'misbehaving', as it is not in their national interests to criticize these 'rogue' countries and organizations. The institutional analysis of corporate governance framework shows that legal institutions, at least in Europe and North America, uphold shareholder primacy. At the same time, the international and regional moves to push sustainability and the CSR agenda to the fore have resulted in a plethora of national laws and judicial decisions that encourage, and in many cases require, corporations to act in the interests of a wider community of stakeholders and to consider their longer-term interests and the environmental and social impact of their actions.[60]

As the world is only emerging from the impact of the COVID-19 pandemic and the continuing geopolitical instability in many regions in the world, the focus of shareholder value maximization in the mainstream corporate governance literature is likely to remain 'unquestioned' for a while to come. Nevertheless, we have to recognize that if it is unquestioned, it will be to the detriment of wider stakeholder interests and at the peril of future corporate

---

[58] R.A. Aguilera, I. Filatotchev, H. Gospel, and G. Jackson, 'An Organizational Approach to Comparative Corporate Governance: Costs, Contingencies, and Complementarities' (2008)19 (3) *Organization Science* 475.

[59] I. Filatotchev and C. Nakajima, 'Internal and External Corporate Governance: An Interface Between Organization and Its Environment' (2010) 21 (3) *British Journal of Management* 591.

[60] See, for example, s. 172, Companies Act 2006 of the UK.

malfeasance, failures and crises.[61] In the meantime, some scholars are pushing for a more joined-up approach to corporate governance and responsibility.[62]

An emerging research agenda

One area that is worthy of note in the context of the present discussion is the increasing attention to matters relating to ESG. As has been observed, ESG has taken the various international fora by storm.[63] Much in the media space is filled with reference to ESG, and yet perhaps not many know the origin of the term 'ESG'. As the present author has discussed elsewhere,[64] the term ESG was coined by a group of financial institutions, invited by the then United Nations Secretary-General Kofi Annan, 'to develop guidelines and recommendations on how to better integrate environment, social and corporate governance issues in asset management, securities brokerage services and associated research functions', in a joint report, *Who Cares Wins*,[65] published by the United Nations in 2004. The participating 18 financial institutions from nine countries endorsed the report on the basis that 'better consideration of environment, social and governance factors will ultimately contribute to stronger and more resilient investment markets as well as contribute to the sustainable development of societies'.[66]

---

[61] For further discussion on corporate accountability and responsibility post-financial crisis, see C. Nakajima and W. Harry, 'Is the Desire to Embed Corporate Social Responsibility within Organizations at a Crossroads?' (2012) 42(3) *International Studies of Management & Organization* 3.

[62] See, for example, I. Filatotchev and C. Nakajima, 'Corporate Governance, Responsible Managerial Behavior, Corporate Social Responsibility: Organizational Efficiency versus Organizational Legitimacy' (2014) 28(3) *Academy of Management Perspectives* 289.

[63] See, for example, G. Kell, 'The Remarkable Rise of ESG' (11 July 2018) *Forbes*. On history of ESG, see, for example, E. Pollman, 'The making and Meaning of ESG' (September 2022) European Corporate Governance Institute Working Paper No 659/2022, and B. Atkins, 'Demystifying ESG: Its History and Current Status' (8 June 2020) *Forbes*.

[64] I. Filatotchev, C. Nakajima and G.K. Stahl, 'Bringing "S" Back to ESG: The Role of Organizational Context and Institutions' 56 *Journal of Financial Transformation* 51.

[65] United Nations Global Compact and Swiss Federal Department of Foreign Affairs, *Who Cares Wins: Connecting Financial Markets to the Changing World* (2004).

[66] *Ibid.*, at ii.

There is a growing consensus amongst business leaders and investors that environmental, social, and governance factors are 'at the core of business' as they can 'have long-term consequences on a company's financial performance'.[67] Since the birth of the term 'ESG' in 2004, much discussion has taken place and many initiatives have been led globally by various bodies, such as the United Nations and its agencies and other intergovernmental organizations, as well as national governments, standard-setting bodies, business and professional associations, rating agencies, and NGOs.[68] Nevertheless, researchers and practitioners increasingly recognize that social responsibility is more nebulous and difficult to gauge than the other two criteria, i.e., 'E' and 'G'. Assessing aspects of social justice and evaluating the company's social impact without adequate data and accepted methodologies appear to be challenging. More importantly, 'E', 'S', and 'G' policies are not orthogonal – they are inter-related: decarbonization strategies may have to recognize the need for a 'just transition' that takes into account the interests of those affected. More importantly, a formal recognition of stakeholder interests increases complexity in accountability, a core principle of 'good governance'.[69]

There is increasing recognition amongst scholars in organizational theory that the quest for compliance with core principles of ESG is not only a response to various corporate scandals and realization that business leaders may be acting irresponsibly vis-à-vis the environment and key stakeholders more often than previously thought,[70] but also a result of the changes and new demands in the global marketplace, such as increased stakeholder activism and institutional pressures.[71] Although there is a substantial and rapidly growing body of research in the fields of responsible leadership and ethical decision-making,[72]

---

[67]   UNEP, *Translating ESG into Sustainable Business Values* (2010) United Nations Environment Program Finance Initiative, Geneva, at 7.

[68]   C. Nakajima, 'The Pandemic, COP26 and Sustainability' (2021) *The Company Lawyer* 42, 217.

[69]   I. Filatotchev, C. Nakajima and G.K. Stahl, 'Bringing "S" Back to ESG: The Role of Organizational Context and Institutions' 56 *Journal of Financial Transformation* 51.

[70]   M. Brown and L. K. Treviño, 'Ethical Leadership: A Review and Future Directions' (2006) 17 *The Leadership Quarterly* 595.

[71]   D. Crilly, 'Predicting Stakeholder Orientation in the Multinational Enterprise: A Mid-Range Theory' (2011) 42 *Journal of International Business Studies* 694.

[72]   N.M. Pless, T. Maak, and D.A. Waldman, 'Different approaches toward doing the right thing: mapping the responsibility orientations of leaders' (2012) 26 *Academy of Management Perspectives* 51, and Stahl, G.K., and M. Sully de Luque, 'Antecedents of Responsible Leader Behavior: A Research Synthesis, Conceptual Framework, and Agenda for Future Research' (2014) 28 *Academy of Management Perspectives* 235.

this research, for the most part, has not focused on contextual factors influencing managerial decision-making in the ESG area, and surprisingly little attention has been devoted to how institutional and organizational contexts may impact on the firm's strategy in the 'S' sphere, and the way it is implemented.

The importance of corporate governance in maintaining business integrity is recognized amongst international policymakers, and some have gone as far as to state, 'The prevention of business crime should be at the centre of corporate governance',[73] and contributions that good corporate governance makes to economic growth have been established by scholars[74] as well as policymakers, as discussed above.

More recently attention has been paid to the role of global institutions such as the aforementioned UN Global Compact and the institutionalization process of codes of conduct for global businesses and their value chains.[75] It has been argued that this exposes companies to 'multiple institutional logics',[76] and it is unclear how this exposure affects the legitimation process and its implications for ESG. While companies face a heightened level of institutional complexity resulting from heterogeneity and fragmentation of formal and informal rules, the recognition of the importance of ESG as a matter of public policy among intergovernmental organizations[77] has produced a plethora of international and regional agreements which, in turn, have encouraged governments to introduce national legislation. It is arguable that the resulting laws and regulations, imposing on companies increasing and wide-ranging obligations concerning environmental, social, and governance issues, have formalized what

---

[73] Angel Gurría, Secretary-General of OECD, 2 December 2014, as quoted in OECD, *Corporate Governance and Business Integrity: A Stocktaking of Corporate Practices* (2015) OECD, Paris.

[74] For example, F. B. Cross and R.A. Prentice, *Law and Corporate Finance* (2007) Edward Elgar, Cheltenham, at 7, drawing on the work of Nobel laureate economist, Douglass C. North, *Institutions, Institutional Change and Economic Development (Political Economy of Institutions and Decisions)*, Cambridge University Press, Cambridge.

[75] I. Ioannou and G. Serafeim 2012, 'What drives corporate social performance? The Role of Nation-level Institutions' 43 *Journal of International Business Studies* 834, and T. Kostova and S. Zaheer 1999, 'Organizational Legitimacy under Conditions of Complexity: The Case of the Multinational Enterprise' (1999) 24 *Academy of Management Review* 64.

[76] G. Bell, I. Filatotchev and R. Aguilera, 'Corporate Governance and Investors' Perceptions of Foreign IPO Value: An Institutional Perspective' (2014) 57 (1) *Academy of Management Journal* 301.

[77] D. Petkoski and N. Twose (Eds.), *Public Policy for Corporate Social Responsibility* (2003) World Bank Institute, Washington DC.

were once corporate voluntary actions to legal requirements.[78] For example, in areas previously identified as matters of voluntary industry or business standards – namely environment, labour, corporate governance, money laundering, bribery and corruption, human rights, and corporate reporting[79] – a complex web of national legislation can now be found providing for protection, prevention, and control. Equally, it has been observed that legislation influences the substance, implementation, and communication of ESG, and that current normative ESG may constitute 'pre-formal law'.[80] Furthermore, in many instances, laws may impose sanctions, regardless of culpability, when breached (e.g., environmental protection). It is also the case that many of the legislative developments have extra-territorial application, whereby one country's laws may have jurisdiction over individuals and corporations outside of the country.[81]

The debate surrounding the categorization of ESG and the quest for acceptable metrics continue, and the broad nature of the 'S' factor poses an additional challenge to policymakers at international, regional and national levels as well as to the business and investment sectors alike. While an agreement on at least some of the core elements that constitute the 'S' might be helpful, it is arguable that businesses should strive 'to do the right thing' for all stakeholders, instead of defining ESG categorization and metrics.[82] However, doing 'the right thing' ultimately requires human judgement. As has been previously observed, 'There is a relentless pressure to replace judgement with formulae... This rests in part on the fallacy that numbers are more precise and accurate than words. As anyone who has compiled a set of accounts knows, almost every number is a judgement.'[83] It is, therefore, respectfully submitted that increasing input from scholars in the relevant disciplines, and, in particular, those in law, would

---

[78]   I. Filatotchev and C. Nakajima, 'Corporate Governance, Responsible Managerial Behavior, and Corporate Social Responsibility: Organizational Efficiency versus Organizational Legitimacy?' (2014) 28 *Academy of Management Perspectives* 289.

[79]   W. Cragg and K. McKague, *Compendium of ethics codes and instruments of corporate responsibility* (2007) York University.

[80]   K. Buhmann, 'Corporate Social Responsibility: What Role for Law? Some Aspects of Law and CSR' (2004) 6 *Corporate Governance* 188.

[81]   I. Filatotchev and C. Nakajima, 'Corporate Governance, Responsible Managerial Behavior, and Corporate Social Responsibility: Organizational Efficiency versus Organizational Legitimacy?' (2014) 28 *Academy of Management Perspectives* 289.

[82]   J. Twentyman, A. Jolly, and S. Franklin, 2021, 'Putting the "s" into ESG,' Slaughter and May, https://my.slaughterandmay.com/insights/client-publications/putting-the-s-into-esg (accessed 8 November 2022).

[83]   J. Charkham and A. Simpson (1999) *Fair shares: the future of shareholder power and responsibility*, Oxford University Press, Oxford, at 207.

be much desired in order to steer the global community in such a way as to deter and prevent economic crime in order to further strengthen our joint efforts towards achieving sustainable development goals and beyond.

8   FATF measures and the combating of corruption in developing countries

Louis de Koker

1   Introduction

This chapter considers the efficacy of anti-money laundering, counter-terrorist and counter-proliferation financing (AML/CFT/CPF) measures in relation to corruption, the implications they may hold for developing countries, and research questions for the future. Particular attention is given to the anti-corruption enhancements to the Financial Action Task Force standards, especially the introduction of the concept of 'politically exposed persons', the increased emphasis on beneficial ownership, and the need for improved governance of financial intelligence units. To consider impact, both positively and negatively, the chapter draws extensively though not exclusively on recent South African examples. South Africa is an important reference country in relation to the FATF and anti-corruption. The country faced significant state capture challenges in the past decade. These developed after South Africa became one of the few developing countries to be invited to join the Financial Action Task Force. It has held the presidency of the FATF and played a leading role in the development of the current global standards. While South Africa's AML/CFT/CPF framework did not prevent large-scale corruption, elements of the framework, and especially risk-based de-banking, did play a helpful role to reign in some of the major role players in South Africa's state capture.

2   Anti-corruption and AML

During the early part of the twentieth century, views still prevailed that corruption was endemic in certain societies, primarily the colonies of

Western powers.[1] Early post-colonial scholars were reluctant to engage in anti-corruption research, concerned that their research may be viewed as colonial and imperialistic.[2] Even international financial institutions were reluctant to identify and engage corruption as a challenge. Some economists initially argued that economic corruption may actually hold economic benefits, for example by allowing bribers to navigate red tape that may otherwise impede the free market.[3] Those views were gradually discredited by multidisciplinary research that highlighted the harmful impacts of corruption on development.[4] Since the late twentieth century, global institutions have accepted that corruption generally undermines development of nations and that it should be combated, even as a 'war on corruption'.[5]

Corruption, generally defined for purposes of this chapter as the use of public office for private gain,[6] includes a broad spread of activities, ranging from small rent-taking actions by civil servants to grand corruption and state capture. Each of these may impact differently on countries and societies.[7] Public services that should be rendered for free, for example, may be provided at a price extorted from citizens, impacting on their personal and economic wellbeing.[8] Public procurement costs can be corruptly inflated to divert public funds for private gain.[9] Public management inefficiencies can arise when management decisions are not focused on advancing public policy benefits but rather on corruptly maximizing opportunities for personal benefit.[10] Proceeds of corruption may not be reinvested in the local economy but may rather be exported and invested in safe havens or remain abroad where they can be enjoyed without undue exposure to domestic law enforcement authorities.[11] Governance mechanisms that should ensure integrity may be deliberately weakened and even corrupted to protect the corrupt political elite.[12]

---

[1]   Sajó & Kotkin, 2002, p. 25.
[2]   Rothstein & Varraich, 2017, pp. 10–12.
[3]   Theobald, 1990, p. 116; Rose-Ackerman, 2006, p xiv.
[4]   Theobald, 1990, p. 125.
[5]   Robinson, 1998, p. 2; Krastev, 2004, 19–20; Bracking, 2007, pp. 3–4.
[6]   Theobald, 1990, p. 2; Campos & Bhargava, 2007, p. 9; Arnone & Borlini, 2014, p. 1; Piquero & Albanese, 2011, pp. 190–193.
[7]   Bracking, 2007, p 4.
[8]   Campos & Bhargava, 2007, p. 1; Rothstein & Varraich, 2017, p. 1.
[9]   Bel, Estache & Foucart, p. 136; Ware et al, 2007, pp. 295–296.
[10]   Theobald, 1990, p. 125.
[11]   Theobald, 1990, p. 126; Global Witness, 2009.
[12]   Theobald, 1990, p. 126.

Consensus regarding the precise impact of corruption continues to be undermined by a lack of agreement about the most appropriate definition of corruption. It is debatable whether agreement on a universal definition that would cover all acts viewed as corrupt in different countries and societies is achievable.[13] Despite this lack of consensus, there is agreement that financial transparency can provide support for effective anti-corruption measures,[14] at least those that involve transactions that may flow through the financial system or otherwise expose corrupt wealth. Where corruption occurs, transparency combined with record-keeping may support efficient investigation and prosecution of corruption. Seizure and confiscation of procedure corruption may diminish the attractiveness of corrupt activities. The enhanced risk of detection and prosecution and the complexity of safely receiving and enjoying proceeds of corruption may act as inhibitors.

Despite their value as anti-corruption measures, the standards of the Financial Action Task Force (FATF), the global intergovernmental standard-setting body for anti-money laundering and later counter-terrorism and counter-proliferation financing, were initially designed and adopted in 1990 to combat drug-trafficking.[15] Among others, the Recommendations required countries to criminalize the laundering of proceeds of drug-related offences and to adopt laws compelling their financial institutions to identify and verify the identities of customers, keep record of transactions and report transactions that were suspected of involving proceeds of crime to a national financial intelligence unit (FIU), which each country had to establish. These units had to process the intelligence and make it available to support investigation and prosecution of related crimes nationally and internationally. Countries were furthermore required to maintain appropriate financial regulation and supervision and to render cross-border assistance in criminal investigation and prosecution by foreign agencies.

In 1996 the application of the FATF standards broadened to proceeds of all serious offences. While this amendment extended the application of the standards to serious corruption offences, a focused discussion commenced regarding specific measures to enhance the FATF standards to support the combating of corruption. These discussions took place in the context of negotiations of the text of a UN Convention on Corruption, a text that built, in turn, on other

---

13   Rothstein & Varraich, 2017, p. 45.
14   Levi, Dakolias and Greenberg, 2007.
15   De Koker & Turkington, 2016.

international agreements, such as the 1997 *OECD Convention on Combating Bribery of Foreign Public Officials in International Business Transactions.*

The *UN Convention against Corruption* was adopted by the UN General Assembly in October 2003 and entered into force in December 2005.[16] In June 2003, however, a few months before the adoption of the Convention, the FATF adopted a revised set of Recommendations. These extended the original recommendations in a number of ways, e.g., they expanded the regulatory scope beyond financial institutions to designated non-financial businesses and professions deemed to be particularly vulnerable to money laundering and terrorist financing abuse. These included real estate agents, lawyers and accountants. FATF also enhanced the customer due diligence obligations of regulated institutions by requiring increased effort to identify beneficial owners, e.g., those persons who own or control corporate entities and/or the person on whose behalf a transaction is being conducted. These were particularly relevant provisions in relation to corruption, as proceeds of corruption are often shielded by using front companies or agents.

The 2003 Recommendations also introduced the concept of a 'politically exposed person' (PEP),[17] defining them as:

> individuals who are or have been entrusted with prominent public functions in a foreign country, for example Heads of State or of government, senior politicians, senior government, judicial or military officials, senior executives of state-owned corporations, important political party officials. Business relationships with family members or close associates of PEPs involve reputational risks similar to those with PEPs themselves.[18]

The definition was clearly stated as not intended to cover middle-ranking or more junior individuals in the foregoing categories. While this definition has its limitations, it does include a range of senior officials who are particularly vulnerable to corruption.

The 2003 FATF standards required countries to compel their regulated institutions to have appropriate risk management systems to determine whether the customer is a PEP; obtain senior management approval for establishing or continuing business relationships with such customers; take reasonable

---

16   Joutsen, 2011, p. 305.
17   FATF, 2003, Recommendation 12.
18   FATF, 2003, p. 14. See FATF, 2012-2022 and specifically the Glossary for definitions relating to 'politically exposed persons' that still reflect the key elements of the 2003 definition.

measures to establish the source of wealth and source of funds; and conduct enhanced ongoing monitoring of the business relationship.

The 2003 standards complemented a set of special recommendations on terrorist financing, first adopted in 2001 in the aftermath of the 9/11 attacks on the United States, and further enhanced in 2004. In 2012 both sets were incorporated into the current revised set of Recommendations. Importantly, the FATF also introduced a mandatory risk-based approach in 2012, requiring countries and regulated institutions to undertake risk assessments to inform risk-based regulation, supervision and compliance. In this process FATF also refined its risk-based approach in relation to PEPs, explicitly differentiating between foreign PEPs, who should always be managed as higher-risk customers, and domestic PEPs, who may not all pose a higher risk.

The FATF standards complement financial measures envisaged in the 2003 *UN Convention on Corruption*. The Convention binds signatory countries to adopt a range of preventive measures, criminalize specified acts and enforce domestic anti-corruption laws and support international law enforcement, asset recovery, and technical assistance, and facilitate information exchange. Article 14 specifically requires state parties to adopt a range of money laundering control measures to 'deter and detect all forms of money-laundering, which regime shall emphasize requirements for customer and, where appropriate, beneficial owner identification, record-keeping and the reporting of suspicious transactions'.

The benefits of effective AML/CFT/CPF measures to strengthen anti-corruption measures are clear, at least in theory, and leading nations have therefore agreed to implement the FATF standards and, by signing the UN Convention, also bound themselves to implement such measures. In practice it has, however, proved much harder to secure these benefits. Furthermore, the implementation of AML/CFT/CPF measures have also come at a cost, especially for nations ravaged by corruption.

This chapter considers current development in relation to the use of anti-money laundering measures to combat corruption and the impact on developing countries with a view to identifying and contextualizing research questions for the future. It complements a paper on a research agenda on anti-money laundering and corruption published more than a decade ago.[19] The adoption

---

[19]   See De Koker, 2011. That agenda included sets of questions around the appropriateness and effectiveness of the use of measures designed to combat drug

of revised FATF Recommendations in 2012, and subsequent revisions to the Recommendations, assisted in addressing some of the concerns but, in turn, they have also opened the door to additional questions. Most of the questions identified in 2011 remain relevant to the research agenda. This chapter will not revisit them but rather complement them by focusing on additional aspects that emerged in the past decade or emerged with even greater clarity in relation to developing countries in this period.

3   Effectiveness of AML measures to combat corruption

Much time, money and effort have been spent on implementing AML/CFT/CPF controls globally. Implementation is still uneven, with many countries and institutions, especially those with more limited resources and capacity, struggling to meet basic requirements effectively.[20] While a focus on the flow of money should deliver anti-corruption benefits, it is not clear that the benefits outweigh the costs. The general belief of AML/CFT/CPF stakeholders is that the benefits will be evident once the FATF measures are fully implemented. A firm, objective evidence base for that belief is, however, lacking. The key measures were designed to combat drug trafficking. The large sums involved in drug trafficking in the 1980s combined with the general profile of drug traffickers increased the effectiveness of such measures in relation to drug trafficking. Corruption, however, is very different in nature and measures designed to combat drug trafficking may not be equally effective against corrupt actors in all countries and contexts globally.[21]

The anti-corruption focus is furthermore on bribe-takers rather on bribe-payers and on the significant corporate benefits that may have attained corruptly by large public companies. Where corporate bribe-payers were prosecuted, sentences were not particularly significant and confiscation of the actual corporate

---

offences to effectively and efficiently combat corruption; how best to protect the integrity of AML agencies when they threaten powerful political forces that may wish to weaken them; whether the focus of the measures on bribe-takers rather than bribe-payers are appropriate to deliver the desired anti-corruption benefits; the need for impact assessments to determine whether the measures are actually delivering anti-corruption results effectively and efficiently, etc.

[20]   De Koker & Turkington, 2015; Pol, 2018; Financial Action Task Force, 2022a.
[21]   De Koker, 2011, pp. 348–349; Pol, 2018.

benefit attained has been rare. Will a more even-handed approach deliver better anti-corruption results?

In June 2021 news broke of Operation Trojan Shield (also called Operation Ironside), a collaboration by law enforcement agencies from several countries. The FBI and the Australian Federal Police led a sting operation and distributed encrypted devices and services to more than 300 criminal syndicates operating in more than 100 countries, leading the criminals to believe that the services were fully secure and impenetrable to law enforcement. This enabled law enforcement to intercept millions of messages sent through the messaging app ANOM. In June 2021 a globally coordinated wave of 800 arrests began, resulting in significant disruption to criminal activity and prosecutions, which included prosecutions for corruption.[22]

This was an innovative law enforcement operation that delivered the types of results that were initially expected to be delivered by AML measures. The impact of the operation on organized crime and on their trust in smartphones and encryption remains to be studied. Importantly, however, the results of this targeted operation and the costs of the operation can be compared with the results and costs of AML measures. Is a focus on financial flows as effective and efficient as a focus on the digital communications of criminals? Can elements of these approaches be combined to provide more effective measures against corruption? How can we increase the efficiency of AML measures in the digital future, while preserving privacy? Studies responding to these questions and outlining actual costs and benefits may inform the shaping of improved anti-corruption approaches.

4   Politically exposed persons

While the PEP concept holds great anti-corruption value in theory, it is accompanied by a range of practical challenges. At the base lies differences about the scope of the concept due to the inherent vagueness of the FATF definition of a PEP.[23] This causes increased complexity for regulated institutions, especially those that operate in more than one jurisdiction that have to navigate the views of different regulators and supervisors.

---

[22]   US Attorney's Office Southern District of California, 2021.
[23]   Chaikin and Sharman, 2007, pp. 34–53; Choo, 2008; Gilligan, 2009; Wolfsberg Group, 2017; Greenberg et al., 2010, pp. 25–32; Menz, 2020.

FATF clearly classifies foreign PEPs as higher-risk customers, while the Wolfsberg Group, an influential association of 13 global banks, advises financial institutions to consider a range of country-related factors before classifying a person as a PEP.[24] Unlike the FATF standards, the Wolfsberg Principles, for example, advise that heads of supranational bodies, members of parliament or national legislatures, senior members of the diplomatic corps, e.g., ambassadors, *chargés d'affaires* or members of boards of central banks, and city mayors and governors or leaders of federal regions may also be considered to fall within the definition but, equally, may be excluded in countries or organizations where the risk of corruption or abuse is considered to be relatively low.[25]

Further scope for different approaches by regulated institutions arises in relation to the degree of closeness of family members or associates to bring them within the scope of the definition. The Wolfsberg Group advises that much depends on context, as not all close family members or close associates may pose the same level of risk. For their purposes, however, close family would generally include a PEP's direct family members, their spouse, their children and their spouses, parents and the siblings of the PEP, while close associates will include a PEP's widely and publicly known close business colleagues or personal advisers, in particular persons acting in a financial fiduciary capacity.[26] What 'direct' entails and whether a known relationship is 'widely' or 'publicly' known introduce space for significant personal judgement calls by compliance officers.[27]

Are there any proven benefits to leaving key aspects of the PEP definition vague?[28] Does it improve compliance or nudge overcompliance by regulated institutions?[29] Will there be regulatory, law enforcement and/or compliance benefit in a higher level of global standardization of PEP definitions, or is it best to leave flexibility at a country and institutional level? Is it possible to pilot

---

[24]   Wolfsberg Group, 2017, p. 5.
[25]   Wolfsberg Group, 2017, p. 4.
[26]   Wolfsberg Group, 2017, p. 4.
[27]   How long a person remains a PEP after leaving their PEP-related function is also not set in stone. The UK's Money Laundering, Terrorist Financing and Transfer of Funds (Information on the Payer) Regulations 2017, reg 35, provides that they should continue to be treated as a PEP (i) for 12 months from the date on which they ceased to perform that function; or (ii) for such longer period as a firm considers appropriate to address risks of money laundering or terrorist financing in relation to that person.
[28]   Choo, 2008.
[29]   De Koker & Symington, 2014.

different approaches and compare their outcomes? Should the definition be broadened, or are better results achieved by applying narrower definitions?

Since the introduction of PEP standards, regulated institutions have asked for government support to identify PEPs. The EU's Fifth Money Laundering Directive, therefore, requires Member States to 'issue and keep up to date a list indicating the exact functions which, according to national laws, regulations and administrative provisions, qualify as prominent public functions'.[30] Few countries have done so, however. In practice, most large institutions that can afford to buy access to commercial PEP databases, rely on data supplied by PEP data vendors, such as World-Check, later acquired by Thomson Reuters/ Refinitiv. They provide publicly available data on higher-risk customers, including PEPs. That service is, however, not without its own risks and complexities. In 2017, for example, Thomson Reuters paid substantial damages to Finsbury Park Mosque for incorrectly linking the mosque to terrorism in its World-Check profile of the mosque.[31]

Much of the global discussion has focused on large, high-capacity regulated institutions. What can be done, however, to provide smaller institutions with appropriate tools to effectively and efficiently identify and manage customers who are PEPs? How can a public–private partnership be broadened to ensure that all regulated institutions are able to fulfil what is in essence a public function, without causing undue harm to innocent holders of high office, their family members and associates?[32]

While questions about the design of the PEP framework are important, there are also key questions arising in relation to actual implementation of the PEP measures. These were not implemented with great urgency by all large financial institutions. In 2009, for example, Global Witness produced a report entitled *Undue Diligence* naming a few global banks who were still continuing business relationships with corrupt regimes, whether wittingly or unwittingly.[33] Various large leaks of confidential documents, such as the Panama Papers (2016), Paradise Papers (2017), FinCEN Files (2020), and Pandora Papers (2021),[34] reflect the criminal use of shell companies to evade AML control measures of banks, often aided wittingly or unwittingly by banks. Is sufficient action being taken against banks and other regulated institutions that may be

---

[30]   EU's Fifth Money Laundering Directive, Article 20a, para 1.
[31]   Sherwood, 2017.
[32]   Kang, 2018; Shalchi, 2022; Financial Action Task Force, 2022c.
[33]   Global Witness, 2009.
[34]   BBC, 2021.

facilitating PEP-related corruption? On the other hand, is too much attention being given to what does not work rather than the elements that have worked, and why they worked? The relevance of questions like these are illustrated by anti-corruption de-banking successes in South Africa.

4.1   De-banking of PEPs

De-banking, also known as de-risking or the risk-based refusal of services, refers to a response by AML/CFT/CPF-regulated institutions to refuse to render services to higher-risk customer segments and to terminate any existing services that are being rendered. De-banking is an intended outcome of the FATF's risk-based measures in those cases where a bank or regulated institution finds that it is unable to mitigate the ML/FT/PF risk associated with a specific customer. While the risk-based AML/CFT/CPF framework primarily requires regulated institutions to identify and manage their ML/FT/PF risks, some institutions decided to rather avoid the risk by not having business relationships with certain higher-risk customers, i.e., to de-bank these customers.

Large-scale risk-based refusals of services to whole industries, segments or even regions were unintended consequences of the standards. The first such refusals were evident in relation to money service businesses in the USA.[35] Despite warnings that denials of service may increase where the FATF's measures are viewed as primarily intended to avoid doing business with higher-risk customers, and may be more pronounced where the costs of risk mitigation measures exceed the profitability of the relevant relationships,[36] the FATF adopted a mandatory risk-based approach in 2012. This contributed to a wave of de-banking, especially of smaller banks in higher-risk regions, remittance service providers, charities, bitcoin companies and even foreign missions.[37]

De-banking has impacted negatively on developing countries, often limiting their access to the global financial system, and undermining remittance flows that may be vital to the economies and the people of developing countries.[38] While the FATF and other global leaders have issued statements decrying

---

[35]   Bester et al., 2008, pp. 158–162.
[36]   De Koker, 2011, p. 368.
[37]   De Koker et al. 2017, pp. 127–128.
[38]   Ratha et al, 2015, p. 11; Collin et al, 2015; Durner and Shetret, 2015; Artingstall et al, 2016; The Commonwealth, 2016; Erbenová, et al, 2016; De Koker et al, 2017; Chatain et al, 2018.

large-scale de-banking, limited practical steps have been taken to address large-scale de-banking.[39]

In the discussions of de-risking, limited attention has been given to some of the crime-combating benefits of de-banking. In South Africa some of these benefits may be identified in the containment of Gupta-linked state capture activities.

An early South African example of de-risking is the de-banking of John Bredenkamp and entities related to him by Standard Bank, one of South Africa's largest banks. Bredenkamp and a number of entities owned or controlled by him were listed as 'specially designated nationals' by the US Department of Treasury's Office of Foreign Asset Control (OFAC) as part of the imposition of US sanctions on Zimbabwe. Bredenkamp was apparently listed by the OFAC as he was said to be a close business associate of President Mugabe of Zimbabwe. He was, furthermore, alleged to be involved in a range of high-risk activities, including grey-market arms trading. Bredenkamp disputed these allegations and approached the court for relief. Standard Bank argued that, whether or not the allegations were correct, a continuing relationship with Bredenkamp would give rise to legal, reputational and business risk, and therefore they decided to terminate the accounts. Bredenkamp pursued the matter to the South African Supreme Court of Appeal, where the court held in 2010 that a bank has a right to terminate a contract with its clients on reasonable notice or as agreed and can do so without providing reasons for the termination.[40] Importantly, the Court held that a bank is also entitled to terminate the relationship with a client on a basis of reputational and business risks and that courts should be reluctant to second-guess that decision. Bredenkamp's appeal was therefore dismissed.

In 2012 ABSA Bank began closing the accounts linked to Fana Hlongwane, a businessman and former adviser to a minister of defence after a Commission of Inquiry looking into possible corruption requested the bank to provide it with relevant account information. Hlongwane approached the court for assistance to gain access to a comprehensive list of bank documents relating to the

---

[39]   Financial Action Task Force, 2021a.
[40]   *Bredenkamp and Others v Standard Bank and Another* [2010] 4 SA 468 (SCA). See also *Bredenkamp and Others v Standard Bank of South Africa Ltd and Another* 2009 (6) SA 277 (GSJ).

closure of the account to inform his decisions about potential legal remedies, but the application was refused.[41]

South Africa's most serious cases relating to PEPs involve the Gupta family and their companies, notably the Oakbay Group of companies.[42] The Gupta family was widely reported as friends of the then President Jacob Zuma and his family. They were the subject of a 2016 Public Protector investigation and report[43] followed by a judicial commission of inquiry, the Zondo Commission.[44] The 2016 report of the Public Protector addressed alleged unlawful conduct by the then president, his son, Gupta family members and several related parties and companies. As a result of the increasing publicity around the Oakbay Group, KPMG and large South African banks began to withdraw their services from persons and entities linked to the group. After being requested to intervene, and a political tussle at cabinet level,[45] the Minister of Finance approached the court for declaratory relief that he is not by law empowered or obliged to intervene in the relationship between the Gupta-linked entities and the relevant banks, regarding the closing of the bank accounts.[46] In the course of those proceedings, the South African Financial Intelligence Centre (FIC) disclosed a list of 72 'suspicious transactions' to the value of R6.8 billion (approximately USD400 million) concluded by the members and associates of the Oakbay Group that were reported by regulated institutions to the FIC. The minister's litigation was supported by affidavits by other large South African banks detailing their concerns about Gupta-related accounts.

The minister's application failed. The Court held that that matter dealt with the exercise of executive authority and that it was not appropriate for a member of the National Executive to draw the judiciary into the exercise of his executive functions.[47] Despite the failure of the formal application, the publicity around the matter and the FIC's information legitimized the withdrawal of banking

---

41   *Hlongwane and Others v Absa Bank Limited and Another* (75782/13) [2016] ZAGPPHC 938.
42   Madonsela, 2018; Judicial Commission of Inquiry, 2022.
43   Public Protector of South Africa, 2016.
44   Judicial Commission of Inquiry, 2022.
45   Momoniat, 2021, para 65–68.
46   *Minister of Finance v Oakbay Investments (Pty) Ltd and Others; Oakbay Investments (Pty) Ltd and Others v Director of the Financial Intelligence Centre* [2017] 4 All SA 150 (GP) para 2.
47   *Minister of Finance v Oakbay Investments (Pty) Ltd and Others; Oakbay Investments (Pty) Ltd and Others v Director of the Financial Intelligence Centre* [2017] 4 All SA 150 (GP) para 82.

services by the largest South African banks and publicized the reporting of a significant number of suspicious transactions relating to the Oakbay Group.

The Bank of Baroda, the last remaining bank of the Gupta Group, followed suit. Concerned about their reputational risk and also about 36 suspicious and unusual transactions of over R4.25 billion, which its Gupta-related corporate clients transacted with it during a 10-month period, they informed their clients that their banking services would be terminated. The Gupta Group's application to prevent this action also failed.[48] De-banking caused severe operational challenges for the group, exacerbated by the withdrawal of other professional services too. The group's key entities, for example, were forced to de-list from the Johannesburg Stock Exchange after failing to secure a transfer secretary and sponsor, and auditing companies also refused to render services for fear of reputational risk.[49] In February 2018, eight companies in the Oakbay Group were placed in voluntary business rescue, as the termination of their banking facilities rendered them commercially insolvent.[50]

De-banking was successful in the Gupta case to prevent further grand corruption. The action taken by banks and other commercial stakeholders contained the companies. The Gupta family fled South Africa and in 2022 South Africa commenced extradition proceedings against the Gupta brothers, Atul and Rajesh. De-banking in this case, however, was politically sensitive and banks and other professionals were under pro-Gupta political pressure to continue to provide their financial and professional services, once they communicated their decisions to terminate the services.[51]

De-banking success was therefore not guaranteed, nor were the de-banking actions immediate. For many years South African banks, auditors and other commercial stakeholders provided services that enabled state capture by the Guptas. These services were rendered because they were profitable. Red flags were raised much earlier, especially in the media, but service delivery continued regardless. Most terminations only began after the publication of the Public Protector's report. Importantly, enabling commercial relationships extended further than South Africa. In many cases relationships with the Gupta entities and transactions impacted negatively on the reputations of the national and international providers, for example it led to the resignation of

---

48   *Annex Distribution (Pty) Ltd and Others v Bank of Baroda* 2018 (1) SA 562 (GP).
49   News24, 2017.
50   *Oakbay Investments (Pty) Ltd v Tegeta Exploration and Resources (Pty) Ltd and Others* [2021] ZASCA 59.
51   News24, 2016.

key KPMG executives in South Africa[52] and the collapse of Bell Pottinger, the British PR firm, and it forced McKinsey, the global consultancy firm, to launch an investigation into its work in the country and repay some of its fees.[53] The involvement in state capture activity in relation to the South African Revenue Service by US management consultancy Bain & Company was also highlighted by the Zondo Commission. The company repaid its consultancy fee with interest. As a result of advocacy by a former Bain partner and whistle-blower, Athol Williams, and Lord Peter Hain, the UK government in 2022 barred Bain for three years from tendering for British government contracts.[54]

De-banking of PEPs and parties and entities related to them tends to be politically sensitive. Despite a slow and uneven start, it appeared to have had a positive impact on containing the Gupta-related corruption in South Africa. Interestingly, it did so even though South Africa's statutory PEP regime only took effect in 2017 when amendments to the Financial Intelligence Centre Act 38 of 2001 entered into force. Yet politics may have scuppered the Gupta-related anti-corruption actions by companies and, importantly, politics still remains relevant in relation to corruption and de-banking allegations.[55]

The Gupta case raises a range of questions regarding PEP-related matters. How can entities be protected when terminating services to powerful politicians based on corruption risks? How can undue influence by companies be prevented, for example, where threats of termination of services are used not to combat corruption but rather to influence political decisions? Should the FATF focus on specific regulated institutions to be broadened to capture global consultancies whose work may support corrupt activities? Would empirical risk assessment requirements assist in addressing concerns about improper termination of services as well as about unintended de-risking and de-banking consequences? Should de-banking and de-risking be conceptually differentiated? These will be relevant research inquiries to pursue in the future.

---

[52] Sweney, 2017b.
[53] Chanson, 2022.
[54] Kollewe, 2022.
[55] Lechman, 2022.

5   Beneficial ownership and beneficial ownership registers

As discussed in section 4 above, the 2003 version of the FATF standards sharpened the focus on beneficial ownership and required countries to ensure that their authorities could obtain up-to-date and accurate information about the person(s) behind legal persons and arrangements. These measures were strengthened and clarified in 2012, and explained in further guidance.[56]

The desire to have greater transparency about the actual controllers of legal persons and arrangements and those who benefit from these structures is perfectly understandable. Criminals have been able hide their wealth in companies and trusts while exercising their control indirectly through nominee directors and shareholders. They have been able to use thinly capitalized shell companies to perpetrate crime. They are able to benefit from these arrangements while law enforcement and third parties may be unaware of their links with the entity or unable to prove such links, where they were suspected. Beneficial ownership became even more abused after the Second World War as tax havens adopted laws that would hide control of entities registered in that jurisdiction and in some cases even criminalized the disclosure of information regarding their beneficial ownership.[57]

The FATF's beneficial ownership standards require measures compelling regulated institutions to collect more information from their clients regarding beneficial ownership. Meanwhile, FATF pressure increased on governments to ensure that beneficial ownership data is available to law enforcement agencies. While there has been good progress in relation to identification of companies, for example with the Global Legal Identifier and other initiatives,[58] progress in relation to beneficial ownership transparency has been slow. According to the FATF's 2022 review, only 52% of assessed jurisdictions had adequate beneficial ownership transparency laws and regulatory structures in place, but effective implementation of these was limited: only 9% of countries were assessed as meeting the FATF's effectiveness criteria in this regard.[59]

---

[56]   E.g. Financial Action Task Force, 2019; Financial Action Task Force, 2022b.
[57]   Blum, et al., 1998.
[58]   Leung et al., 2022.
[59]   FATF, 2022a, p. 32.

5.1   Complexity of identification of beneficial ownership

The FATF defines a beneficial owner as the natural person or persons who ulti-mately control a customer and/or the natural person on whose behalf a trans-action is being conducted.[60] 'Ultimate control' refers to situations where those natural persons exercised that control indirectly through a chain of ownership or control.[61] Only a natural person can be an ultimate beneficial owner, but more than one natural person can be the ultimate beneficial owner of a specific legal person or arrangement.[62]

The FATF recognizes the practical challenges in actually identifying ultimate beneficial owners despite taking reasonable measures.[63] Where there is doubt about whether a person with a controlling ownership interest in a legal person is the ultimate beneficial owner, or where no natural person exerts control through ownership interests, a regulated institution is guided to identify the natural persons (if any) exercising control of the legal person or arrangement through other means. According to the FATF, the meaning of a 'controlling ownership interest' depends on the ownership structure of the company. Importantly, it allows it to be based on a threshold, e.g., any person 'owning more than a certain percentage of the company (e.g. 25%)'.[64] Where no natural person is identified in that role, the natural person who holds the position of senior managing official should be identified and recorded as holding this position.[65]

A 2018 joint report by the FATF and the Egmont Group of FIUs analysed more than 100 case studies for data on concealment of beneficial ownership. In the majority of case studies, use was made of complicated direct and indi-rect ownership structures, often chains of ownership with legal persons and arrangements across multiple countries.[66] Globally there are few restrictions

---

[60]   Financial Action Task Force, 2012–2022, p. 119.
[61]   Financial Action Task Force, 2012–2022, n70.
[62]   Financial Action Task Force, 2012–2022, n72.
[63]   Financial Action Task Force, 2012–2022, n72.
[64]   Financial Action Task Force, 2012–2022, n35.
[65]   Financial Action Task Force, 2012–2022, n72.
[66]   Financial Action Task Force & the Egmont Group of Financial Intelligence Units (2018), para 56.

on complex ownership structures. The FATF itself views the complexity as justified and beneficial ownership as readily ascertainable:[67]

> Complex ownership and control structures are not, in and of themselves, unlawful. Often, these corporate structures serve legitimate purposes and facilitate a wide range of commercial activities, entrepreneurial ventures, and the management of personal finances. ... Complex ownership structures can simplify business transactions for companies that regularly trade transnationally, provide services to international clients, or conduct parts of a company's operations (such as manufacturing or research and development) in another country. Often complex control structures are used by family businesses, by government-owned or operated public or commercial business ventures, and by publicly traded companies to structure their affairs. In these instances, a financial institution, legal/accounting professional, or other service provider will be in a position to readily ascertain the beneficial ownership of the structure. These structures are generally transparent to relevant authorities and present minimal vulnerabilities for disguising beneficial ownership.

The statements that these structures are generally transparent to relevant authorities or that service providers could readily ascertain the beneficial ownership of these structures were not supported by any evidence provided in the report. Given what is known after the Panama Papers, Pandora Papers and similar releases of confidential company formation information,[68] it is difficult to defend statements about general transparency to the authorities. It is clear, however, that the FATF believes that the complex corporate ownership and control structures can serve important purposes and that the abuse of corporate structures can be adequately addressed by improved regulation of corporate and legal professionals and by the availability of beneficial ownership information to government agencies, for example by means of beneficial ownership registries or disclosure by the companies themselves.

Progress on effective implementation of measures such as these, however, has been slow. The FATF's 2021 stocktake review found, for example, that in more than 70% of countries the non-financial sector (e.g., trust and company service providers, lawyers and accountants) is poorly implementing mitigation measures.[69] Despite these challenges, the FATF put even more emphasis on beneficial ownership transparency in its 2022 revision of it standards.

It is appropriate to ask whether the design of the FATF's beneficial ownership concept and transparency around shareholding and shareholding-linked

---

[67] Financial Action Task Force & the Egmont Group of Financial Intelligence Units (2018), para 57.
[68] BBC, 2021.
[69] FATF, 2021, p. 29.

voting rights provide the most appropriate solution to the corporate transparency problem that the FATF wishes to address. Are there alternative solutions that are required to support improved beneficial ownership transparency?

Those who are focused on beneficial ownership registers and declarations as a solution to the problem tend to underestimate the subtleties inherent in corporate law concepts relating to control. They tend to equate shareholding with control and also assume that control is always sufficiently clear and static to be recorded in a register. That is not necessarily the case. The registry-based tests for control often reflect shareholding and voting rights. Shareholder and voting agreements may, however, amend voting rights, even conditionally and temporarily, and may allow voting rights to be exercised by third parties as proxies. Such agreements are often private agreements and may even be informal and temporary. Preference shares may be non-voting shares and may therefore be overlooked when voting rights are considered, but these shares may actually have voting rights when the preference dividend has not been paid or depending on other conditions in company documents. By structuring dividend payment cycles or triggering voting conditions, these non-voting shares may be able to cast controlling votes at key meetings. Control is furthermore exercised by those who attend the company meeting, provided that quorum requirements are met. Where shareholders vote by show of hands, each shareholder has one vote, regardless of the number of shares held. Control exercised at the meeting by those present voting by hand may therefore show little resemblance to theoretical power and control reflected by a company's public shareholding information. Many shareholders may not attend key meetings and many small companies may not have any in-person meetings at all.

Control over different aspects of a company is furthermore divided between the board of directors and the general meeting of shareholders. The board makes the day-today decisions and directors are not necessarily required to hold any shares in the company. Decisions relating to transactions may be taken by the board. Where such a decision is relevant from a money laundering perspective, the composition of the board and its meeting rules are more important to understand than shareholding and voting rights of the shareholders of the company. Depending on the type of decision, it may actually be taken by a manager with delegated authority, while neither the board nor the general meeting may have specific knowledge of the matter. Corporate control may further be shielded by using nominees or simply by controlling the board from the outside as a so-called shadow director.[70] Whether a person is a shadow director or not is a factual question to be considered in view of all of the facts. It is possible that board members may not even appreciate at that time that their decisions are influenced by a shadow director.[71]

While long-term control over a company may hold money laundering benefits for criminals, for example facilitating the holding and control of real estate, short-term control over key decisions of companies may also be used to advance criminal objectives, for example the opening of a bank account that can be controlled by third parties. Company documents and structures can be carefully crafted to trigger such control when required. Compliance officers and law enforcement therefore need a sophisticated understanding of the type of decision that is relevant to their enquiry and decision-taking mechanisms and dynamics within the particular company.

In addition, it is important to recognize the challenges inherent in interpreting complicated corporate documentation. This is illustrated by the 2022 South African judgment in *Nedbank Limited v Houtbosplaas (Pty) Ltd and Another.*[72] A leading judge, now retired, set up an estate planning scheme involving two companies and one trust each for each of his four daughters. Each of the four trusts held one ordinary share and one preference share in each of the two companies, while the judge held one preference share in each of the companies. According to the memoranda of association of the companies, the holders of preference shares will not be entitled to cast a vote when voting upon a resolution that may result in their personal enrichment. However, it recognized the right of the preference shareholders to vote on any resolution relating to the compensation of directors or any other matter within the normal scope of the powers of the company.

---

[70] Nielson & Sharman, 2022.

[71] For UK and Australian approaches to a shadow director, see *Buzzle Operations Pty Ltd (in liq) v Apple Computer Australia Pty Ltd* [2011] NSWCA 109 para 181–243. S 251 of the Companies Act 2006 (UK) states that: '"shadow director" in relation to a company, means a person in accordance with whose directions or instructions the directors of the company are accustomed to act. A person is not to be regarded as a shadow director by reason only that the directors act on advice given by him in a professional capacity.' Whether an adviser is giving advice in a professional capacity or whether a professional adviser may be exceeding that capacity are factual questions. See Jamieson & Hughes, 2012.

[72] *Nedbank Limited v Houtbosplaas (Pty) Ltd and Another* [2022] ZASCA 69 (19 May 2022).

Nedbank, the banker of the two companies, demanded to see the trust deeds of the four trusts, arguing that each trust held at least 25% of the votes in each company, thereby meeting a regulatory threshold for beneficial ownership that then applied under the South African Money Laundering Regulations. Their legal counsel took the position that the votes of the preference shares should be ignored and that each of the four trusts, holding one ordinary share each, therefore met the 25% shareholding threshold. The North Gauteng court rejected their interpretation and pointed out that the preference shares are voting shares in terms of the companies' memoranda in all cases except decisions that may enrich the holders of the preference shares or benefit their estates.[73] Nedbank appealed against this decision, but the Supreme Court of Appeal rejected their argument on similar grounds. As the preference shares were voting shares, each trust only held two votes out of the nine that could be cast, with the former judge exercising one vote. As each trust could only exercise 22% of the votes, none of the trusts crossed the 25% voting threshold.

It is not clear what would have been recorded in relation to beneficial ownership of these companies in an official beneficial ownership register, as South Africa has not yet established one. The challenge of identifying beneficial ownership correctly, even by the company concerned, should not be underestimated. In the *Houtbosplaas* matter, the key facts were publicly available and the dispute centred merely on their interpretation, with the bank disputing the founder's view. Where criminality is concerned, criminals and their advisers will attempt to hide actual control in obtuse documents and processes that are designed to mislead readers and complicate the interpretation of key provisions. Few institutions and fewer governments have the capacity to closely read and correctly interpret complicated corporate documents of large numbers of companies.

Given these complexities, financial institutions welcome beneficial ownership registries as they limit their due diligence enquiries. Criminals, on the other hand, may also welcome beneficial owner registries, especially where these may officially capture wrong information about the actual control of corporate entities, effectively shielding criminal control from standard customer due diligence enquiries. In these cases, however, incorrect beneficial ownership data will undermine rather than strengthen the fight against crime and corruption. Are there better ways to address or at least limit beneficial ownership challenges?

---

[73] *Nedbank Limited v Houtbosplaas (Pty) Ltd and Another* [2020] ZAGPPHC 220 (17 March 2020).

5.2   Alternative solutions

While the FATF accepts that corporate control requires a level of complexity to meet a wide range of commercial objectives, it has not subjected that approach to critical analysis. International corporate groups and individuals operating global business enterprises may require a significant amount of corporate law flexibility and complexity. Most users of the corporate form, however, have little need for that level of flexibility. There are, therefore, approaches that can ring-fence complexity.

Corporate law regimes of countries are normally focused on the public company, i.e., the company that may have an unrestricted number of share-holders and that can, if further requirements are met, have their securities listed on a stock exchange. In addition, these company regimes also allow for private limited companies. These are companies that may have one member and a restricted maximum number of members, for example, 50 non-employee shareholders. Most of these companies, however, only have one or a handful of shareholders. Due to their small size and limited number of stakeholders, they do not require a particularly complex corporate law regime.

Statistics provide a helpful lens. In the UK, for example, in June 2022 Companies House had 5,064,188 companies registered for England and Wales. Of these, only 5,951 were public companies.[74] The complexity of company legislation is therefore mainly aimed at serving around 6,000 companies of the more than 5 million registered companies in the UK, 93% of which are private companies, with the remainder being smaller pockets of specialized entities. Some private companies may require a level of complexity too, but in the vast majority of private companies, control tends to be simple and clear.

This absurdity of regulating the majority of small companies with measures designed for large companies was recognized in South Africa, as well as the fact that small companies lacked the capacity to consistently comply with complex company law requirements. In 1984, therefore, the government adopted the Close Corporations Act 69 of 1984.[75] This Act enabled the registration of a radically simplified business form for single entrepreneurs and small groups of not more than 10 members. The law was enabling, comprehensive, yet easy to navigate and allowed stakeholders to enforce the key provisions of the Act without resorting to government agencies. Close corporations did not have shares, but members' interests, and these were held by members who had to be

---

74   Companies House, 2022, Table 1.
75   Cilliers et al., 2000.

natural persons, bar a few limited exceptions. Juristic persons were not allowed to be members, whether directly or through a nominee or other structure. Trust *inter vivos* were also excluded from membership. Membership interests were furthermore accompanied by management rights with no separation between members and management.

The key information of close corporations was publicly available at the Registrar of Companies and Close Corporations. Members' interests were publicly registered and were owned by those in whose names they were registered. Nominee ownership was not recognized. Beneficial ownership was therefore transparent, as attempts to own members' interests indirectly or informally was not legally recognized or enforceable.

As no turnover restrictions applied, this business form was also attractive to family businesses that operated large, national business enterprises. Private companies were allowed to transform into close corporations and vice versa, provided that the conditions of the target business form were met. Close corporations could therefore grow their businesses and, if and when required, transform into private or public companies.[76]

The close corporation was hugely successful. From 1985 to 2008, 2,014,122 close corporations were registered, compared with 453,361 companies.[77] The initial plan in the 1980s was to replace private companies with close corporations, should they prove successful, leaving the complicated Companies Act 61 of 1973 to regulate public companies.

The simplicity of the close corporation's ownership and control was, however, gradually eroded. The Close Corporations Amendment Act 25 of 2005, for example, enabled a trustee of a trust *inter vivos* to be a member of a close corporation under certain conditions. The government's intention was to make the close corporation more suitable for estate planning. The implication of enhanced estate planning functionality for tax evasion and financial crime abuse did not receive sufficient attention. Over time, this amendment led to a proliferation in close corporations with complex trustee membership.

When the South African government had an opportunity to reform company law – at a time when South Africa's arms deal corruption pressures were high – it was decided to reposition private companies as the entity of choice for small

---

[76]   Henning, 2000.
[77]   Henning, 2009, p. 22.

business and to roll back close corporations by not allowing registration of new corporations. The general motivation was that the proposed new Companies Act 71 of 2008 – again focused primarily on large public companies – has been sufficiently simplified for private companies.[78] That position was not supported by published empirical research on user capabilities, including their capability to successfully navigate and comply with the new rules.

If South Africa retained the original close corporation framework, it would have lessened the opportunity for abuse of South African corporate business forms by criminals. It would have ring-fenced ownership complexity in the company form, which would have been mainly used by a far smaller number of large companies. The government would have been able to add further regulatory requirements to the company form to prevent abuse, without concern that additional red tape would have an unnecessarily negative impact on small businesses that use a corporate form.

The decision to terminate close corporation registration contributed to South Africa's mediocre performance in its 2021 FATF mutual evaluation.[79] The report found that South Africa had around 2.1 million legal persons in South Africa in 2019, with the vast majority being private companies, and that there were approximately 10 million directors, of whom 2.5 million were foreign directors. By then, the number of close corporations had dwindled to approximately 355,000.[80] The report found that competent authorities were only to a limited extent able to access beneficial ownership information, if at all, and that access to such information was not timely.[81] South Africa was also found to lack a comprehensive mechanism to ensure that all legal persons keep accurate and up-to-date information on beneficial ownership and that South Africa had no beneficial ownership register.[82] In 2021, consultation commenced on amendments to improve transparency of beneficial ownership. Proposals were subsequently published as part of the General Laws (Anti-Money Laundering and Combating of Terrorism Financing) Bill, published in August 2022.[83]

South Africa's experience with close corporations provides a rich seam for research on corporate integrity and the use of beneficial ownership measures

---

[78] Henning, 2009; Henning 2010.
[79] Financial Action Task Force, 2021b.
[80] Financial Action Task Force, 2021b, para. 99.
[81] Financial Action Task Force, 2021b, para. 411.
[82] Financial Action Task Force, 2021b, p. 197.
[83] General Laws (Anti-Money Laundering and Combating of Terrorism Financing) Bill B 18—2022.

to combat corruption and other crime risks. By providing a well-designed, transparent corporate form for small business, a country can limit the usage of the more complex company form to the large complex businesses that require greater flexibility. That enables the country to implement appropriate company law measures to support transparency of beneficial ownership and the legitimate use of the company form without the standard regulatory concerns that most entities would not be able to comply with enhanced control measures. This would be a cheaper and more beneficial strategy than merely relying on beneficial ownership registries and customer due diligence checks by regulated institutions. These have not proved effective to date and, for the reasons outlined above, are unlikely on their own to respond adequately to the integrity requirements of the FATF. Alternative solutions will need to be crafted for each jurisdiction to lower and limit unnecessary corporate beneficial ownership complexity levels. Providing a more appropriate, transparent corporate business form for small businesses will, however, support economic growth while also limiting the abuse of corporate beneficial ownership.

6   AML/CFT/CPF governance

Appropriate AML/CFT/CPF measures can support anti-corruption action. It is, however, important to recognize that the AML/CFT/CPF measures and the relevant agencies themselves may be undermined by corruption, to minimize their support for anti-corruption action.[84] The agencies may also be ensnared in the politics around enforcement action against senior politicians and their legitimacy may be undermined if they do not have appropriate governance measures in place to protect their integrity.[85]

Corrupt politicians may, for example, wish to infiltrate their national FIU or ensure that it is controlled by them. Control and placement of the South African FIC became controversial during the country's state capture phase. Senior politicians wanted to move the independent FIC away from the Ministry of Finance into the 'more pliant justice, crime prevention and security (JCPS) cluster ministers – where the Guptas could control any suspicious transaction-record report'.[86] The attempts to weaken AML/CFT controls, however, went further. South Africa was in the process of adopting a new bill

---

[84]   Chaikin and Sharman, 2007, pp. 18–33, 69–72; Tang and Ai, 2010.
[85]   De Koker, 2011.
[86]   Van Wyk, 2022; Momoniat, 2021, para. 239.

to amend its Financial Intelligence Centre Act 38 of 2001. The bill responded to its 2009 FATF mutual evaluation report and set out its first binding PEP measures. Parliament adopted the bill, but its signing by the president was delayed by politicians linked to state capture. It was eventually signed after the president appointed a new minister of finance viewed as more sympathetic to his cause.[87] Even then, the commencement of the Act was delayed with arguments that the PEP provisions are discriminatory and therefore unconstitutional.[88] Attempts were also made to change the composition and reporting lines of South Africa's FATF delegation.[89] When those attempts failed, the Gupta family tried to buy their own bank, perhaps, as was alleged, to control the reporting of any suspicious transactions by that bank.[90]

Operational independence as well as accountability and transparency to the extent appropriate to its intelligence functions are critical elements of effective FIUs.[91] How can these aspects best be safeguarded, especially in countries where the rule of law is under pressure? Are there some measures that have proved more effective than others to ensure operational independence? Once the FIU is adequately protected, where are the other vulnerabilities in the framework and how can they best be protected against political interference and influence? Research on case studies in different countries will help to build more resilient AML/CFT/CPF frameworks and agencies.

7   Conclusion

Important questions relating to the application of AML/CFT/CPF measures to combat corruption in developing countries have not received appropriate research attention yet. Research exploring what works and what does not – and why not – and how measures and systems can be designed and supported to work better in countries and regions globally, will assist in building integrity and governance frameworks that are more resilient and more efficient at combating the scourge of corruption. This chapter highlights a few key research questions that should be added to the broad anti-corruption research agenda in this space.

---

[87]   Momoniat, 2021, para. 271.
[88]   Momoniat, 2021, para 238.
[89]   Momoniat, 2021, para. 281–282.
[90]   Momoniat, 2021, para. 318.
[91]   De Koker, 2011; Egmont Group, 2018.

References

Arnone, M. & L.S. Borlini (2014), *Corruption: Economic Analysis and International Law*, Cheltenham: Edward Elgar.

Artingstall, D., N. Dove, J. Howell & M. Levi (2016), *Drivers & Impacts of Derisking*, A report for the Financial Conduct Authority, Shamley Green: John Howell & Co.

BBC (2021), 'Pandora Papers: Your guide to nine years of finance leaks' available at https://www.bbc.co.uk/news/business-41877932 (accessed 15 July 2022).

Bel, G., A. Estache & R. Foucart (2014), 'Transport infrastructure failures in Spain: Mismanagement and incompetence or political capture' in Søreide, T. & A. Williams (eds) *Corruption, Grabbing and Development: Real World Challenges*, Cheltenham: Edward Elgar, 129–139.

Bester, H., D. Chamberlain, L. de Koker, C. Hougaard, R. Short, A. Smith & R. Walker (2008), *Implementing FATF Standards in Developing Countries and Financial Inclusion: Findings and Guidelines*, Washington, DC: The FIRST Initiative, The World Bank.

Blum, J.A., M. Levi, R.T. Naylor & P. Williams (1998), 'Financial havens, banking secrecy and money laundering', *Crime Prevention and Criminal Justice Newsletter*, Double issue 34 and 35, UNDCP Technical Series, 8, available at https://www.imolin.org/imolin/finhaeng.html (accessed 15 July 2022).

Bracking, S. (2007) 'Political development and corruption: Why 'right here, right now'?' in Bracking, S. (ed.) *Corruption and Development: The Anti-Corruption Campaign*, Palgrave Studies in Development, Houndsmill: Palgrave Macmillan, 1–27.

Campos, J.E. & V. Bhargava (2007), 'Tackling a social pandemic' in Campos, J.E. & S. Pradhan (eds), *The Many Faces of Corruption: Tracking Vulnerabilities at the Sector Level*, Washington, DC: The World Bank, 1–25.

Chaikin, D. & J.C. Sharman (2007), *APG/FATF Anti- Corruption/AML/CFT Research Paper*, Asia/Pacific Group on Money Laundering and Financial Action Task Force FATF/PLEN(2007)37, Sydney: Asia and Pacific Group on Money Laundering.

Chaikin, D. & J.C. Sharman (2009), *Corruption and Money Laundering: A Symbiotic Relationship*, New York: Palgrave Macmillan.

Chanson, R. (2022), 'South Africa: Consulting firms, including McKinsey, under fire in "state capture" probe', *The Africa Report*, 12 April, available at https://www.theafricareport.com/ 193472/ south -africa -consulting -firms -including -mckinsey -under-fire-in-state-capture-probe/ (accessed 15 July 2022).

Chatain, P.L, E. Van der Does de Willebois, I. Gonzalez del Mazo, R.D. Valencia, A.M. Aviles, K. Karpinski, S. Goyal, C. Corazza, P. Malik & I. Endo (2018), *The Decline in Access to Correspondent Banking Services in Emerging Markets: Trends, Impacts, and Solutions Lessons Learned from Eight Country Case Studies*, Washington, DC: World Bank.

Choo, K-K.R. (2008), 'Politically exposed persons (PEPs): risk and mitigation', *Journal of Money Laundering Control*, 11(4), 371–387.

Cilliers, H.S., M.L. Benade, J.J. Henning, J.J du Plessis, P.A. Delport, L. de Koker & J.T. Pretorius (2000), *Corporate Law*, Durban: Butterworths.

Collin, M., L. de Koker, M. Juden, J. Myers, V. Ramachandran, A. Sharma & G. Tata (2015), *Unintended Consequences of Anti-money Laundering Policies for Poor Countries*, Washington, DC: Centre for Global Development.

Companies House (2022), *Official Statistics – Companies Register Activities: 2021 to 2022*, 30 June, available at https://www.gov.uk/ government/ statistics/ companies

-register -activities -statistical -release -2021 -to -2022/ companies -register -activities -2021-to-2022 (accessed 15 July 2022).

De Koker, L. (2011), 'Applying anti-money laundering laws to combat corruption' in Graycar, A. & R.G. Smith (eds), *Handbook of Global Research and Practice in Corruption*, Cheltenham: Edward Elgar, 340–358.

De Koker, L. & J. Symington. (2014), 'Conservative corporate compliance: Reflections on a study of compliance responses by South African banks', *Law in Context*, 30, 228–256.

De Koker, L. & M. Turkington (2015), 'Anti-money laundering measures and the effectiveness question' in Rider, B. (ed.) *Research Handbook on International Financial Crime*, Cheltenham: Edward Elgar Publishing, 520–532.

De Koker, L. & M. Turkington (2016), 'Transnational organised crime and the anti-money laundering regime', in Hauck, P. & S. Peterke (eds), *International Law and Transnational Organised Crime*, Oxford: Oxford University Press, 241–263.

De Koker, L., S. Singh & J. Capal (2017), 'Closure of bank accounts of remittance service providers: Global challenges and community perspectives in Australia', *University of Queensland Law Journal*, 36(1), 119–154.

Durner, T. & L. Shetret (2015), *Understanding Bank De-risking and its Effects on Financial Inclusion – An Exploratory Study*, Oxford: Oxfam International.

Egmont Group (2018), *Understanding FIU Operational Independence and Autonomy*, Egmont Center of FIU Excellence and Leadership (ECOFEL), available at https:// egmontgroup .org/ en/ content/ newpublication -understanding -fiu -ope rationalin dependence-and-autonomy (accessed 15 July 2022).

Erbenová, M, Y. Liu, N. Kyriakos-Saad, A. López-Mejía, G. Gasha, E. Mathias, M. Norat, F. Fernando & Y. Almeida (2016), *The Withdrawal of Correspondent Banking Relationships: A Case for Policy Action*, IMF Staff Discussion Note, Washington, DC: IMF.

Financial Action Task Force (2003), *FATF Forty Recommendations*, Paris: Financial Action Task Force.

Financial Action Task Force (2012–2022), *FATF Forty Recommendations*, Paris: Financial Action Task Force.

Financial Action Task Force & the Egmont Group of Financial Intelligence Units (2018), *Concealment of Beneficial Ownership*, Paris: Financial Action Task Force.

Financial Action Task Force (2019), *Best Practices on Beneficial Ownership for Legal Persons*, Paris: Financial Action Task Force.

Financial Action Task Force (2021a), *High-Level Synopsis of the Stocktake of the Unintended Consequences of the FATF Standards*, Paris: Financial Action Task Force.

Financial Action Task Force (2021b), *Anti-Money Laundering and Counter-Terrorist Financing Measures – South Africa: Mutual Evaluation Report*, Paris: Financial Action Task Force.

Financial Action Task Force (2022a), *Report on the State of Effectiveness and Compliance with the FATF Standards*, Paris: Financial Action Task Force.

Financial Action Task Force (2022b), *Public Statement on Revisions to R.24*, Paris: Financial Action Task Force.

Financial Action Task Force (2022c), *Partnering in the Fight Against Financial Crime: Data Protection, Technology and Private Sector Information Sharing*, Paris: Financial Action Task Force.

Gilligan, G. (2009), 'PEEPing at PEPs', *Journal of Financial Crime*, 16(2), 137–143.

Global Witness (2009), *Undue Diligence: How Banks Do Business with Corrupt Regimes*, London: Global Witness.

Greenberg, T.S., L. Gray, D. Schantz, C. Gardner & M. Latham (2010), *Politically Exposed Persons: A Guide on Preventive Measures for the Banking Sector*, Washington, DC: The World Bank.

Henning, J.J. (2000), 'Close corporation law reform in Southern Africa', *Journal of Corporation Law*, 26, 917–950.

Henning, J. J. (2009), 'The South African close corporation under the Companies Act of 2008', *Amicus Curiae*, 80, 22–28.

Henning, J.J. (2010), 'The impact of South African company law reform on close corporations: Selected issues', *Acta Juridica*, 1, 456–479.

Jamieson, N., & K. Hughes (2012), 'The identification of shadow directors under English law: What guidance might Buzzle provide?', *Butterworths Journal of International Banking and Financial Law*, 27, 364–366.

Joutsen, M. (2011), 'The United Nations Convention Against Corruption' in Graycar, A. & R.G. Smith (eds), *Handbook of Global Research and Practice in Corruption*, Cheltenham: Edward Elgar, 303–318.

Judicial Commission of Inquiry into the Allegations of State Capture, Corruption and Fraud in the Public Sector including Organs of State (Zondo Commission) (2022), *All the Recommendations*, Final Reports, Vol 6(4), Johannesburg: Commission of Inquiry into State Capture.

Kang, S. (2018), 'Rethinking the global anti-money laundering regulations to deter corruption', *International & Comparative Law Quarterly*, 67(3), 695–720.

Kollewe, J. (2022), 'Bain & Co barred from UK government contracts over "grave misconduct" in South Africa', *The Guardian*, 3 August, available at https://www .theguardian.com/business/2022/aug/03/bain-and-co-barred-from-uk-government -contracts-over-grave-misconduct-in-south-africa (accessed 10 August 2022).

Krastev, I. (2004) *Shifting Obsessions: Three Essays on the Politics of Anticorruption*, Budapest: Central European University Press.

Lechman, R. (2022), 'Why have the banks not shut down Ramaphosa's accounts?' *IoL*, 20 June, available at https://www.iol.co.za/business-report/companies/why -have-the-banks-not-shut-down-ramaphosas-accounts-c17c095a-8fa9-4ba1-8c37 -17ac7abf5533 (accessed 15 July 2022).

Leung, D., B. Nolens, D. Arner & J. Frost (2022), *Corporate Digital Identity: No Silver Bullet, But a Silver Lining*, BIS Papers No 126, Basel: Bank for International Settlements.

Levi, M., M. Dakolias & T.S. Greenberg (2007), 'Money laundering and corruption', in Campos, J.E. & S. Pradhan (eds), *The Many Faces of Corruption – Tracking Vulnerabilities at the Sector Level*, Washington, DC: The World Bank, 389–426.

Madonsela, S. (2018). 'Critical reflections on state capture in South Africa', *Insights on Africa*, 11(1), 113–130.

Menz, M. (2020), 'Show me the money – managing politically exposed persons (PEPs) risk in UK financial services', *Journal of Financial Crime*, 28(4), 968–980.

Momoniat, I. (2021), *Statement of Mr Ismael Momoniat*, Judicial Commission of Inquiry into the Allegations of State Capture, Corruption and Fraud in the Public Sector including Organs of State, Sandton.

News24 (2016), 'Gupta's Oakbay employees march to banks with demands', available at https://www.news24.com/Fin24/guptas-oakbay-employees-march-to-banks-with -demands-20160426 (accessed 15 July 2022).

News24 (2017), 'Firms snub Oakbay, forcing it to officially delist from JSE', available at https://www.news24.com/Fin24/breaking-firms-snub-oakbay-forcing-it-to -officially-delist-from-jse-20170711 (accessed 15 July 2022).

Nielson, D.L. & J.C. Sharman (2022), *Signatures for Sale: How Nominee Services for Shell Companies are Abused to Conceal Beneficial Owners*, Stolen Assets Recovery Initiative, Washington, DC: World Bank Group.

Piquero, N.L. & J.S. Albanese (2011), 'The relationship between corruption and financial crime' in Graycar, A. & R.G. Smith (eds), *Handbook of Global Research and Practice in Corruption*, Cheltenham: Edward Elgar, 189–202.

Pol, R. (2018), 'Uncomfortable truths? ML = BS and AML = BS2', *Journal of Financial Crime*, 25(2), 294–308.

Public Protector of South Africa (2016), *State of Capture*, Report No 6 of 2016/17, Pretoria: Office of the Public Protector of South Africa.

Ratha, D.K., S. De, E. Dervisevic, S. Plaza, K. Schuettler, W. Shaw, H. Wyss, S. Yi & S.R. Yousefi (2015), *Migration and Remittances: Recent Developments and Outlook*, Migration and Development Brief, No. 24, Washington DC: World Bank.

Robinson, M. (1998), 'Corruption and development: An introduction' in Robinson. M. (ed.), *Corruption and Development*, London: Frank Cass, 1–14.

Rose-Ackerman, S. (2006) 'Introduction and overview' in Rose-Ackerman, S. (ed.), *International Handbook on the Economics of Corruption*, Cheltenham: Edward Elgar, xiv–xxxviii

Rothstein, B. & A. Varraich (2017), *Making Sense of Corruption*, Cambridge: Cambridge University Press.

Sajó, A. & S. Kotkin (2002), 'Understanding and misunderstanding corruption: Part 1 – Introduction' in Sajó, A. & S. Kotkin (eds), *Political Corruption in Transition: A Sceptic's Handbook*, Budapest: Central European University Press, 23–32.

Shalchi, A. (2022) *Politically Exposed Persons Regime*, Research Briefing, London: House of Commons Library.

Sherwood, H. (2017), 'Finsbury Park mosque wins apology and damages from Thomson Reuters', *The Guardian*, 1 February, available at https:// www .theguardian .com/ uk -news/ 2017/ feb/ 01/ finsbury -park -mosque -wins -apology -and -damages -from -reuters (accessed 15 July 2022).

Sweney, M. (2017a), 'Bell Pottinger goes into administration amid South Africa scandal', *The Guardian*, 12 September, https://www.theguardian.com/media/2017/ sep/12/bell-pottinger-goes-into-administration (accessed 15 July 2022).

Sweney, M. (2017b), 'KPMG chiefs in South Africa quit amid Bell Pottinger scandal', *The Guardian*, 15 September, available at https:// www .theguardian .com/ media/ 2017/ sep/ 15/ bell-pottinger-fallout-deepens-kpmg-chiefs-south-africa (accessed 15 July 2022).

Tang, J. & L. Ai (2010), 'Combating money laundering in transition countries: the inherent limitations and practical issues', *Journal of Money Laundering Control*, 13(3), 215–225.

The Commonwealth (2016), *Disconnecting from Global Finance De-risking: The Impact of AML/CFT Regulations in Commonwealth Developing Countries*, London: The Commonwealth Secretariat.

Theobald, R. (1990), *Corruption, Development and Underdevelopment*, London: Palgrave Macmillan.

US Attorney's Office Southern District of California (2021), 'FBI's encrypted phone platform infiltrated hundreds of criminal syndicates: Result is massive worldwide takedown', available at https://www.justice.gov/usao-sdca/pr/fbi-s-encrypted-phone -platform-infiltrated-hundreds-criminal-syndicates-result-massive (accessed on 15 July 2022).

Ware G.T., S. Moss, E. Campos & G.P. Noone (2007), 'Corruption in public procurement: A perennial challenge' in Campos, J.E. & S. Pradhan (eds), *The Many Faces of Corruption – Tracking Vulnerabilities at the Sector Level*, Washington, DC: The World Bank, 295–334.

Van Wyk, P. (2022), 'Zuma, Cabinet and Abrahams weakened systems to stop money laundering – now SA is paying the price', *Daily Maverick*, 3 July, available at https://www.dailymaverick.co.za/article/2022-07-03-zuma-cabinet-and-abrahams -weakened -systems -to -stop -money -laundering -now -sa -is -paying -the -price/ (accessed 15 July 2022).

Wolfsberg Group (2017), 'Wolfsberg Guidance on Politically Exposed Persons (PEPs)', available at https://www.wolfsberg-principles.com/sites/default/files/wb/Wolfsberg -Guidance-on-PEPs-May-2017.pdf (accessed on 15 July 2022).

9 Comparative perspectives in fighting organized crime

Antonello Miranda

1 Introduction

The fight against organized crime is a field where the application of comparative methodology finds, at least in appearance, its ideal terrain.

This fact is obviously reinforced by the circumstance that, regardless of the peculiarities of each type of crime or criminality and regulatory response, globalization on the one hand and digitalization on the other, and the universal spread of the web, have made crime itself and the fight against it more than international, even transnational.

However, this very phenomenon forces us to review the general approaches and even the idea one has of legal comparison. Indeed, in many countries there is an idea and consideration of comparative law that is anchored in rather rigid stereotypes dating back to the last century. Comparative law of the German matrix, which is also widespread in English-speaking countries, often limits itself to observing the rules present in the various legal systems without, however, ever going into the depths of the 'real' explanation of any differences or similarities. Sometimes one looks at the 'circulation of a model' or observes a hypothetical legal transplant but hardly ever grasps the reasons why the model has been successful (or not). Still worse is when the 'comparatist' only does the work of reading foreign law without interpreting the socio-political and economic background that necessarily characterizes it.

Instead, crime has also gone beyond the international dimension to the transnational one, where it is not enough to fight it on an 'international' level, but it is necessary to act through the legal systems, through the individual legal systems, taking into account all those aspects that, although not explicit in each system, actually operate concretely in all of them.

2 Comparative methodology and the fight against organized crime

If you will allow me to make a bold comparison, here we are faced with something reminiscent of the *lex mercatoria*, i.e., those rules that were consolidated in practice and which, put in competition with each other, ended up being followed by all 'merchants' and in all markets regardless of nationality and even of the 'official' recognition of the same rules practised.

Crime operates irrespective of the nationality of the criminal or of the places where he or she acts, and this is why, especially today, fighting it requires not only synergies and international cooperation but also 'alternative' solutions that can actually and concretely operate everywhere, beyond the actual regulatory 'recognition' by each system.

In other and perhaps simpler words, to struggle against transnational crime, it is not enough to invoke national rules that are often useless, if not downright harmful, nor to think that problems can be solved through rules of international law that are often difficult to devise and very slow to enact. National rules, even the most rigid ones, are valid within the borders of the state that issues them.

International rules take a long time to be approved and accepted and are not always actually effective, because they depend on the concrete application of single legal systems. This is why the use of the 'classical' comparative method is, at least, inadequate. Studying a legal solution adopted in one country and thinking of transplanting it in another legal system without taking into account the systemic differences and the evolution of the specific legal system or, worse, without considering the cultural, social, economic and, above all, political background of each country, is the best way to obtain no results, as well as to err in the reconstruction and evaluation of the legal datum. Today, at least in Italy, legal comparison takes into account not only the single normative data (national, European, international) but also, and above all, studies the connections between the legal rules and normative choices of every 'society', reconstructing the political–social datum too and therefore the effective operation of the rules.

Another weak point of the 'traditional comparative' approach to the criminal phenomenon (and not only to law in general) is the lack of awareness of the substantial diversity in the way the law is conceived in the various systems of the world. This happens even among the great legal authors, who tend to make classifications of various kinds but who, at the end of the day, do not realize that just those taxonomies are the product of a 'Western' vision of law (and jurists) that is not present in other systems. Just as it is not so easy to 'export democracy', it must be admitted that one cannot study legal systems through the spectacles of the Western jurist: one would end up seeing, as in *The Wizard of Oz*, everything emerald green, but only because one wears lenses of that colour.

Instead, one must take these differences into account, not thinking that the very fact that a certain rule, a certain solution works in the USA or the UK or France or Estonia or Italy means that others must 'import' it or would like to 'import' it. Examples of more or less forced 'exports' of rules can be found everywhere in the world and in recent history. No one or very few look at the concrete fruit of these exports, and above all very few ask themselves why 'rejection' or legal irritation very often occurs in the receiving countries.

If a given society decides to follow a model or is 'contaminated' by an alien model, it does so regardless of the actual 'transplant' by the legislator. This is the case of the 'bleeding' of the rules, i.e., the discolouration of the national regulatory structure due to the 'stain' or discolouration produced by alien rules actually operating in the same society: in this way, the presence of 'alien' behaviour and rules spreads over the national regulatory structure, effectively altering it and giving rise to something new and different, even in the presence of the 'old' legislative rules, but also in the presence of new regulatory and behavioural elements that have not been yet 'verbalized' or transposed into law.[1]

---

[1] Let me give an example to clarify the concept: in Palermo, my town, there is now a large Pakistani community of Islamic religion. Some of them have begun to engage in small business activities, gaining some stability. Obviously, these people (regularly immigrants) rented premises, someone bought an apartment in a condominium, etc. Of course, to do their business, to purchase a house, to rent a room, to buy and resell goods, they must comply with the Italian legal provisions ruling these relationships. But alongside this 'normal' doing, the relations within the community are often governed by the specific rules of that social group. If the owner of the rented premises is Pakistani, as the tenant is, regardless of the Italian rules, the agreement is often regulated 'in the Islamic way' and according to the habits of that group, as in a sort of parallel reality. Obviously, since it is not possible to keep the two realities separate forever, they end up meeting each other and so alien rules 'lose colour' by bleeding on the canvas of local and indigenous norms.
     Thus they change the way in which they negotiate, change the opening hours, change the competition with large shopping malls of small family businesses, change the 'food' and product 'rules' (I am thinking of halal food), change the

The point (and in this once again the Italian comparative school, or rather the 'Sicilian' school, has been in the vanguard) is that Western legal systems, those of both common law and civil law that refer to the 'Western Legal Tradition', have in common an idea of law that no one else in the world has. For us, law is something that is self-generating and self-justifying, something that is free, indeed completely free from dependence on religious, moral or ethical precepts, something in which nothing is created, nothing is destroyed, but everything is transformed by society and without the legislator's interference except to a limited extent and in particular situations.

To put it more simply, law, in the Western legal tradition, is secular and above all self-sufficient: it is secular because the legal rules were born spontaneously and evolved with society without, however, depending on or descending from the 'will' of a God (or a philosophy or a political creed, or ethical or moral issues); it is self-sufficient because, as I said before, it is able to fill any gaps through its own principles and with its own mechanisms and instruments.

To make this clear to an English-speaking audience, I would say that this is absolutely evident when, faced with the absence of statutes or precedents, the courts rely in their discretionary decision not on pure arbitrariness but on 'values', i.e., on those principles that the legal system itself has matured and consolidated over time and that constitute the cornerstones of the system: accordingly there is no need to decide by drawing inspiration from religious precepts that cannot be questioned precisely because they are 'the word of God', nor even less so from political-ideological or philosophical principles or 'external' to the legal system; one decides through principles that are immanent in law.

After all, whoever buys bread or drugs for a jurist concludes a contract, regardless of whether that agreement, that exchange of what for what, may be more or less morally or ethically or religiously correct and just; and even if one looks at it from the point of view of 'criminal law' (or as I prefer to say, criminal leg-

---

cost of labour and the commitment to work. It goes without saying that in this situation we should ask whether and to what extent the host legal system can tolerate bleeding (by declaring hybridization and thus integrating its own system) or cannot use 'bleach' to wash its regulatory pattern.

See: Miranda, A (2018) 'The Bleeding of Legal Rules Between Rights and Limits, in the Age of Migration Flows and the Crisis of the Nations', in Colombo, G (ed.) *Hybridizations, Contaminations, Triangulations: Itineraries in Comparative Law Through the Legal Systems of Italy and Japan*, special Issue of *The Italian Law Journal*, 23, ss.

islation), that contract remains what it is: I am thinking of the Italian anti-drug legislation that allows the sale of 'modest quantities', so that the buying and selling of x grams of drugs would be as lawful as buying a sandwich, while buying xxx grams of drugs would no longer be lawful; if tomorrow our legislator changed its mind and increased or decreased the amount of drugs on free sale, from the point of view of the contractual 'essence' of the buying–selling relation, nothing would change. To put it in terms more comprehensible to a common lawyer, I would say that if I buy bread or buy drugs, I am technically concluding a contract with the presence of a consideration; perhaps one could object that if the sale were prohibited the consideration would be vitiated, but even in this case the boundary is blurred, too blurred.

Finally, it must also be admitted that however much behaviour may be forbidden (perhaps it would be better to say sanctioned, because in theory in criminal law, at least in the case of the Italian criminal code, there are no 'prohibitions' but indications of sanctions in the case of behaving in a certain way: it is not forbidden to kill a man but it is postulated that murder will be punished with imprisonment), then it must be seen whether in practice this behaviour is 'admitted' by social practice. It is somewhat questionable to look only at the 'legal' or 'legislative' datum in the narrow sense when then in reality, despite the provision of the sanction or the use of the 'force of the state', the people or a good part of them follow and put into practice precisely that 'forbidden' or sanctioned behaviour. The comparatist knows that 'law' or rather the legal rule does not end with the prediction of the legislature or the precedent of a court, but one must also observe what practices are followed by the people, what rules are 'established' in society regardless of their 'recognition' by the state.

These observations lead us to consider that society moves and acts by obeying or disobeying the rules, not so much when certain behaviours are explicitly foreseen and permitted and others forbidden; it moves and acts by obeying or disobeying the rules when there is a 'convenience' to do so: a convenience that is not only and exclusively economic (it is useless to think of a simple cost–benefit analysis) but of 'pleasure', enjoyment, satisfaction, 'improvement of the quality of life', even if not material and not contingent and immediate. No one obeys rules unless there is a convenience (it is worth reaffirming, NOT necessarily of an economic nature[2]) to do so.

---

[2] I am thinking, for example, of certain mafia bosses who have operated and unfortunately still operate in Sicily and the USA. The case of Salvatore 'Totò' Riina is emblematic: he spent his life in hiding and living in very precarious and even uncomfortable conditions; the wealth that mafia trafficking allowed him to accumulate was not the 'purpose' of his activity, or rather, it was a 'surplus',

Therefore today, the comparatist who tackles aspects of the fight against crime must on the one hand keep the regulatory elements and legislative instruments very clear, but must also check the efficiency and effectiveness of the regulatory and legislative choices with respect to their possible application, both in the initial context and in the contexts subject to possible transplantation. Ignoring the political datum or the datum of the social and economic composition of the countries involved in the criminal phenomenon means only making blunders, if not actually ending up damaging even the healthy part of society and, as an old adage goes, throwing the baby out with the bathwater.

It goes without saying that the legislator should be animated by the best of intentions. However, often the law, the statutory law, looks at the contingent situation without thinking that the sanction or remedy may be even more harmful than the evil it is intended to cure.

This is why, in my opinion, the comparatist should rediscover the 'alternative' role of law in general and private law in particular. Finding means and solutions, other than the simple criminal 'punitive' system, that make it more 'convenient' and 'satisfying' to follow the rules instead of breaking them is, in my opinion, the best way to actually fight crime.

It is not possible in this work to analyse *funditus* each crime-fighting situation to verify empirically whether what is stated here is accurate. However, in my opinion, we can focus on two aspects of the fight against organized crime where a transnational criminal phenomenon has been responded to at an international level or a model has been 'conceived' that has then been exported and revisited to some extent in other jurisdictions. I am referring to the case of 'trafficking in human beings' for the first hypothesis and to the issue of 'compliance' and compliance with its standards for the second hypothesis.

---

because the real driving force was the 'convenience' that came from his absolute command of 'Cosa Nostra'. Evidently, in his case, the risk of being arrested or killed was compensated not by the 'wealth' (which was neither used nor flaunted) but by the 'enjoyment' he derived from exercising his power. Obviously, wealth also served to protect his family, but it was not the 'personal' and mainspring of Riina's (and other mafiosi in general) criminal actions. Similarly, it is not an 'economic' choice of those who, as terrorists, decide to commit suicide: the promise of an after-life benefit and the possibility of annihilating themselves in the arms of the Uri amidst rivers of honey and other delights, has nothing economic or real about it, but it is still a prospect of improvement which, to some extent, evidently appeals (besides the advantages of another nature, also economic, which one can obtain from one's criminal action).

3 Trafficking in human beings and the alternative use of comparative law

In the 1970s in Italy the idea of 'the alternative use of law' spread among many young jurists and judges. To tell the truth, that season was not distinguished, at least in my opinion, by great political achievements and particularly revolutionary results for the world of law; on the contrary, if one looks back at that period, one realizes the absurdity of certain rulings and theories.

However, one must also admit that those who, like me, believed in the possibility of 'using' the law in an alternative way also hoped to be able to give new answers to the changing needs of society, which in those years was drastically moving. And in the end something of that experience remained, if only in the confirmation of the idea, widespread among comparatists, that the 'law of private individuals' is much more deeply rooted, shared and close to the 'people' than even the best laws (criminal, administrative and so on) of the state can be. For a comparatist of the Palermo school, then, private law, or rather the law of the *cives*, is the 'rule of law' on which the civil life of a society is founded.

I understand that this may seem strange to younger readers, steeped in pan-constitutionalism or neo-positivism, but private law has its own 'intrinsic strength' and 'independence' from external factors that makes it (in almost all its aspects) impervious to the forcing of the legislature: private law, at least in the sense that is proper to it in the Western legal tradition or, more correctly, in the European tradition, is, as I said before, 'secular and self-sufficient' and the legislature's infamous stroke of a pen is not enough to send it to the scrap heap. Private law is then, if you like, 'liberal' in the sense that it is based on the position of equality of the subjects and provides for corrective and protective interventions whenever a distortion or alteration of the equalitarian scheme appears.

This is certainly not the place to reconstruct and explain the assumption in question. But it must at least be said that, I have become increasingly convinced, when faced with the dark side of the law, i.e., the negative effects that often occur as a consequence of interventions, albeit in good faith and with the best of intentions, by the legislature and when faced with the proliferation of laws and statutes, especially in the administrative sphere and again in the face of the often ineffectiveness of 'merely punitive and afflictive' rules and sanctions in general, that there was and is room for a reading, an interpretation, a new and alternative use of private law also in the wake of the experiences of other legal systems.

'Power to the Imagination' was a well-known slogan of the 1970s; imagination in the use of private law, I maintain today, because it is not enough to punish or threaten sanctions, it is not enough to try to envisage the imposition of behaviour in the most classic 'Bentham's dog' manner if nothing is done in practice to ensure that it is more convenient to follow the rules than to violate them, if nothing is done to increase the degree of 'enjoyment', of 'pleasure' in following the rules.

From this point of view, I believe that trafficking in human beings is precisely one of the most striking cases of a system of rules designed to achieve positive and virtuous results but which clashes with factual reality, sometimes ending up being a remedy worse than the evil it was intended to combat, and leaving room for a different use of the rules of private law that might instead encourage 'social' acceptance by improving their effectiveness and efficacy. And it is on this that I would like to focus my attention.

Looking at things from the point of view of the Italian and European situation as well as internationally, I am immediately reminded of a book on Malaysian pirates that I read as a boy. In that book, describing the struggle between the United Kingdom, the Honourable East India Company and the pirates, the author, E. Salgari, speculated that in order to discourage mutiny and murder in England, it was more effective to have the convicts whipped with the 'cat-o'-nine-tails' (i.e., a heavy, physically painful punishment) than hanged (i.e., capital punishment).

I do not know whether the story is true or a legend, but I think it is emblematic of reality: sometimes some simple punishments are more effective than others, and particularly heavy punishments, even if so 'final' as the death penalty, make little or no impression on people who do not value their lives and the lives of others.

As I will say in a moment, this is, in my opinion, the focal point on criminal legislation (Italian, English, European or world-wide is not important) against human trafficking; in fact, no national criminal legislation has *in se ipsa* the capacity to solve the problem and eradicate or limit the phenomenon. The point is more political than (strictly speaking) legal. If we look at the various national legislations, we can see that almost all the countries of the 'Western legal tradition' have rules against human trafficking, and the Palermo Protocol (the first international agreement aimed at combating the phenomenon on a global scale) has established a sort of international guideline or harmonized legislation that provides for the best criminal laws. But today, quoting a Bob Dylan song, despite so many years of ironclad punitive rules, it seems that 'times are NOT yet changing'. In fact, human trafficking is strong and seems to be a lucrative and extremely organized international business, sometimes with the complicity or compliance of the public authorities (as happened with Libya, then Turkey, then Belarus… etc.).

Of course, I do not intend to ignore the pedagogical role of legislation, but I think that statutes and acts are usually enacted more as a response to public opinion or rather to what the legislature and the government think should or can be the majority opinion.

As it turned out in a similar issue, such as artificial insemination, human trafficking implies the need to protect the victims in the first place and to prevent or at least limit trafficking, i.e., irregular immigration.

In such cases, merely repressive legislation is ineffective, as was amply demonstrated both by the first versions of Articles 600, 601 and 602 of the Italian Criminal Code in force until 2003, and by subsequent amendments.

While trafficking in human beings and smuggling identify a new phenomenon, i.e., the irregular immigration of persons who are in a particular condition of subjection to the criminal organization and who are both victim and offender, the old Italian regulations were only focused on the fight against slavery, i.e., the 'acquisition' of the 'ownership' of a human being, a completely different phenomenon in the strict sense.

Until the 2003 legislative reform of the immigration regulations, the Italian legislator had dealt with the matter in a fragmentary manner and with frequent amendments, overlapping of regulations and competences; the difficulties in interpreting the regulations depended on the confusion of the provisions, and the absence of a system of general and common principles and guidelines that could be used in uncertain cases. Here, of course, central and complex issues such as the protection of human rights, respect for the person, public safety, immigration control and the care of women and children have entered the legal debate. Often, however, the principles relating to these issues came into conflict to such an extent that there was a need, again from a legal and systematic point of view, to give them a hierarchical order, or at least to set a scale of values.

This debate gave rise to the new Italian immigration legislation that implemented (or at least tried to) the principles on which EU immigration policy is based. In fact – although since the mid-1980s, some European governments had thought of regulating immigration matters with common actions, considering this to be the best and most efficient solution for their state interests (Schengen agreements) – with the Treaty of Amsterdam (1997), the EU institutions were entrusted with the competences concerning immigration issues and the conditions of treatment of immigrants present on EU territory, introducing a regulation that was previously a matter left to the Member States and to European intergovernmental cooperation. In this way, issues concerning visas, asylum, immigration control, and other policies related to the free movement of immigrants became EU competences.

In matters of the admission, entry, stay and expulsion of immigrants, Italian provisions therefore had to be aligned with the commitments and guidelines of EU law. The European Union, especially after 11 September 2001, has defined and created step by step a real 'stronghold', characterized by strict border controls on the entry of non-EU immigrants and the free movement of EU citizens.

The objectives of the EU's immigration policy were (and are) aimed at combating illegal immigration and limiting legal immigration as much as possible; in order to control the external borders (by means of close cooperation between the Member States' police forces), the EU intended to make the 'stronghold Europe' impenetrable – it would open its doors only to non-EU immigrant workers, only if legally admitted, only if requested, only if needed and, I would say, only if useful because, after all, they are 'qualified'. The political issues of returns/repatriations/expulsions/outplacements and the 'externalization' of border controls are still the EU's overriding concerns. Furthermore, EU Member States agree on the adoption and implementation of swift measures to order the deportation of irregular immigrants trying to enter EU territory.

These are the priority objectives of EU immigration policy, but despite the statement that the development of 'a common immigration policy', including the definition of the conditions of entry and residence of aliens and measures to combat illegal immigration, is a constituent element of the European Union's objective of creating an area of 'freedom, security and justice' with respect for fundamental rights 'without discrimination on grounds of sex, race, colour, ethnic or social origin, genetic features, language, religion or belief, political or other opinion, membership of a national minority', Directive 2004/81/EC (not applicable to the United Kingdom, Ireland and Denmark) provides only and simply for the granting of a 'reflection period' and a residence permit of up to six months in the territory of the Member State (at the discretion of national law), also limited to 'third-Country nationals who are or have been victims of offences related to trafficking in human beings even if they entered the territory of the member state illegally' and only if they actively cooperate against trafficking in human beings or action to facilitate illegal immigration.

On the other hand, the directive states that the residence permit may be withdrawn at any time, in particular 'if the competent authority considers that the victim's cooperation is fraudulent or illegal' or 'on grounds of public policy and protection of national security' or 'when the competent authorities decide to discontinue the proceedings'. In these cases, the ordinary rules for foreigners apply, resulting in the imposition of an expulsion order.

As a result, immigrants often suffer inadequate treatment (to put it mildly) in the Member States' temporary reception (detention) centres, without taking into account their needs, demands, rights, and the requests of the most vulnerable categories of immigrants. Moreover, they are sent back out of the EU territory without attention to the concrete case and without a proper investigation of the situations they have fled from and where they would be forced to return to.

Unfortunately, this seems to be a general trend: for example, more than 12 years ago, on 1 September 2010, the Algerian government enacted a new criminal law that provided for imprisonment of up to 10 years for 'passeurs' and up to six months for those who tried to leave the country illegally. I know that 'hindsight is full of pits', but even at that time it was easy to imagine what would be the fate of thousands of desperate people who every month reach Algeria or Libya (i.e., the 'camp' organized by traffickers and where people are subjected to all kinds of violence) from sub-Saharan African countries. This is news today and is there for all to see.

From these European Union provisions emerges the intention to balance two different goals, which may also be inconsistent in their implementation. The first (priority) is the restrictive control of migration flows to EU territory from third countries and the fight against illegal immigration. The second is the consideration of immigrants with special needs (such as children and women) in the application of measures to combat illegal immigration. The intention to implement strict return and expulsion policies is also evident.

In Italy, it was almost impossible to comply with this European indication to combat human trafficking only with the general provisions against 'slavery', which were completely incapable of striking the phenomenon, also due to the difficulties of interpretation and reconstruction.[3] Following political and legal criticism from the most influential Italian authors, the Parliament on 11 August 2003 approved a new statute 'against trafficking and smuggling in human beings' by revising and improving the old Articles 600–602.

The new wording of Article 600 stipulated:

> Whoever: a) exercises over another person powers and prerogatives such as those exercised by a master or; b) places or maintains a person in a state of continuous subjection or submission, forcing him or her to work or engage in sex (in any form) or begging or any other service that enables his or her exploitation, shall be punished by imprisonment for a minimum of eight years and a maximum of 20 years.

The penalty is increased by 50% if the victim is a minor or if the acts are related to prostitution or trafficking in human organs.

The most interesting improvement consists in the definition of the 'state of continuous subjection or submission', which should be the consequence of any kind of 'violence, intimidation, threat, coercion, fraud, abuse, undue influence or exploitation of any situation of physical or psychological inferiority or any situation of need, or any kind of promise of money or other advantages to parents or those exercising parental authority' over the victim. This rule refines the old one by considering all types of subjection or submission without differ-

---

[3]   The problem is to catch the slave traders (and if I remember correctly, very rarely in the last 15 years has anyone been convicted of this charge) and to protect the 'slaves' by encouraging them to denounce their situation. At the same time, the rule does not allow the victim to be admitted as a legal immigrant or benefit from similar facilities.

The interpretation of these rules was very difficult: to what extent can we consider that one man was the 'property' of another? Are we to perceive ownership as perpetual and continuous or is it possible to have temporary 'ownership'? Can we consider as a 'slave' the woman who under psychological or other subtle forms of pressure has been forced (but with some sort of consent, usually from her family) to prostitute herself for one or two months until she can pay for the 'services' of illegal immigration?

The rules had been too general and at the same time were intended to cover a crime far removed from human trafficking offences. Thus the judiciary, which in Italy must, at least formally, obey and strictly enforce the laws, failed to overcome the limits of those rules: for example, at least until 1997, judges accepted as 'slavery-like conditions' only the few strictly and peremptorily provided for by the 1956 Geneva Convention. Since 1999, only the Court of Cassation has considered it possible to extend the provision of Articles 600–602 on 'de facto slavery' to all the different forms of 'modern slavery', taking the list of the Geneva Convention as a mere and non-mandatory exemplification.

entiating between physical and psychological inferiority (both of which are not to be understood in the medical sense but as a 'cultural and cognitive disparity', i.e., submission to certain religious rules or traditional or tribal customs) and between absolute or temporary possession of the victim. It is only necessary that the victim lies in a 'state of helplessness' for an adequate continuous period of time.

Article 601 extends the provisions of Article 600 to those who engage in human trafficking by:

> persuading and fraudulently inducing or coercing, threatening, abusing, intimi-dating, etc … another person to … illegally enter, reside in or leave Italian territory under the same circumstances as those explained in Article 600.

This is the first of the 36 new articles of the penal code that provided for 'trans-national' offences, i.e., offences committed in more than one state or com-mitted in a state other than the one in which the effects occur. This is a very important point because it thus becomes possible to prosecute the trafficker of human beings in Italy even if the persuasion or inducement was exercised in a foreign state and even if the material fact of 'introduction, stay or departure' has not taken place.

The new version of Articles 600–602 gave the judiciary the possibility of considering all types of human trafficking as crimes. But of course, these regu-lations have not proved to be an extremely effective tool to combat trafficking: in fact, their relevance only comes to light after the event.

To improve the tools for an adequate and timelier fight against human traf-ficking, the law has extended the applicability of anti-mafia rules to human trafficking. This makes it possible for the victim of human trafficking to benefit from all the provisions, guarantees and protections that Italian law grants to the person 'cooperating with justice' (i.e., the *pentito*), witnesses and their parents and relatives. The idea is that it is necessary to protect and reward the victim for cooperating with the authorities also by allowing a limited possibility of regular immigration to curb the link and dependence on the human trafficker.

Consequently, a new confiscation hypothesis is introduced that is not limited to the profits and income from the crime but extends to all assets of the offender. In addition, a new set of alternative punishments is provided for, such as the closure of the business or company or the revocation of the administrative licence to operate a business whose activity is in some way connected to human trafficking. Whether it is possible to extend the application of these rules to include the liability of bankers and professionals, as is the case of terrorism or mafia and money laundering, is a question of fact and a matter of debate for judges and jurists. In my opinion, there is room for a similar interpretation of the new rules by emphasizing how this instrument can be more effective than others in limiting the phenomenon. It is a way to cut off or at least make it more difficult to make money and profit from irregular or criminal activities.

Finally, thanks to a 2001 law reinforced by the 2003 provisions, the liability of the legal person is recognized. This regulation is particularly important first of all because it is perfectly in line with European Union regulations and not least because, with the provision of this liability of the legal person, it is now possible to hit and stop those companies or associations that, under the cloak of apparent legitimacy, run their business on minors or organ transplants.

As in the most classic of *pochades*, we have two pieces of news: the good news is that Italy has complied with EU rules and equipped itself with instruments to combat human trafficking. The bad news is that after almost 20 years, we still do not have the possibility to fully implement these provisions. Trafficking is still strong and human traffickers seem to be 'on duty'. Moreover, as during the prohibition era, we have a kind of rebound effect: the more criminal laws or penalties are increased, the higher the risks for exploiters and the higher the prices on the black market. The consequences on human trafficking during the 'war in Libya' were emblematic and have unfortunately been constantly repeated until today.

I understand the 'political' reasons for passing these regulations. There is a strong public demand for security and protection against crimes. Of course, people who come to our countries must respect our rules, and if the foreigner commits a crime, they must be punished. However, I fear that there is often a great risk of confusing the criminal with the victim of human trafficking.

I am aware that each country has a peculiar and very narrow view of the problem, and I can imagine that Germany is more interested in preventing irregular immigration from Turkey and Eastern countries than in preventing irregular immigration from North Africa or China to Italy. I can imagine that in the UK the problem of combating the prostitution of hundreds of young Belarusian or Moldovan girls is substantially limited and far removed from the Italian problem of preventing the thousands of irregular immigrants who work underpaid and without any (legal) protection. It is obvious that the problems that Germany and the UK face are completely different from those faced by Spain, France or Italy – the latter need to control their coastlines, a very difficult task. So in reality there is again a contradiction between the 'appearance' of law (every country in Europe says it wants to 'protect and regulate' immigration) and the actual 'substance' of reality: in fact, no country wants to keep 'economic' immigrants, regular or irregular (France's negative approach against 'regularized' immigration of Tunisians from Italy, for example during the Libyan war is evident).

In my opinion, this is the main reason why the 'national' and otherwise merely 'repressive' approach to the general problem is weak and impotent. What is needed is a different frame involving massive international cooperation and collaboration with weak and developing countries; irregular immigration must also be combated not only with a narrow 'penal' or statutory approach but in a 'multidisciplinary' manner using the tools offered by international law, economics, sociology and especially the alternative use of private law.

The problems of immigration are far from being solved: the undifferentiated arrest and deportation of thousands of people is an unrealistic prospect even from a simple and cynical 'cost–benefit' balance sheet. Moreover, a simple and dramatic consequence of the potential increase in risks for criminal organizations trafficking in human beings always involves the concrete and actual increase in costs and prices (in a very broad sense) for migrants: this is the 'dark side of the law'. Even in a 'good law' there is a dark side and sometimes the actual consequences of the application of a rule are unpredictable and even worse than the event it is intended to correct or combat.

In my opinion, the point is all about tackling the phenomenon on the one hand by obviously increasing control over irregular immigration (and this is only possible in the context of broader cooperation between states), but on the other hand by increasing the possibilities of legal entry into our countries and at the same time trying to eliminate or help eliminate the real causes of emigration. I suggest, perhaps provocatively, abolishing all kinds of restrictions and limits on immigration, naturally also trying to create better living conditions in the immigrants' countries of origin and above all to help train their managerial and entrepreneurial classes: Russian (and before that Soviet) influence on Afro-Asian countries is also the result of the training of the cadres and managerial classes of those countries at the Peoples' Friendship University in Moscow, once Lumumba University.

For us Italians, for example, it would be very important to resume training the managerial and entrepreneurial classes of countries such as Somalia, Eritrea or Ethiopia, from which most migrants come to our territory; doing hairy charity by sending a few doctors to work in dilapidated hospitals for a month and then leaving is not an intelligent choice; it would be different if we helped to train doctors and architects who could build hospitals and work in them. But here, as always, it is a matter of political choices. Moreover, if only we made the visa system work better, we could achieve the goal of better controlling the flows and at the same time reduce the use of the black market and trafficking. Or one could take a cue from the Estonian model of granting electronic residency to anyone (with appropriate controls) who applies for it.

Let us assume for a moment that immigration is a positive phenomenon from an economic point of view: in Italy, despite the crisis and an incredible 30% youth unemployment, practically all the heavy work in agriculture or small businesses or in general the heaviest activities are carried out by immigrants. Let us assume for a moment that immigrants hope to return to their countries of origin as soon as possible and hope to bring their skills, assets and lifestyle to a higher level. Would it be impossible to think that a more pro-regulatory approach to legal immigration aimed at the emergence of exploitation and the provision of educational support would lead to a decrease in irregular immigration and a decrease in criminal activities related to human trafficking?

I have already said, but the results are there for all to see, that the merely 'punitive' approach is useless. In my opinion, there is room – and it is more effective – to use 'private' law in the fight against human trafficking. Let me try to briefly give some examples: among the big problems of human trafficking were and are the 'illegal adoptions' of children, the purchase of children from surrogate mothers and the sale of human organs. Of course there was a criminal law response, but it did not prove sufficient. In Italy, we have improved our legislation on international and domestic adoption by simplifying procedures and making it easier to make affiliation agreements. At the same time, we improved our laws on donation and transplantation. The consequence in both cases has been a drastic reduction in the illegal adoption market and the 'black market' for organs.

The same can be said for the phenomenon of 'surrogate mothers': I do not have the space here to speak about it *funditus*, but I believe that the appeal (also by the Italian Supreme Court) to the principle that the mother is the one who gives birth (and who would therefore have exclusive parental responsibility), would lead to a decisive and drastic reduction in the phenomenon.

Another example comes to us from the Immigration Act (2008) and precisely from Article 12 (5*bis*), according to which:

> whoever rents or leases a house or flat to an irregular immigrant shall be punished with arrest up to 3 years.

And Article 22(12), according to which:

> the employer of the irregular worker shall be punished by arrest of up to 1 year and a fine of €5,000 for each irregular worker.

These prohibitions were by no means surprisingly successful, as expected. We all know, authorities and judiciary included, of the incredible situation of exploitation and degradation in which the hundreds if not thousands of people, mostly economic migrants and illegal immigrants, live in Villa Literno or in the countryside around Ragusa or in the rich industrial north. It does not seem to me that despite 20 years of 'repressive' legislation much has been achieved – quite the contrary.

Instead, I think that regulations providing economic and tax incentives to employers or to those who rent houses and flats to foreign migrants could be far more effective in inducing emersion from clandestinely, also giving the possibility of a real improvement in the living conditions of migrants and a concrete possibility of their stable return to their countries of origin. In the same direction, the rules on consumer protection and freedom of competition could be rebuilt to prevent speculation and distortion of the free market. I mean, for example, that a company or employer that employs irregular workers in the black market is violating the rules of competition (it is a clear example of unfair competition against companies or employers that employ regular workers, pay taxes, pay health insurance, etc.). From the point of view of consumer protection, 'irregular' work could be challenged on the basis of the consumer's right to obtain a service or product that respects the producer's 'promises' (also ethically and morally correct): for example, if I want to eat a 'real Neapolitan pizza', it is a violation of my consumer right if the pizza is not prepared as a 'real Neapolitan pizza', i.e., by a 'regular' and 'licensed' pizza maker and with the original ingredients and according to the original recipe.

In this, the diffusion of soft law, i.e., contracts stipulated between traders and between entrepreneurs who agree to display 'a quality certification' on condition that they abide by certain rules (no payment of 'pizzo' – protection money – no use of black-market workers, precise commitments and specific good practices of safety, healthiness, etc.) with relative 'clauses' on 'quality certification' etc., with relative 'penalty clauses' of compensation for damages to the benefit of the group and with the further condition of expulsion from the group, can, in my opinion, work better than any penal or repressive rule; the English experience of 'private associations' can be a comfort on this.

Also from this perspective we could reconstruct the rules on cohabitation and even the traditional concept of 'family' or the rules on private work: I am referring to the case of caregivers, domestic helpers and domestic servants (who in Italy are usually irregular immigrants, and obviously underpaid or exploited).

In these cases, it will be more useful to provide incentives and rewards for the conclusion of 'regular' contracts with migrants instead of fighting, uselessly, against, for instance, simulated marriages: in Modena, some time ago, the mayor denounced the growing number of 'surprise' civil marriages between very elderly Italian men and very young foreign women initially (irregularly) hired as maids or nurses. As a famous English judge said, 'this is probably immoral or reprehensible but … it is real life and it is absolutely normal'. And if we want to successfully combat human trafficking, we cannot ignore reality. Once again, the issue is more political than legal.

It may be because he who goes with the lame learns to limp, and therefore my long association with fellow economists, sociologists and political scientists has altered my perception, but I believe that, in order to address these complex issues, there is room, indeed a need, for legal doctrine to reopen the season of the political nature of law by rediscovering the egalitarian and protective function that is at the basis of the civil 'liberal theory of law' and is the foundation of European civilization.

4   To comply or not comply … this is the question

The rules of so-called 'compliance' (which we have emblematically represented, but not only, in the Italian Act no. 231/2001) represent one of the most striking cases of a system of rules 'worldwide'[4] intended to obtain positive and virtuous results but which clashes with factual reality, sometimes ending up being a remedy worse than the evil it was intended to combat and leaving room for a different use of the rules of private law that could instead incentivize 'social' acceptance by improving its effectiveness and efficacy.

Like most of my generation, I now rarely go to the cinema. Of course, I am very fond of (action) films, but framed between television and the internet, it is so easy to find an alternative, and being lazy I only go out if the film is interesting

---

[4]   Even if the 'model' is as usual Western or precisely Anglo-American. See the English Bribery Act that is a kind of 'specimen' or format to follow.

to my wife. However, some time ago one of my wife's chosen films caught my attention. First of all because of the title – 'Compliance' – and, second, because of the plot, which was also interesting from a 'legal' point of view. The story is simple on the surface: Sandra is a middle-aged manager in a fast-food restaurant; Becky is a teenage counter girl who really needs the job. One stressful day (too many customers), an overt police officer calls, accusing Becky of stealing money from a customer's purse, which she vehemently denies. Sandra, overwhelmed by her managerial responsibilities, carries out the officer's order to detain Becky. This choice begins a nightmare that tragically 'blurs the boundaries between experience and prudence, legality and reason'. The film is based on a true story and is about how unreasonable obedience to authority can sometimes be dangerous.

In my opinion, this is just a starting point for a general discussion on 'compliance' with rules and the risk that blind and narrow submission to rules (sectorial and overconfident) can create more problems than it would eliminate. This is, I believe, the case with 'compliance', which today is one of the most complex aspects of law, so complex that it is sometimes out of control. Compliance is also a global phenomenon: most countries have had rules on compliance and some book of good intentions is almost in progress.

But could we define 'compliance' in a common way? Could we have a 'common standard' of compliance? Although I am not a 'digital native', I understand the power of the 'Web' and its unbeatable mass of information, and also the fascinating and 'fatal attraction' for ordinary people. Like most of my students … I searched the web for the word 'compliance' and got a reference to 360,000,000 webpages. If one refines the search to 'regulatory compliance', the result is 'only' 160,000,000 webpages, while 'legal compliance' scores 330,000,000 webpages, 'risk assessment' 170,000,000 webpages, and 'governance' 462,000,000 webpages. Of course, it is almost impossible to extract a single meaning of compliance from this mass of information, although in a very general way compliance means 'to comply with stated requirements, rules or standards'.

At the organizational level, it is achieved through management processes that ascertain the appropriate requirements (as defined in laws, regulations, contracts, strategies, policies, best practices, etc.), assess the status of compliance, evaluate the potential risks and costs of non-compliance versus the likely costs of achieving compliance, and then select, fund, and initiate any corrective action that appears to be necessary. However, in my opinion, this is obviously a general and basic characteristic of legal norms and the rule of law: according to the Italian legal system – but this is absolutely the same in every 'civil law system' – we should all obey and 'respect' legal norms (*ignorantia legis non excusat*). Every legislator, not surprisingly, wants his rules to be obeyed and no legislator (usually…) thinks they are useless.

Legal compliance is the process of ensuring that an organization follows laws, regulations, standards and business rules in order to not infringe the rules, at the same time fighting the crimes and avoiding the 'collusion'. The definition of legal compliance includes the understanding of and adherence to codes of ethics within entire professions or activities so that it is, as I will discuss later, almost impossible to act or work without the risk of doing something wrong or 'incorrect'. The common idea is that:

> if a strong legal governance component is in place, risk can be accurately assessed and the monitoring of legal compliance be carried out efficiently.[5]

In order to be compliant with the law, the 'complier' should manage its policies so that they are: (1) consistent with the law, and (2) comprehensive with respect to the law.

The role of legal compliance has also been expanded to include the self-monitoring of ungoverned behaviour with industries and corporations that could lead to workplace indiscretions: it is important to keep in mind that if a strong legal governance component is in place, risk can be accurately assessed and legal compliance monitoring can be done efficiently.

In conclusion, we can say that compliance has two meanings: (1) the daily round to comply with a set of rules, and (2) the procedures adopted to prove that an organization complies with a set of rules when failure to do so is blameworthy. The point is that in searching for compliance rules and their reconstruction, it seems that they have progressively shifted towards the meaning of a generic but strict adherence to rules.

We can draw inspiration from the guidance rules suggested within the English Bribery Act 2010[6] (a good example also for 'general and speculative' civil law systems). This act and the 'guidance' rules are clear and precise and, *prima*

---

5   World Heritage Encyclopedia, Legal Governance, Risk Management and Compliance; see also, Miller, GP (2014) 'The Law of Governance, Risk Management and Compliance' (Aspen Casebook) Aspen Publisher.
6   See <http://www.legislation.gov.uk/ukpga/2010/23/pdfs/ukpga_20100023_en.pdf>.

facie, seem to be a very useful tool to avoid the risks of non-compliance with the rules. Thus, for efficient compliance, we must follow at least these arguments:

1. Proportionate procedures
2. The involvement of the organization's top management
3. Risk assessment procedures
4. Due diligence of existing or potential associated persons
5. Communication of the organization's policies and procedures and training in their application
6. The monitoring, review and evaluation of misconduct and/or corruption prevention procedures.

Other topics to be followed are:

1. The provision of gifts, hospitality and promotional expenses; charitable and political donations; or requests for facilitation payments
2. Direct and indirect employment, including recruitment, terms and conditions, disciplinary action and remuneration
3. Management of business relations with all other associated persons, including pre- and post-contractual arrangements
4. Financial and commercial controls such as proper accounting, review and approval of expenditure
5. Transparency of transactions and disclosure of information
6. Decision-making, such as procedures for delegation of authority, segregation of duties and avoidance of conflicts of interest
7. Enforcement, detailing disciplinary processes and sanctions for violations of the organization's compliance rules (e.g., anti-corruption)
8. The reporting of irregular or illegal procedures, including 'speak up' or 'whistle blowing'
9. The detail of the process by which the organization plans to implement its procedures for preventing misconduct (negligent or intentional), e.g., how its policy will be applied to individual projects and different parts of the organization.

Let me give a brief description, according to the Bribery Act, of the 'meaning and content' of each main topic.

With regard to proportionate procedures, an organization's procedures for preventing even inadvertent violations of the law by persons associated with it are proportionate to the risks it faces and the nature, scale and complexity of the organization's activities; they are also clear, practical, accessible, effectively implemented and enforced. Of course this is easier said than done ... the suggestion is perhaps clear but how in the 'real world' it is actually possible to follow it and how much the costs of implementing those procedures are not only unclear but probably, with all the good intentions of the legislator, unpredictable.

As far as high-level commitment is concerned, those at the top of an organization are in the best position to promote a culture of integrity in which violation of legal rules and/or corruption are unacceptable. The purpose of this principle is to encourage the involvement of senior management in determining procedures to prevent misconduct and/or corruption. Whatever the size, structure or market of an organization, senior management's engagement in the prevention of misconduct and/or corruption is likely to include communication of the organization's anti-corruption stance, and an appropriate degree of involvement in the development of non-compliance prevention procedures. Again, in my opinion, despite the (almost) clear wording of the law, this is a very weak point because there is clearly a big difference between the organizational structure of Fiat Chrysler Automobiles and the small grocery store near my home.

With regard to risk assessment, the purpose of this topic is to promote the adoption of risk assessment procedures that are proportionate to the size and structure of the organization and the nature, scale and location of its activities. The organization assesses the nature and extent of its exposure to potential external and internal risks of breaches of regulations on its behalf by persons associated with it. The assessment should be periodic, informed and documented. Risk assessment procedures (that enable a business organization to accurately recognize and highlight the risks it faces, whatever its size, activities, customers or markets) usually reflect certain basic characteristics. These are:

1. Supervision of risk assessment by senior management.
2. Adequate resources – this should reflect the scale of the organization's business and the need to identify and prioritize all relevant risks.
3. Identification of internal and external sources of information that will enable risk assessment and review.
4. Due diligence investigations.
5. Accurate and appropriate documentation of the risk assessment and its conclusions.

Once again, it is clear that there is a difference depending on the different 'size' and market of the company: I mean, for example, that there is obviously a difference if they are a small business in the local market or a large-scale manufacturer operating in the international market. And, of course, the costs of risk assessment are also different depending on the size and target market of the company. During the 'assessment phase' the risks commonly encountered are: (1) country risk; (2) sector risk; (3) transaction risk; (4) business opportunity risk; (5) business partnership risk; and some internal factors, such as: deficiencies in employee training, skills and knowledge; bonus culture that rewards excessive risk-taking; lack of clear financial controls; lack of a clear message from top-level management (if any, and still it seems that the law was designed for large companies but not for small ones, which are, in most countries in Europe and even in the United Kingdom, the vast majority).

The country risk is very important and most of the time underestimated by small businesses: I am thinking, for example, of the current situation in Sicily, where a number of small businesses thought of 'relocating' part of their activities to North African countries just before the outbreak of the 'Arab Spring' or the fall of the Libyan regime. Usually the entrepreneur thinks that everything is simple and that the personal knowledge of a 'friend' is the right key to start a business, saving money for the consultant and the lawyer. In reality, those operating in external markets (but sometimes also those operating in the domestic market) should at least be aware of the perceived high levels of corruption, the absence of effectively implemented anti-corruption legislation, the inability of the foreign government, the media, the local business community and civil society to effectively promote transparent procurement and investment policies and (in a certain society) a somewhat widespread idea that complying with the law may be unnecessary and/or unprofitable. Of course, and again, the 'prevention' of this risk is a 'cost' and perhaps decisive depending on the size of the company.

In terms of sectorial risk, of course some areas are riskier than others. As it is easy to understand, the sectors with the highest risk are the mining and energy industries and the large infrastructure sector, such as in Italy, especially, construction, transport or motorway construction and maintenance companies, and more generally all 'mixed' activities involving a 'private company' working in agreement with the public administration. In Italy, until recently there was a great risk of corruption and non-compliance and a new law was enacted to combat the phenomenon: according to Article 319-quater of the Italian 'Criminal Code' entitled 'Undue inducement to give or promise benefits', i.e., 'Undue influence to give or promise benefits':

> a public official or a person in charge of a public service who, abusing his position or powers, induces someone to give or promise money or another type of benefit illegitimately to him or a third party, may be punished by imprisonment from one to three years

(Of course, it is the same if a person induces the public official to act illegitimately by promising or giving money or another benefit.)

Despite its appearance, this rule, like others in the field of compliance, if applied 'strictly' can be a cure worse than the disease. It is complex to understand what exactly 'other benefits' means, and it is really difficult to separate the normal discretionary activity of the public administrator from 'undue influence'; moreover, what kind of 'undue influence' is it? If I am a public administrator and I have a close friend who is the CEO of an excellent construction company and I have to decide to do a public construction and the choice of the contractor is for my friend's company, which offers the best price and the best guarantees and the best work, can I be guilty of 'undue influence' if I spent my holidays aboard my friend's yacht? And if in this case I, in order to avoid any 'judicial problems' for me, prefer to choose a different company that is less good, less convenient than my friend's, am I acting in the interest of the people and the administration of the state? A real risk of throwing the baby out with the bathwater is evident.

As with sectorial risks, it is clear that certain types of transaction give rise to higher risks, e.g., charitable or political contributions, licences and permits, and public procurement transactions. Again, it depends on the different concrete situation: I understand that the rules against corruption apply to everyone and for everyone, but there is a concrete difference between a large company giving 'off the record' a large sum of money to support the electoral campaign of a candidate to be elected mayor of Rome and a ticket for a football match in the third division or a bottle of (local) wine offered as a gift by a grocer to the mayoral candidate of the very small parish of 'Castlerock'.

Commercial opportunity risks may arise in high-value projects or with projects involving many contractors or intermediaries; or with projects that are apparently not undertaken at market prices, or that do not have a clear legitimate purpose.

Regarding commercial partnership risk, some relationships may involve a higher risk, for example, the use of intermediaries in transactions with foreign public officials; consortia or joint venture partners; and relationships with politically exposed persons where the proposed commercial relationship involves, or is related to, an important public official.

The organization applies due diligence procedures, taking a proportionate and risk-based approach, to persons who perform or will perform services for or on behalf of the organization, in order to mitigate identified risks of misconduct or corruption. Due diligence procedures are both a form of corruption risk assessment and a means of mitigating a risk. Indeed, the aim is to encourage organizations to put in place due diligence procedures that adequately inform the application of proportionate measures to prevent people associated with them from corrupting or committing misconduct on their behalf. A high degree of care should be taken where local law or convention mandates the use of local agents in circumstances where it may be difficult for a commercial organization to extricate itself from a business relationship once established. The importance of thorough due diligence and risk mitigation prior to any engagement is critical in such circumstances. One more relationship with particularly important due diligence implications is a merger of business organizations or an acquisition of one by another.

In terms of communication, the organization must seek to ensure that its policies and procedures for preventing misconduct are embedded and understood throughout the organization through internal and external communication, including training, which is proportionate to the risks it faces. According to the Bribery Act 'guidance':

> communication and training discourage bribery by associated persons by improving awareness and understanding of a business organisation's procedures and the organisation's commitment to their proper application. Making information available helps to monitor, evaluate and review corruption prevention procedures more effectively. Training provides the knowledge and skills necessary to employ the organisation's procedures and address any corruption-related problems or issues that may arise.

Of course:

> the content, language and tone of communications for internal use may vary from those for external use in response to the different relationship the public has with the commercial organization. The nature of communication will vary greatly among commercial organizations in compliance with the different corruption risks faced, the size of the organization and the scale and nature of its activities.

Codes of conduct and participation in pro-compliance activities can reassure existing and future associates as well as 'customers' and can act as a deterrent to misconduct and corruption on the one hand and add value to the organization itself on the other. Training should be tailored to the specific risks associated with specific posts (e.g., higher-risk functions such as purchasing, contracts, marketing and distribution, working in high-risk countries).

From a concrete and realistic point of view, despite the stringency of anti-corruption regulations and their strict enforcement, even if all standards are perfectly followed, only compliance will not make a company safe. But why? There are a number of answers:

1. Research in the field of business behavioural ethics has shown that most initial ethical transgressions in business go unnoticed, even by those who commit them. We rationalize our bad behaviour to such an extent that we do not realize that we are crossing ethical boundaries until it is too late.
2. Compliance is mainly based on controlling employees' behaviour and decisions through a strict set of rules and laws, like 'a policeman's culture': too much control can actually backfire and important information is hidden. A flaw in compliance programmes is that they assume that misconduct comes from bad people, rather than good people doing bad things. Moreover, as has been criticized, 'the question still remains: how should leaders react to lawsuits? Hiring compliance officers may seem like a good thing for public relations, but does this actually address the real problem? If we look at this through the lens of a company fresh from a TCPA violation, they don't need compliance officers, but rather a way to prevent non-compliant leads from entering their system in the first place.'[7] Consequently, it makes much more sense to invest in prevention so that your representatives are only calling consumers who have given consent, rather than compliance officers who can only react when problems occur. But, again, even prevention is not enough to avoid negative consequences and, of course, it is a 'cost' to bear.
3. Are we sure that companies (and people) are really interested in following the rules? And are we sure that all rules are fair, good and really efficient? Even the racial laws were enacted (in Italy and Germany) by a parliament, but I don't think any of us think that those who did not comply with them were 'criminals'. In my opinion (I am not a politician but I am not naive enough to realize that statutory law should obey politics and not the other way around), it is necessary for people and society to perceive the rules as efficient and convenient to follow.
4. Moreover, even if a law is enacted with the 'best of intentions', there is always a 'dark side of the law' and sometimes (especially for criminal laws) too many laws and a 'strict interpretation' can be, as I said, a worse remedy than the disease. In Sicily there is a proverb that says: 'we love the wind in church but ... not so much as to blow out the candles.' This is the 'paradox of the Google car' that respects all the rules of the road but when it interacts with the people, it crashes because those who follow may not understand the logic behind the computer driver's decision.

---

[7]   See <http://leadid.com/blog/answering-the-compliance-question>.

5. Compliance is no longer confined to the narrow 'economic' or 'commercial' terrain or the fight against corruption. Compliance is a large and general phenomenon involving all people in a modern society. Employment law, individual rights, civil liability, professional duties and responsibilities, environmental law, even the new and dramatic human migration, are confronted with the need to 'reasonably' comply with rules that are too sectorial and sometimes without a 'systematic approach'.

Compliance is a general phenomenon not only or mainly limited to corruption, fraud against public administration and institutions, money laundering, insider trading, etc. Compliance is a general phenomenon widespread in all fields of modern human activity, so that it is no longer a problem for large companies, but is now a phenomenon that also affects the small business and even every professional or 'normal person' during their 'struggle' to comply with the 'jungle' of rules. In my opinion, too many complex and 'single' rules to comply with (the 'statutorification' or 'orgy of statute making') mean increasing risks of unintentional violation and/or liability. Thus professional activities such as the doctor, dentist, accountant, biologist, researcher, but also traditional activities such as farmers, food producers, manufacturers, retailers, small businesses, etc., may be under the blue sky of law and regulation (only partially against mafia, corruption, terrorism, etc.). This also means higher (transaction) costs, which in rich times are passed on to the end consumer, but in lean times should be borne by the individual professional. In this case, higher costs sometimes mean choosing between bankruptcies and 'circumventing' the rules.

From this point of view, I think it is interesting to note that the great economic crisis, at least in Italy and Sicily, has produced a 'virtuous' effect by pushing small businesses and small professionals to denounce mafia blackmail. Of course, it is impossible for them to suddenly become courageous; the point is that they have been squeezed between the impossibility of earning money from their work and the need to pay taxes, insurance, etc., and, on top of that, the 'pizzo' (the demand for the threat of money) of the mafia. In this case, the choice is between bankruptcy and filing for extortion. All people are subject to sometimes 'crazy' European and national rules.

It is not unusual to find rules like this (probably fake[8]):

> In the ordinance on (unground) nuts (other than ground nuts), the expression nuts refers to those nuts, other than ground nuts, that would not qualify as (unground) nuts (other than ground nuts) due to being (unground) nuts...

Those who know the European directives can easily agree with me.

In Italy (but it seems to be the same in most European countries), the over-production of rules and the 'network' of 'alternative' decisions of the administrative courts that overlap with the decision of the ordinary courts are making it extremely difficult every day to comply with *all* rules, even if a subject is correct and honest; thus, for example, there is no 'public selection' or 'contract with the public administration' that is not questioned and scrutinized by the administrative court with the logical consequence of waiting years and years for a decision. The recent compliance regulation (Italian Act no. 231/2001) is inspired by the just principle of stopping the 'violation of the rules' for corruption, fraud against the public administration, health and safety, environmental law, money laundering, organized crime offences and food and product safety offences; but the 'criminal model', i.e., only punitive, was weak (although necessary, of course) so the legislator provided for a 'collaborative model' by discussing with stakeholders to 'collaborate' with the authorities to prevent the possible violation of the rules. In other words, there is the possibility, for example, for a contractor to 'discuss' the risks of rule violations and, after the suggested measures have been taken, to obtain a 'legality rating', i.e., a document certifying that the contractor has made every effort to comply with the law. The procedure, in spite of good intentions, is of course not straightforward, but in fact there is a sharp increase in applications for the 'rating'; this is a clear demonstration that the collaborative approach is perhaps better than the 'punitive' ones alone.

Now we can try to fix, if there are any remedies, and look for developments. As far as remedies are concerned, in my opinion we should look for:

1. New 'policies' that make it more 'convenient' to follow the law
2. Collaboration (better than the criminal and punitive approach alone)
3. Mediation (mediation culture is crucial, especially when there is a transnational issue or people from different cultures are involved)
4. Information/training – the training of compliance experts is nowadays a necessity due to the complexity of compliance in every different system

---

[8]   Some said that this is a satirical opus of the UK magazine, *Private Eye*.

and also for issues that are considered 'sensitive' by national, European and international rules (I am thinking, for example, of the complexity of Islamic finance and so on). Similarly, the dissemination of information on all aspects of compliance and related topics is extremely important: if procedures and controls are clear, ascertained and known, this obviously leads to better compliance.

In conclusion there is a need to spread the culture of legality, but at the same time there is a need for the rules to be *clear, simple, easy to use, concrete* and, above all, *convenient to follow*. In a simple cost–benefit analysis, no one will comply with a law if it is cheaper to violate it. This is not a 'criminal risk' but an 'economic risk': a criminal calculates the risk of being imprisoned and it is part of the 'costs' – a mafioso knows, and doesn't care, that he will probably be killed, but he cares a lot if he cannot make money from his criminal activity. A common man (Clapham's common man) obeys and respects the law as long as it is convenient or at least a 'zero game'.

The collaborative and mediative approach and dialogue between law and institutions and private actors seems to be better than the traditional 'punitive approach'. The 'benefits' for those who follow the rules should be increased so that this makes it more 'convenient' and 'rewarding' to comply. In this field there is, in my opinion, room for an 'alternative use of private rules' instead of the 'usual' criminal rules, i.e., using the ordinary civil rules on civil liability, anti-trust, competition law, etc., to 'hit' those who gain an economic advantage against those who, on the contrary, are fair, honest, and precise. This means that the legislator (and the jurist) should understand that sometimes it is better to 'mediate' a concrete solution instead of insisting on a 'difficult' application of useless criminal or 'strict' rules.

Of course one cannot generalize, but this is the 'mastery' of politics over legislation. My father, who was a mathematics professor, told me: 'A railway station for an engineer is the place where *trains* leave; for an architect it is the place where *people* leave.' As a jurist, I think we should think less about the (rigid application and reconstruction of) rules and more about the real needs of people!

This is the only way to avoid a gap between law and reality, blurring the boundaries between experience and prudence, legality and reason, and fight all over the world organized crime in a more effective way.

Index